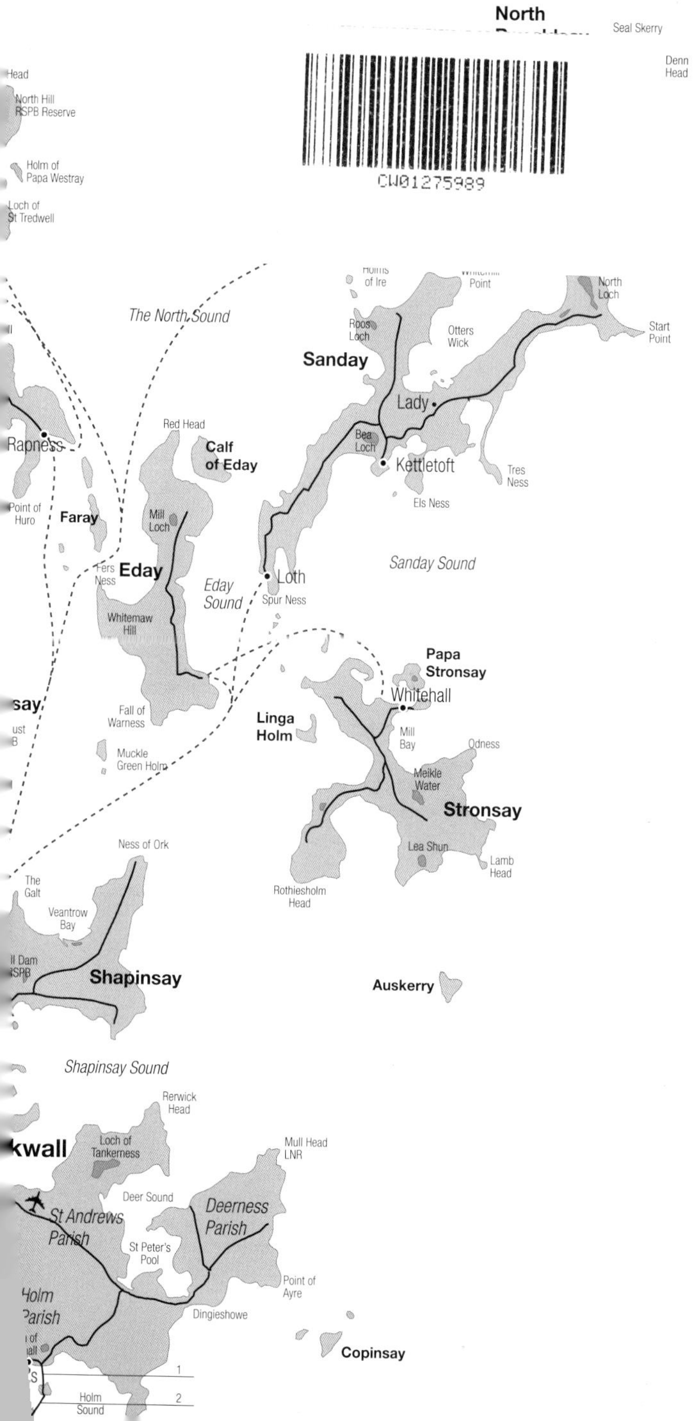
North
Seal Skerry
Denn Head
Head
North Hill RSPB Reserve
Holm of Papa Westray
Loch of St Tredwell
Holms of Ire
Point
North Loch
Start Point
The North Sound
Roos Loch
Otters Wick
Sanday
Lady
Bea Loch
Kettletoft
Tres Ness
Els Ness
Red Head
Calf of Eday
Rapness
Point of Huro
Faray
Mill Loch
Fers Ness
Eday
Eday Sound
Loth
Spur Ness
Sanday Sound
Whitemaw Hill
Papa Stronsay
Whitehall
say
Fall of Warness
Linga Holm
Mill Bay
Odness
Muckle Green Holm
Meikle Water
Stronsay
Lea Shun
Lamb Head
Ness of Ork
Rothiesholm Head
The Galt
Veantrow Bay
Shapinsay
Auskerry
Shapinsay Sound
Rerwick Head
kwall
Loch of Tankerness
Mull Head LNR
Deer Sound
Deerness Parish
St Andrews Parish
St Peter's Pool
Point of Ayre
Holm Parish
Dingieshowe
Copinsay
1
2
Holm Sound

The **Orkney** Book of **Wildflowers**

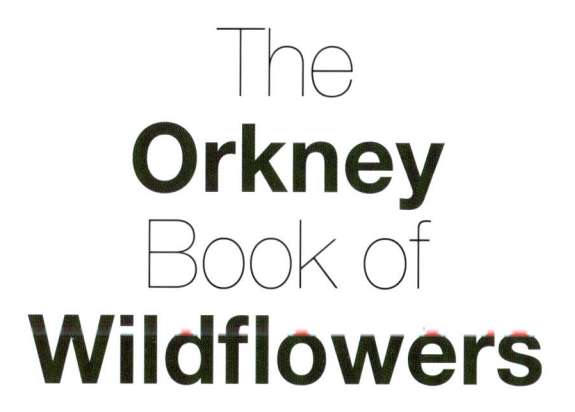

Wildflowers by habitat – from shore to hilltop

Pocket Edition

by Tim Dean • Illustrated by Anne Bignall

First published in 2014 as a tabletop version
with this subsequent revised Pocket Edition published in 2019
by The Orcadian (Kirkwall Press)
Hell's Half Acre, Hatston, Kirkwall, Orkney, KW15 1GJ
Tel. 01856 879000 • Fax 01856 879001 • www.orcadian.co.uk

Book sales: www.orcadian.co.uk/shop/index.php

Text Tim Dean © 2019
Artwork Anne Bignall © 2014

ISBN 978-1-912889-00-6

All rights reserved. The contents of this book may not be reproduced in any
form without written permission from the publishers, except for short extracts
for quotation or review

Printed in Orkney by The Orcadian, Hatston Print Centre,
Hell's Half Acre, Kirkwall, Orkney, Scotland, KW15 1GJ

The Author and the Artist

With a yearning to know, Tim started with I-Spy books and graduated via Brooke Bond tea cards, Observer's books and Collins Guides. Later, with a yearning to share, Tim began to write his own. The Orkney Book of Wildflowers follows on from The Natural History of Walney Island (1990), Birdwatching Walks in Cumbria (1998) and The Orkney Book of Birds (2008). From conception to the bookshelf is always a lot longer than it should be, but alongside the books, his days are spent sharing Orkney's natural heritage with other souls. Tim and Susan have a 13 year old daughter, Eleanor, who likes taking photographs of Opposite-leaved Golden-saxifrage and Pink Purslane.

With an inkling to see and create, Anne started with mud pies in Suffolk woods and graduated via slightly later editions of the I-Spy guides and Observer books to those acknowledged above. At the same time, Anne began wielding pencils. The Orkney Book of Wildflowers follows on from waiting one million tables, working as an illustrator, teaching art and painting her own nature-based work. The latter is still undertaken, but at a pace comparable to tectonic plate movement, in order to accommodate her current day job working for the North Isles Landscape Partnership Scheme. Anne lives in Kirkwall with Mark; they spend a great deal of time planting things.

About this book

The Orkney Book of Wildflowers has been converted into a Pocket Edition – no easy task. A feature of this Pocket Edition is that now the habitats are colour-coded so that wildflowers in each of those habitats can be found quickly. Simply identify your habitat, flick to the appropriate colour and in theory, the wildflower you are looking for will be there.

Dedicated to our understanding families

Acknowledgments

Our grateful thanks to John Crossley, Callum Flaws and the crew of the MV Eynhallow, Tommy Gibson, Martin Gray, Tracy Hall, Rosemary McCance, Eric Meek, Peter Radband, Auntie B Rendall, Jenny Taylor, Rod Thorne, Phillip Weiss and the late Elaine Bullard. Special thanks to Julian Branscombe for his peerless proof-reading and James Miller for his encouragement. We are indebted to Drew Kennedy for his skill in transforming an A4 landscape coffee-table book to a pocket-sized edition. He has achieved this miracle without compromising either text or illustrations.

Contents

Introduction	ix
The importance of plants in Orkney	xvi
Some of the best of Orkney's habitats and wildflowers	xix
The chosen localities	xxii
Habitats and their wildflowers (page number refer to species text)	1

Sand and shingle shores   **2**
Oysterplant   4
Sea Campion   5
Curled Dock   6
Cleavers   6
Sea Rocket   7
Sea Mayweed   8
Perennial Sow-thistle   8
Silverweed   9
Oraches   10
Sea Sandwort   11

Salt marshes   **12**
Scurvygrass   14
Sea Arrowgrass   15
Annual Sea-blite   16
Sea Plantain   16
Common Saltmarsh-grass   17
Saltmarsh Rush   17
Sea Milkwort   18
Lesser Sea-spurrey   18
Greater Sea-spurrey   19
Sea Aster   20
Glassworts   20

Dunes, links and dry grasslands   **22**
Wild Pansy   24
Sand Sedge   24
Lady's Bedstraw   25
Marram   26

Lyme Grass   27
Grass-of-Parnassus   28
Mouse-ear Hawkweed   28
Cowslip   29
Field Gentian   30
Autumn Gentian   31
Yellow Rattle   32
Common Twayblade   32
Yarrow   33
Lesser Burdock   34
Red Bartsia   35
Common Ragwort   36
Red Clover   37
Hardheads   38
White Clover   38
Bugloss   39
Common Bird's-foot-trefoil   40
Curved Sedge   41
Bulbous Buttercup   41
Selfheal   42
Sea Bindweed   43
Lesser Meadow-rue   43

Lowland freshwater – lochs, burns, marshes and wet grasslands   **44**
Marsh Marigold   46
Ragged Robin   46
Water Mint   47
Meadowsweet   47
Great Willowherb   48

v

Lady's Smock	49
Marsh Willowherb	50
Marsh Pennywort	50
Bogbean	51
Bog Pimpernel	52
Tufted Forget-me-not	52
Water Forget-me-not	53
Soft Rush	54
Sneezewort	54
Marsh Ragwort	55
Common Marsh-bedstraw	56
Water-cress	56
Yellow Iris	57
Lesser Spearwort	58
Marsh Arrowgrass	58
Marsh Cudweed	59
Marsh Thistle	60
Butterbur	60
Monkeyflowers	62
Marsh Cinquefoil	63
Early Marsh-orchid	63
Amphibious Bistort	64
Mare's-tail	64
Northern Marsh-orchid	65
Water-crowfoots	67
Greater Bird's-foot-trefoil	68
Brooklime	68
Marsh Horsetail	70
Water Horsetail	70
Meadow Buttercup	71

Sea cliffs, coastal grasslands and coastal heaths — 72

Sea Spleenwort	74
Thrift	74
Buck's-horn Plantain	75
Scots Lovage	76
Kidney Vetch	76
Common Dog-Violet	77
Scottish Primrose	78
Wild Thyme	79
Cat's-ear	79
Autumnal Hawkbit	80
Roseroot	81
Spring Squill	82
Sea Ivory	83
Eyebright	83
Mountain Everlasting	84
Alpine Meadow-rue	85
Crowberry	86
Goldenrod	86
Carnation Sedge	87
Devil's-bit Scabious	88
Glaucous Sedge	88
Common Sorrel	89

Arable fields, waysides and disturbed ground — 90

Daisy	92
Spear Thistle	92
Creeping Thistle	93
Dandelion	94
Smooth Sow-thistle	95
Prickly Sow-thistle	95
Corn Spurrey	96
Field Pansy	96
Field Forget-me-not	97
Creeping Buttercup	98
Lesser Trefoil	98
Field Horsetail	99
Colt's-foot	100
Common Hemp-nettle	100
Stinging Nettle	101
Shepherd's-purse	102
Red Dead-nettle	103
Northern Dead-nettle	103
Hybrid Woundwort	104
Charlock	104
Sun Spurge	105
Sweet Rocket	106
Germander Speedwell	107
Field Speedwell	107
Oxeye Daisy	108
Sweet Cicely	108

Hogweed	109
Scentless Mayweed	110
Cow Parsley	110
Groundsel	111
Bush Vetch	112
Meadow Vetchling	112
Fumitories	113
Tufted Vetch	114
Broad-leaved Dock	114
Tansy	115
Pineappleweed	116
Bitter-cresses	116
Common Chickweed	117
Greater Plantain	118
Ribwort Plantain	119
Common Mouse-ear	119

Plantation woodlands — 120

Wood Anemone	124
Ground-elder	124
Daffodil	124
Pink Purslane	125
Salmonberry	125
Few-flowered Garlic	126
Lesser Celandine	130
Snowdrop	130
Ground-ivy	131
Polypody	131
Hybrid Bluebell	132
Opposite-leaved Golden-saxifrage	132

Wild woods and dales — 134

Primrose	138
Red Campion	138
Valerian	139
Foxglove	139
Broad Buckler-fern	140
Wild Roses	143
Water Avens	146
Rosebay Willowherb	146
Wood Sage	147
Great Wood-rush	147
Blaeberry	150
Bracken	150
Honeysuckle	151
Wood Horsetail	151
Wild Angelica	152

The peat hill – heaths and blanket bogs — 154

Bell Heather	156
Cross-leaved Heath	157
Ling	157
Hard Fern	158
Tormentil	159
Prostrate Juniper	161
Lesser Twayblade	162
Heath Spotted-orchid	163
Sheep's Sorrel	164
Heath Speedwell	165
Stone Bramble	166
Stag's-horn Clubmoss	166
Fir Clubmoss	167
Heath Milkwort	168
Common Milkwort	169
Heath Bedstraw	169
Heath Rush	170
Fairy Flax	170
Round-leaved Wintergreen	171
Slender St John's-wort	172
Green-ribbed Sedge	172
Lady's-mantles	173
Bog Asphodel	174
Sphagnum	175
Marsh Violet	175
Marsh Lousewort	176
Lousewort	177
Great Sundew	179
Round-leaved Sundew	179
Hare's-tail Cottongrass	181
Common Cottongrass	181
Butterwort	182
Creeping Willow	184

Cloudberry	184
Bog Bilberry	185
Black Bog-rush	186
Yellow Saxifrage	186
Deergrass	187

The high hill and stony tops	**188**
Trailing Azalea	190
Bearberry	190
Purple Saxifrage	191
Alpine Bearberry	192
Moss Campion	193
Dwarf Cornel	194
Common Cow-wheat	194
Mountain Avens	195
Alpine Saw-wort	195
Mountain Sorrel	198

Bibliography 200
Appendices 203

   Appendix A) Location of habitats by parish and island
- i) **Sand and shingle shores** 204
- ii) **Salt marshes** 206
- iii) **Dunes, links and dry grasslands** 206
- iv) **Lowland freshwater – lochs, burns, marshes and wet grasslands** 208
  - a) Lochs (including upland lochs) 208
  - b) Burns 210
- v) **Plantation woodlands** 214
- vi) **Wild woods and dales** 214

   Appendix B) Botanical descriptions of some of Orkney's best sites 218

   Appendix C) Local Nature Conservation
   Sites by parish and island 225
   Index 237

Introduction

Why do it? The route

At the height of summer, Orkney blooms. Whether you are on the cliffs or at the shore, by a loch or on the hill or even just admiring some of the roadside verges, you cannot fail to notice that Orkney is in flower. Maybe you would like to know what these flowers are – the act of putting a name to a species is hugely satisfying. Flower books come in all shapes and sizes but invariably the identification books contain far too many species. In your search for the 'blue pea-like flower that scrambles through the verge and on to the fence' you are faced with a multitude of choices – in '*The Wildflowers of Britain and Northern Europe*' (2003) by Blamey, Fitter and Fitter, you are presented with 121 pictures of members of the pea family, 27 of which are blue. That degree of information is a lot to wade through and potentially off-putting; for some it might be the last time they pick up a flower book. Identification would be so much easier if there was a book that dealt solely with flowers that were likely to be seen in Orkney. Going back to that 'blue pea-like flower', Orkney has 26 members of the pea family, only four of which are blue.

Although hardly scientific, reducing the possibilities seems to work. The same principle was adopted for *The Orkney Book of Birds* which was published in 2008. After Orkney's birds, why not Orkney's flowers? It also seemed logical to emulate the bird book formula; consequently within the pages of *The Orkney Book of Wildflowers*, 230 species have been described. Artist Anne Bignall has painted ten habitats and 221 of these species – all of them, just like the bird book, with readily identifiable Orkney locations. The two will now sit side by side on book shelves – within their pages, captured by pen and gloriously by brush, are some of the county's finest wildlife treasures. There may be more books to come………

What is it?

Wildflower books occur in a variety of formats – none of them are perfect for every reader. One of the commonest formats is a book organised in the standard systematic manner which begins with the Buttercup family and proceeds through the various plant families such as Dock, Heath, Pea, Carrot, and Daisy to Orchid. In an illustrated book this type of format would result in a series of plates depicting an abundance of similar looking plants. If we followed this traditional type of layout for a book about Orkney's wildflowers, Plate 1 would be titled 'Buttercups' and depict Meadow Buttercup, Creeping Buttercup, Bulbous Buttercup, Lesser Spearwort and Lesser Celandine – structurally there is not a great deal to separate these five of the Buttercup family; the abundance of similar yellow flowers could create confusion and the plate may struggle to hold the reader's attention.

Another common format is a wildflower book laid out by colour. Many of these volumes begin with yellow wildflowers and work their way through the rest of the rainbow. By following this style for *The Orkney Book of Wildflowers*, Plate 1 would be titled 'Yellow flowers' and show Meadow Buttercup, Creeping Buttercup, Bulbous Buttercup, Lesser Spearwort and Lesser Celandine – the same five very similar flowers and again a plate of limited appeal.

However, it could be easily argued that both these types of formats have their merits. One of which means that depicting similar wildflowers on the same plate means that plants may be compared and differences distinguished in the one 'helpful' illustration. However, it may be that the resulting illustration of similar plants is prosaic and what is considered to be helpful for identification purposes fails to capture either attention or imagination and may result simply in confusion.

This book follows neither of the above formats. Our five previously mentioned yellow Buttercups now find themselves variously situated in their habitats. Meadow Buttercup and Lesser Spearwort are firmly anchored in the '*Lowland freshwater – lochs, burns, marshes and wet grasslands*' keeping company with Brooklime, Water Horsetail, Butterbur and Marsh Thistle. Bulbous Buttercup now finds itself mixing with Common Bird's-foot-trefoil, Sea Bindweed and Lesser Meadow-rue in the '*Dunes, links and dry grasslands*' and Lesser Celandine shares a plate with Hybrid Bluebell, Snowdrop and Opposite-leaved Golden-saxifrage in the '*Plantation woodlands*' chapter.

Anne's rich illustrations will aid identification and the text describes some of the finer points. However, *The Orkney Book of Wildflowers* is not an identification book – that sort of book is well catered for and often features lifeless specimens set against the starkness of a white page. *The Orkney Book of Wildflowers* is a vibrant celebration of Orkney's flowers. The settings (location and habitat) are as important as the subject and pinpoint the plant in time and place. Inspirational images that fired me as a child included such well known paintings as *Monarch of the Glen* – the grandeur of the setting adds to the majesty of the subject. The backgrounds to every species in the excellent but largely forgotten *The Oxford Book of Birds* were further inspiration – Ospreys fishing over highland lochs, Ptarmigan in flight against snowy Scottish peaks or Choughs on coastal cliffs. These inspiring images had one common denominator – they depicted the species within its habitat – that was the identification clue that I wanted and we wanted the same for *The Orkney Book of Wildflowers*.

The habitats

The Orkney Book of Wildflowers, which is flexible enough to include a few trees, shrubs, ferns, clubmosses, mosses and a lichen, takes us on a journey through various habitats from sea level to the summit of Ward Hill on Hoy (479 metres or 1,571'6"). Within those habitats approximately 1000 species, subspecies and hybrids of wildflowers have been recorded in Orkney. One day there may be an Orkney book that includes all of them and paintings or photographs to accompany. However, that tome is well beyond the scope of this modest volume. For *The Orkney Book of Wildflowers*, 230 of the county's plants have been arranged within their habitats. This is a bold uncompromising statement – if only it had been as easy as that. Broadly speaking a habitat is an environment in which a plant normally occurs – for example Hybrid Bluebells normally occur in woodland and Yellow Iris normally occurs in wetlands. Undoubtedly there are many plants that remain faithful to one habitat – instances of the 'faithful' include Sea Rocket on the shore and Tormentil on the hill – you would be hard pressed to find these plants in any other habitats.

However, there are always exceptions and there are a multitude of plants which are less obliging and capable of straddling the boundaries that help to define these habitats – in effect they are able to grow in a variety of habitats. There are many examples of border-crossing flowers; two of Orkney's favourites, Primrose and the delicate Common Dog-violet, may be found growing among dunes, on sea cliffs, in the hill or in woodland. This multi occupancy caused a few headaches for the author and much soul-searching took place as he wrestled with flowers that had the ability to grow in an assortment of habitats.

Two particularly problematic species were Thrift and Red Campion, flowers most of us are very familiar with – in which habitat chapters would they be most appropriate? Arguably the salt-loving Thrift could sit quite comfortably in three of them: the shore, salt marsh or sea cliff. Initially it was included in the salt marsh chapter alongside plants such as Scurvygrass and Sea Milkwort; but on reflection it was moved to the *Sea cliffs, coastal grasslands and coastal heaths* section where it is now rubbing shoulders with Kidney Vetch and Scottish Primrose. The move was based solely on the probability that more people were likely to be familiar with its carnation-pink flowers in this habitat. Red Campion, in Britain and Ireland, is generally a plant of 'hedgebanks and woods' – in Orkney it is often found on the coast, but among tall herb vegetation quite typical of Orkney's 'treeless woodland – hence in this book it can be found in the *Wild woods and dales* chapter. Could the Thrift dilemma have been rectified easily if, instead of having standard habitats such as the *Sand and shingle shores*, *Salt marshes* and *Sea cliffs, coastal grasslands and coastal heaths*, they were all lumped together under the one heading *Salt influenced habitats*? No, not satisfactorily – this would immediately have created another dilemma evident in any island group – the influence of the sea is far reaching; typical salt-loving plants of the shore may be found well inland – in Orkney it is possible to find Sea Plantain among heather in the hill, eight miles from a tideline.

The Orkney Book of Wildflowers Pocket Edition includes ten habitats as we make a journey from the soft coasts of sand and shingle to the high tops of Hoy. We visit habitats in every parish; we also travel to most of the inhabited islands and some of the uninhabited in the search to find a particular plant in its particular habitat and in a particular locality. The ten chosen habitats have been colour-coded. Coloured tabs at the top right corner of each page will guide you to the specific habitat.

- Sand and shingle shores
- Salt marshes
- Dunes, links and dry grasslands
- Lowland freshwater – lochs, burns, marshes and wet grasslands
- Sea cliffs, coastal grasslands and coastal heaths
- Arable fields, waysides and disturbed ground
- Plantation woodlands
- Wild woods and dales
- The peat hill – heaths and blanket bogs
- The high hill and stony tops

The species

Each species is dealt with in a similar way – a typical example follows:

8) Silverweed (*Potentilla anserina*)   Rose family

Moors, Moorek – *Bread and cheese, Bread and butter, Silver feather, Midsummer silver*

Height to 15cm; flowers June to August. Widespread and abundant in Orkney (27/28); easy to find.

The first line of the species account commences with a **number** – that number corresponds to the illustration of that species on the plate. After the number is its **commonly known name** followed in brackets by its **Latin name** – both these names have been taken from *English Names of Wildflowers* J.G. Dony, F.H. Perring and C.M. Rob (1980). Concluding the line is the plant's **family**.

The second line, where appropriate, contains the **Orkney name** (in bold italics) followed by **other colloquial names** from various parts of Britain.

The third line begins with the plant's **height** or for some trailing species, its **length** followed by its flowering **period** which due to the vagaries of our climate is necessarily broad. Finally the last three pieces of information relate to the plant's **status and distribution** in Orkney, its **abundance** – the number of 10km squares within which it occurs in Orkney - and the **ease with which it may be found**.

No system of categorisation is perfect; there will always be exceptions to the rule. The status and distribution of the wildflowers for *The Orkney Book of Wildflowers* has been calculated using 10km squares of which there are 40 covering Orkney – ten of these squares have less than 3% of land in them and of these, two of them have just 0.1%. *The New Atlas of the British and Irish Flora* has distribution maps for all of Orkney's species and limits itself to 28 ten kilometre squares. The Orkney Book of Wildflowers follows this example. Generally speaking, if the species occurs in more than 15 of those squares it is considered to be **widespread**, if it occurs in less than 15 it is deemed to be **local**.

The abundance of each of the wildflowers has been determined by using the self-same 10km squares and the table below indicates the categories:

> **abundant** - occurring in more than 22 squares
>
> **frequent** - occurring in 15 to 22 squares
>
> **occasional** - occurring in 8 to 15 squares
>
> **rare** - occurring in less than 8 squares

And finally the species is given one of four categories based on how easy or difficult it may be to find.

The categories are:

> **easy to find**
>
> **fairly easy to find**
>
> **not easy to find**
>
> **hard to find**

Again, this is not an exact science and no doubt there are holes in this system through which you could drive a combine harvester. However, the categories are meant to be simple and give a helpful indication of the effort that is needed to find a particular wildflower. I'm sure we can all understand why I've categorised the following as:

> **Daisy** – **easy to find** – it's virtually everywhere
>
> **Oysterplant** – **fairly easy to find** – if you know where to go in South Ronaldsay, Deerness and Sanday, it's conspicuous and accessible
>
> **Common Twayblade** – **not easy to find** – although it is fairly wide in its distribution, it is neither numerous nor conspicuous
>
> **Mountain Avens** – **hard to find** – it occurs solely on Hoy and having the agility of a Mountain Goat and a tight-rope walker's head for heights are both near-essential requirements.

Where some very similar plants occur in the same habitat, a general description of these similar plants precedes the specific descriptions. The heading to the similar plants is asterisked * and italicised. The following are dealt with in this manner:

Oraches	*Wild Roses*
Glassworts	*Ferns*
Forget-me-nots	*Heathers*
Monkeyflowers	*Clubmosses*
Horsetails	*Milkworts*
Water-crowfoots	*Lady's-mantles*
Bitter-cresses	*Sphagnum*
Speedwells	*Sundews*
Fumitories	*Cottongrasses*

The illustrations – by Anne Bignall

The paintings in this book are intended to complement Tim's observations on the wildflowers of Orkney, providing a visual aid to help identify each plant as well as bringing the written descriptions to life by showing the plants growing in their natural surroundings. Although it has been important to depict the flowers accurately, the paintings are not intended as diagrams but as images of the flowers that give some sense of their character and their place in the environment.

As a sister publication to *The Orkney Book of Birds*, the paintings follow the same format. Each flower is shown in its habitat with its Orkney background; some of the locations are iconic, others are less well-known, but they are places where the species can be found. This ensures the book really belongs to Orkney and the reader can gain a good feel for Orkney's habitats, landscapes and character.

At the start of each habitat section of the book, a single illustration shows a scene in Orkney that is a representative example of that vegetation type. In the following pages the individual plants that are typical to that habitat are then shown in collections of either five or six plants per plate, each with their own background.

The paintings are in acrylic which is perhaps a less common choice for plant illustrations. However, given there was less need for fine detail than in more traditional botanical illustrations, it was chosen over watercolour as the favoured medium.

The importance of plants in Orkney

Dock, Heather, Marram, Rush and a hundred other plants – necessity, the mother of indigestion

You only have to look at the stomach contents of Tollund man to realise the gulf between then and now. The well-preserved remains of a four thousand year old man (christened Tollund man) were found in peat in Denmark in 1950. It was possible to tell what he had last eaten. The answer proved to be largely plants such as Fat Hen (*Chenopodium album*), Corn Spurrey (*Spergula arvensis*), Heartsease (*Viola tricolor*), Sorrel (*Rumex acetosa*), Black Bindweed (*Polygonum convolvulus*) and Pale Persicaria (*Polygonum lapathifolium*) – the first four of these species occur in Orkney

We are losing knowledge of Orkney's plants and their uses at a rapid rate. Doubtless much has already been lost but we must be thankful for the information that remains and helps us to thread the Orkney past together. Certain plants of course have always been important – the plants that have sustained Orkney lives be they cereal (*bere*), vegetable (*neep*) or fruit (*blaeberry*) – they still serve the same all important purposes. However, it is evident that in our modern world we have little practical use or edible use for many plants that were previously considered essential components of daily life. These plants had their place in the rhythms of Orkney and nowadays it is difficult to appreciate the importance attached to some of the commonly occurring plants that made Orkney life easier.

It is probable that few plants were considered useless. If it could not be made into something useful, it could be eaten, drunk, taken as a medicine or played with. Indeed, there were plants which fulfilled more than one of these functions. Take for example the ubiquitous dock. It would be fair to say that in the modern day it is not held in the highest regard. Landowners consider it a pernicious weed that reduces the quantity and quality of the grazing sward. In bygone times before the rise of Orkney's agricultural industry, Docks (other than the Curled Dock of the seashore) were possibly far less abundant than they are now. They had a use and were a sought after commodity whose stems were pliable yet robust enough to be woven and fashioned into fish traps known as *fursaclews*. There was often an added bonus in the roots – a maggot which made a tempting bait for sea trout.

Some of Orkney's most useful plants are also some of the most

> *'Everything green that grew
> out of the mould
> Was an excellent herb to our
> fathers of old.'*
>
> Rudyard Kipling *'Our Fathers of Old'*.

abundant. Heather, which covered far more of Orkney than it does now, was indispensable. Young thin stems were plaited into a rope which would support the thatch in roofs, hold down haystacks or made into baskets (*cubbies* or *caesies*) or into door mats (*flackies*). Basket ware found during the excavation of Howe Broch dates from the Iron Age. Cordage, made from Crowberry, a very close relative of Heather and of equal toughness, was unearthed at Skara Brae. A combination of Heather and Crowberry were the two principal ingredients in the manufacture of Orkney baskets for the next 5000 years. Baskets were woven for specific purposes: *cubbies* for holding peats, *luppies* as a measure for meal, *skeps* for sifting meal and *caesies* for carrying.

A number of grasses provided a variety of uses. In the Hebrides, Marram was an integral element of thatching. In Orkney where it is known as *Bent*, it appears not to have been used for this purpose. In heather-less islands such as Sanday and North Ronaldsay, it was manufactured into rope known in Orkney as *simmons*. Its roots were harvested and woven into loops for hanging *caesies* over horses backs and in chair making, the stems were bound tightly together to provide draught-proof backs. However, thatch in Orkney was manufactured from Eelgrass but it was used principally by the poor and lasted little more than two years. And every Orkney house was indebted to the humble Rush: its pith provided the wick for the *cruisie* which for centuries was the only source of light for the long winter nights.

Some of Orkney's plants could be regarded as life savers. During the three months before harvest as the previous year's grain ran out and bread became scarce, the seeds of the yellow-flowered member of the Cabbage family, Charlock, and those of the white-flowered Corn Spurrey were harvested to make life-saving *reuthie* bread. The valuable harvest needed to be protected and around the croft Tansy was strewn under the bases of the corn stacks before they were built to deter mice. Stock were equally valuable and their welfare was always paramount; sheep grazed on Sea Plantain which helped them fatten and improved the quality of the meat, while Nettles were fed to cattle in the belief that they were an aphrodisiac. From the wettest parts of the hill Sphagnum was collected – its absorbency and antiseptic properties combine to form an indispensable dressing for wounds.

Another plant held in high regard was Yarrow from which a tea was derived. Neill in '*A tour through some of the islands of Orkney and Shetland*' (1806) describes it as such: 'At Kirbuster, I observed laid out to dry, at a cottage door, a large collection of the flowering tops of the dwarfy milfoil, which grows on the dry commons, and which is known here by the oddly corrupted name of "*meal and folie*" (the Latin is *Achillea millefolium*). These flowering tops they infuse and drink as tea, this beverage being held in high repute for dispelling melancholy'. Other indispensable herbs included Tormentil which tackled dysentery and diarrhoea and the toothache-curing Yellow Iris which eye-wateringly involved sucking the juice from the roots through the nose.

The most obvious Orkney example of using any and every plant is evident in a 'tonic' that by accounts was in general use in and before the 18th Century as a remedy for what was known in Orkney as '*axes*'. By way of explanation, '*axes*' appears to have been a complaint of the spring described at the time as an 'anguish distemper'. The cure involved a potion of 'Buck's-horn Plantain, Water Plantain (?), Scots Lovage, Wild Daisy, Rocket, roots of Elecampane, Millefoil, roots of Spignelle, Dandelion, Parsley roots, Wormwood, Comfrey, Tansy, Sea Pink, Garden Angelica and a kind of Masterwort'. In Wallace's '*An Account of the Islands of Orkne*' (1700) he relates that half a pint of this concoction is drunk in the morning and evening and that the 'old women talk wonders of it pretending there are so many of the herbs good for the liver, so many for the head and so many for the heart and spleen'. Even at the time Wallace was of the opinion that the 'infallible cure' was sheer quackery.

Some of the best of Orkney's habitats and wildflowers

We all have our own favourite places to see wildflowers in Orkney; among the prime sites are Yesnaby for *Primula scotica*, the hills of Hoy for alpines and Sanday's links for dune flowers. However some of our favourites may also be more modest and might include a small patch of wet grassland with Ragged Robin and Lady's Smock, a flowering roadside verge with a crowd of orchids including both Northern Marsh and Early Marsh, Common Twayblades and even Fragrant Orchid or a sheltered quarry, bright in the springtime with a liberal dotting of Primroses.

Orkney is well-endowed with unparalleled locations in which to see Orkney's habitats and wildflowers. Four of these sites have been designated of international importance and 21 have accolades of national importance. In addition Orkney boasts 247 Local Nature Conservation Sites (LNCs) many of which are considered especially important for their botanical interest and cover virtually all the habitats that this volume deals with (a comprehensive list of these can be found in Appendix C).

Alongside all these sites we have those that are managed by conservation organisations such as the Royal Society for the Protection of Birds and the Scottish Wildlife Trust. Neither must we forget Orkney's two Local Nature Reserves, Mull Head and Happy Valley, the former rich in coastal habitats and the latter a fine example of plantation woodland.

The following list includes nationally and internationally important sites – some of the best in Britain and the best in Europe. Also featured are some of the reserves managed by conservation organisations; a fuller description of some of these sites follows in Appendix B.

What the abbreviations mean…
- Site of Special Scientific Interest (SSSI) – national designation
- Special Area of Conservation (SAC) – European designation
- Local Nature Conservation Sites (LNCS) – local designation
- Local Nature Reserve (LNR)
- Royal Society for the Protection of Birds (RSPB)
- Scottish Wildlife Trust (SWT)

Sand and shingle shores
   Pentland Firth islands (SSSI vascular plants)

Salt marshes
   Central Sanday (SSSI – salt marsh)
   Waulkmill, Orphir (SSSI – salt marsh)

Dunes, links and dry grasslands
   Central Sanday (SSSI – machair, sand dune)
   Northwall, Sanday (SSSI – machair)

Lowland freshwater – lochs, burns, marshes and wet grasslands
   Glims Moss and Durkadale, Birsay (SSSI – fen, marsh and swamp)
   Hoy (SAC – acid peat-stained lochs and ponds, base-rich fen, hard water springs depositing lime)
   Loch of Banks, Birsay (SSSI and RSPB – fen, marsh and swamp)
   Loch of Isbister and the Loons, Birsay (SAC, SSSI and RSPB – fen, marsh and swamp, mire)
   Mill Dam, Shapinsay (RSPB)
   Mill Loch, Eday (SSSI – wetland)
   Northwall, Sanday (SSSI – machair loch)
   Onziebust, Egilsay (RSPB)
   Pentland Firth islands (SSSI vascular plants)
   Rousay (SSSI – freshwater lochs)
   Stromness Heaths and Coast (SAC and SSSI – base-rich fen, freshwater)

Sea cliffs, coastal grasslands and coastal heaths
   Hill of White Hamars, South Walls (SWT – vegetated sea cliff, maritime grassland and heath)
   Holm of Burghlee, Shapinsay (SWT – vegetated sea cliff, maritime grassland and heath)
   Hoy (SAC – vegetated sea cliffs)
   Marwick Head, Birsay (RSPB)
   Mull Head, Deerness (LNR – maritime grassland)
   North Hill, Papa Westray (SSSI and RSPB – maritime cliff)
   Noup Cliffs, Westray (RSPB)
   Rousay (SSSI – maritime cliff)
   Stromness Heaths and Coast (SAC and SSSI – maritime cliff, vegetated sea cliff)
   Ward Hill Cliffs, South Ronaldsay (SSSI – maritime cliff)
   Waulkmill, Orphir (SSSI – maritime cliff)
   West Westray (SSSI – maritime cliff)

Arable fields, waysides and disturbed ground
Brodgar, Stenness and Sandwick (RSPB)

Plantation woodlands
Binscarth, Firth
Gyre, Orphir
Happy Valley, Stenness (LNR)
Hoy Lodge, Hoy
Muddisdale, St Ola
Olav's Wood, South Ronaldsay
The Willows, Kirkwall
Vinquoy Wood, Eday

Wild woods and dales
Burn of Quoys, Hoy (Hoy Trust)
Cottascarth and Rendall Moss, Rendall (RSPB)
Hobbister, Orphir (RSPB)
Berriedale, Hoy (SSSI – upland woodland)
Pegal, Hoy (Hoy Trust)
Waulkmill, Orphir (SSSI)
White Glen, Hoy (RSPB)

The peat hill – heaths and blanket bogs
Birsay Moors, Birsay (RSPB)
Cottascarth and Rendall Moss (RSPB)
Doomy and Whitemaw Hill, Eday (SSSI)
Harray Road End, Firth (SWT – heath)
Hill of White Hamars, South Walls (SWT – heath)
Hobbister, Orphir (RSPB)
Holm of Burghlee, Shapinsay (SWT – heath)
Hoy (SAC and SSSI – alpine and subalpine heaths, blanket bog, dry heaths, wet heathland)
Keelylang Hill and Swartabeck Burn, Orphir and Firth (SSSI – blanket bog, subalpine dry heath)
Mull Head, Deerness (LNR – heath)
Orphir and Stenness Hills, Orphir and Stenness (SSSI – upland assemblage)
Rousay (SSSI – blanket bog, subalpine wet heath)
Stromness Heaths and Coast SAC (SAC and SSSI – dry heath, subalpine heath)
Trumland, Rousay (RSPB)
West Mainland Moorlands, Firth, Harray, Evie and Birsay (SSSI – blanket bog, upland assemblage)

The high hill and stony tops
Hoy (SAC and SSSI – alpine and subalpine heaths)

The chosen localities

Auskerry – 1 species illustration
Sea cliffs – Common Sorrel

Birsay – 10 species illustrations
Shore – Sea Campion
Links – Selfheal
Freshwater – Marsh Marigold, Marsh Willowherb
Sea cliff – Kidney Vetch, Carnation Sedge
Arable – Stinging Nettle
The Hill – Heath Milkwort, Common Milkwort, Black Bog-rush

Burray – Dunes, links and dry grasslands + 8 species illustrations
Links – Red Bartsia, Hardheads, Curved Sedge
Arable – Fumitory, Red Dead-nettle, Northern Dead-nettle
The Hill – Bog Bilberry, Sheep's Sorrel

Copinsay – 1 species illustration
Sea cliff – Thrift

Deerness – 9 species illustrations
Shore – Sea Rocket
Salt marsh – Sea Plantain
Links – Lady's Bedstraw, Common Twayblade
Freshwater – Mare's-tail, Amphibious Bistort
Sea Cliffs – Spring Squill
Arable – Charlock, Tufted Vetch

Eday – 6 species illustrations
Links – Grass-of-Parnassus
Freshwater – Soft Rush
Sea cliffs – Cat's-ear
Arable – Creeping Thistle, Field Horsetail
The Hill – Tormentil

Egilsay – 6 species illustrations
Links – Autumn Gentian, Yellow Rattle
Freshwater – Bogbean, Meadow Buttercup
Arable – Hogweed
The Hill – Lady's-mantle

Evie – 8 species illustrations
Shore – Sea Sandwort
Links – Cowslip
Arable – Broad-leaved Dock
Plantations – Hybrid Bluebell
Wild wood – Primrose
The Hill – Round-leaved Sundew, Heath Spotted-orchid, Stag's-horn Clubmoss

Firth – Plantation woodlands + 9 species illustrations
Salt marsh – Sea Aster
Arable – Oxeye Daisy
Plantations – Wood Anemone, Few-flowered Garlic, Ground-elder, Polypody, Opposite-leaved Golden-saxifrage
Wild Wood – Valerian
The Hill – Hare's-tail Cottongrass

Flotta – Arable fields, waysides and disturbed ground + 4 species illustrations
Freshwater – Lesser Spearwort
Arable – Prickly Sow-thistle, Lesser Trefoil
The Hill – Slender St John's-wort

Glims Holm – 2 species illustrations
Links – Lyme Grass
Sea cliff – Sea Spleenwort

Graemsay – 6 species illustrations
Links – Sand Sedge
Freshwater – Sneezewort
Sea cliff – Goldenrod
Arable – Shepherd's-purse
The Hill – Creeping Willow, Lousewort

Harray – 8 species illustrations
Freshwater – Water Mint
Wild wood – Wild Angelica, Rosebay Willowherb, Red Campion
Arable – Wavy/Hairy Bitter-cress, Common Hemp-nettle
The Hill – Hard Fern, Cloudberry

Holm – 7 species illustrations
Shore – Cleavers
Freshwater – Water Forget-me-not
Sea cliff – Eyebright
Arable – Bush Vetch, Scentless Mayweed
Wild Wood – Wood Horsetail
The Hill – Deergrass

Hoy – Wild woods and dales; The high hill and stony tops + 16 species illustrations
Links – Lesser Burdock, Common Bird's-foot-trefoil
Freshwater – Marsh Pennywort
Sea cliffs – Roseroot
The Hill – Great Sundew, Stone Bramble, Yellow Saxifrage, Prostrate Juniper
High Hill – Bearberry, Purple Saxifrage, Mountain Avens, Trailing Azalea, Dwarf Cornel, Common Cow-wheat, Alpine Saw-wort, Mountain Sorrel

Kirkwall – 4 species illustrations
Salt marsh – Scurvygrass
Arable – Field Speedwell, Groundsel
Plantations – Ground-ivy

North Ronaldsay – Lowland freshwater – lochs, burns, marshes and wet grasslands + 4 species illustrations
Shore – Silverweed
Arable – Sweet Cicely, Germander Speedwell, Dandelion

Orphir – 9 species illustrations
Salt marsh – Saltmarsh Rush, Common Saltmarsh-grass, Glasswort
Sea Cliff – Alpine Meadow-rue
Arable – Field Forget-me-not
Plantations – Lesser Celandine,
Wild Wood – Great Wood-rush, Bracken
The Hill – Marsh Violet

Papa Westray – 5 species illustrations
Shore – Perennial Sow-thistle
Links – Field Gentian
Freshwater – Marsh Ragwort, Marsh Arrowgrass
Sea cliffs – Autumnal Hawkbit

Rendall – 8 species illustrations
Salt marsh – Sea Arrowgrass
Freshwater – Butterbur, Early Marsh-orchid
Arable – Common Mouse-ear
Wild Wood – Foxglove, Water Avens
The Hill – Fir Clubmoss, Sphagnum

Rousay – The peat hill – heaths and blanket bogs
    + 10 species illustrations
Links – Common Ragwort
Freshwater – Bog Pimpernel
Sea cliff – Mountain Everlasting, Crowberry
Plantations – Salmonberry, Snowdrop
Wild Wood – Wild Rose
The Hill – Heath Speedwell, Round-leaved Wintergreen
The High Hill – Alpine Bearberry

St Andrews – 7 species illustrations
Salt marsh – Greater Sea-spurrey
Freshwater – Lady's Smock, Marsh Thistle
Sea cliff – Common Dog-violet
Arable – Spear Thistle
The Hill – Cross-leaved Heath, Common Cottongrass

St Ola – 7 species illustrations
Links – White Clover
Freshwater – Meadowsweet, Brooklime, Water-cress
Sea cliff – Glaucous Sedge
Wild wood – Wood Sage
The Hill – Green-ribbed Sedge

Sanday – Sand and shingle shores + 7 species illustrations
Salt marsh – Sea Milkwort
Links – Wild Pansy
Freshwater – Yellow Iris
Arable – Colt's-foot, Greater Plantain, Common Chickweed
The Hill – Bell Heather

Sandwick – 8 species illustrations
Shore – Sea Mayweed
Links – Marram
Freshwater – Common Marsh-bedstraw, Marsh Cinquefoil

Sea cliffs – Scottish Primrose
Arable – Sun Spurge, Pineappleweed
The Hill – Bog Asphodel

Shapinsay – 5 species illustrations
Freshwater – Greater Bird's-foot-trefoil
Sea Cliff – Wild Thyme
Plantations – Pink Purslane, Daffodil
The Hill – Ling

South Ronaldsay – Salt marshes + 9 species illustrations
Shore – Oysterplant
Links – Mouse-ear Hawkweed, Sea Bindweed, Lesser Meadow-rue
Sea cliffs – Scots Lovage
Arable – Creeping Buttercup, Smooth Sow-thistle, Sweet Rocket
Wild wood – Honeysuckle

Stenness – 9 species illustrations
Salt marsh – Lesser Sea-spurrey
Freshwater – Monkeyflowers, Great Willowherb
Arable – Field Pansy, Daisy, Tansy, Cow Parsley
Wild wood – Blaeberry
The Hill – Fairy Flax

Stromness – 8 species illustrations
Links – Red Clover
Freshwater – Water Horsetail, Marsh Horsetail
Arable – Ribwort Plantain
Wild Wood – Broad Buckler-fern
The Hill – Lesser Twayblade, Marsh Lousewort, Butterwort

Stronsay – Sea cliffs, coastal grasslands and coastal heaths
  + 4 species illustrations
Shore – Orache
Links – Bulbous Buttercup
Freshwater – Northern Marsh-orchid
Sea cliffs – Devil's-bit Scabious

Swona – 1 species illustration
Freshwater – Ragged Robin

Westray – 10 species illustrations
Shore – Curled Dock
Salt marsh – Annual Sea-blite
Links – Yarrow, Bugloss
Freshwater – Tufted Forget-me-not, Brackish Water-crowfoot
Sea cliffs – Buck's-horn Plantain
Arable – Hybrid Woundwort
The Hill – Heath Bedstraw
The High Hill – Moss Campion

Wyre – 5 species illustrations
Freshwater – Marsh Cudweed
Sea cliffs – Sea Ivory
Arable – Meadow Vetchling, Corn Spurrey
The Hill – Heath Rush

Habitats and their wildflowers

Sand and shingle shores

This habitat section relates to the land that adjoins the sea. More specifically it focuses on the beach, the expanse that lies between the high water mark and the cliff face, dune line or field line. Orkney's coastline is long and diverse. Totalling almost 550 miles and amounting to 14% of Scotland's coastline, it ranges from the hard coasts where the full force of the North Atlantic waves meet with towering near vertical cliffs to sheltered, rocky, sandy and muddy soft coasts found in the more enclosed areas of Scapa Flow and the northern isles. There are many miles of hard coast composed of rocky flagstone sculpted by the waves where conditions are not wholly suitable for flowering plants. By comparison, sand and shingle beaches are far less numerous, more diverse and richer in plant life. These beaches include some of the most popular and frequently visited in Orkney. This narrow, salt-influenced ribbon of land is subject to changing, and at times high, degrees of dynamic disturbance from the sea. This zone does not yield large numbers of wildflower species; the section refers to ten of them, six of which – Oysterplant, Sea Rocket, Sea Campion, Orache, Sea Sandwort, Sea Mayweed –are pretty much beach specialists. The remaining four, Cleavers, Curled Dock,

Bay of Wheevi, Sanday with Start Point Lighthouse and Buryan Broch

Silverweed and Perennial Sow-thistle are all abundant especially along the backshore, an area that can be influenced strongly by the adjacent land use. Also they are all well-known colonisers and can be found further inland on ground disturbed by agents other than the sea.

All of the inhabited islands and all of the parishes (with the obvious exception of landlocked Harray) have sand and shingle beaches (soft coasts) on which most of the illustrated plants can be found. The one major exception is Oysterplant which though abundant in certain localities, has a very restricted distribution within the county.

1. Oysterplant at Eastside, South Ronaldsay

1) Oysterplant (*Mertensia maritima*   Borage family
Sea lungwort, Northern shorewort

Height to 50cm; flowers June to August. Local and occasional in Orkney (14/28); fairly easy to find.

This flawless perennial is a northern plant, Norway and Iceland being its citadels in Europe. In Britain it is found almost exclusively in Scotland on the west and north coasts and in the Northern Isles; in England it is virtually extinct. Orkney is undoubtedly the plant's stronghold and it would be no exaggeration to say that there are more plants here than anywhere else in the United Kingdom. It is as special to Orkney as the Scottish Primrose. However, within the county it has a restricted distribution and in recent years has disappeared from former sites most notably the Bay of Skaill in Sandwick and Birsay Bay but may still persist in low numbers on Westray. Nowadays it is most common on the soft coasts of Sanday, South Ronaldsay, Stronsay, Swona, Copinsay and at Newark Bay in Deerness. Plants may occur on beaches, both sandy and stony, where it thrives on surfaces disturbed by waves. It also flourishes at No 4 barrier where it grows along the A961 some 300 metres from the sea and a tyre's width from the tarmac – here wave action is simulated by the blade of an Orkney Islands Council snow plough as it clears the build up of sand after easterly gales. It has even been found growing on those unsightly spoil heaps of earth and rubble that appear all too frequently on Orkney's shores in the name of coastal defence or coastal dump.

Its rambling and leafy sprays radiate from the root like the spokes of a wheel. The leaves are oval, fleshy and grey-blue and its five-petalled

2. Sea Campion at Mar Wick Bay, Birsay

flowers are initially pink before turning a radiant blue. The seeds can survive prolonged immersion in salt water and its dispersion in sea currents enables the plant to colonise new but sometimes temporary sites; seeds have been known to travel at least 450km. Named because its leaves taste of oysters, its rarity should be a warning against collection.

2) **Sea Campion** (*Silene uniflora*) — Campion family

Dead man's bells, Dead man's hatties, Witches' thimbles

Height to 20cm; flowers May to July. Widespread and abundant in Orkney (25/28); easy to find.

Restricted to the coast and occurring from sea level drift line to cliff top grassland, this white-flowered perennial has waxy, oval leaves and an inflated calyx. It is a sprawling plant and likely to be found cascading over shingle or tumbling down near-vertical cliff faces, the latter habit resulting in two of its vernacular names *Dead man's bells* and *Dead man's hatties* – so named because of the inherent danger in attempting to gather a posy. It was never picked and never brought into the house possibly to discourage children from endangering themselves on the cliffs. Because of its ability to tolerate high levels of nutrient enrichment, white cushions of Sea Campion may be abundant in seabird colonies.

3) Curled Dock (*Rumex crispus*)   Dock family
Bullwan, Dillowan, Dowhan, Dockan, Tirso

Height to 100cm; flowers June to October. Widespread and abundant in Orkney (28/28); easy to find.

Docks are not high in the popularity stakes. This particular one though, possibly deserves a little bit more attention given that it tends to occur more often in natural habitats than some of its more unwelcome cousins. It is either an annual or short-lived perennial growing both in Orkney and Britain on disturbed pastures and waste ground; it does occur in a variety of coastal habitats and is abundant especially above the tideline on shingle beaches. Flowering between June and October, it is easily recognised by its spear-shaped leaves which have crisped and wavy edges. When seeding, its tall, tan-brown plumes create a colourful addition to the shoreline flora. It has uses too; eaten in North America by the Paiute, the roots were baked in ground pits; Loudon (1848) considered its bruised roots cured 'the itch'.

4) Cleavers (*Galium aparine*)   Bedstraw family
Goosegrass, Blood-tongue, Cling rascal, Grip-grass, Stickleback, Sticky Willie

Sprawling to 100cm; flowers May to September. Widespread and abundant in Orkney (27/28); fairly easy to find.

In Orkney it is normally confined to waste ground and to the shore, more especially higher up the beach where it crawls over the pebbles, sand and other plants. Its most conspicuous feature is its 'sticky' stems – the 'stickiness' due to the backward-pointing prickles found on the stem, leaves and round fruits which cleaves the plant, in its entirety, to the passer-by – hence Cleavers. The inconspicuous flowers are greenish-white and the linear leaves are set in a whorl.

3. Curled Dock at Rapness pier, Westray

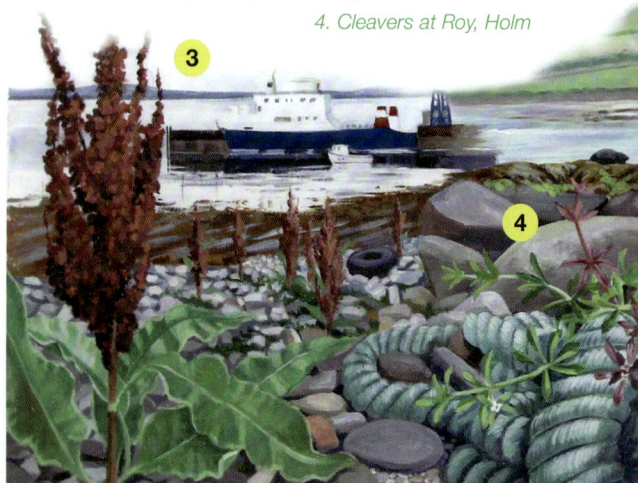

4. Cleavers at Roy, Holm

Historically Cleavers has had many uses; the leaves and stems have been employed to strain milk and a really strong solution can curdle milk. The fruits can be roasted and infused in water and it has long been utilised as an herbal for piles, skin diseases, scurvy and ulcers. Another widespread name is *Goosegrass* – both adult geese and goslings can be fed on chopped plants. It is also a plant of childhood – we can all remember covering each other's clothing with *Sticky Willie* but how many of us engaged in the game known as Bloody Tongues in which tongues that were not quick enough were caught (and cut!) by *Sticky Willie*?

5) **Sea Rocket** (*Cakile maritima*)   Cabbage family
Strandby

Height to 40cm; flowers June to October. Local and frequent in Orkney (13/28); fairly easy to find.

This is a sweetly scented annual with fleshy and untidy sprawling stems, succulent, shiny, toothed and hairless leaves and four-petalled flowers of mauve, pink or sometimes white. The water in its cells helps to dilute the salt, with which it comes into contact, either from sea spray, or even inundation on a high spring tide. In Orkney it occasionally occurs in the fore dunes and on shingle but it is most common and most likely to be found on sandy beaches where it is frequently seen along the nutrient-rich, winter-storm tideline – the Orkney name, *Strandby*, aptly describes this preference. The flowers, especially in late summer, are often a first source of nectar for migrating butterflies as they make landfall in the county and its seeds, which are resistant to salt water, are dispersed by tides.

5. Sea Rocket at Sandside Bay, Deerness

6. Sea Mayweed at the Noust of Bigging, Sandwick

6) Sea Mayweed (*Tripleurospermum maritimum*)　　　Daisy family

Height to 50cm; flowers July to September. Widespread and abundant in Orkney (28/28); easy to find.

In Orkney, the *'white daisy of the shore'* can be found in a variety of coastal habitats including drift lines of open sand and shingle and on cliff tops. With its white-rayed flower-heads, yellow discs and fine pointed thread-like leaves, its appearance is very similar to a near relative the Scentless Mayweed (page 110). However there are fine differences: Scentless Mayweed is much more likely to be found inland, is less persistent and has leaves which feel softer. It is quite probable that the species hybridise especially where agricultural land meets the coast.

7) Perennial Sow-thistle (*Sonchus arvensis*)　　　Daisy family

Dog thistle - Milkweed, Milky dickle, Hare's lettuce, Hare's house, Hare's palace, Rabbit's meat, Rabbit's victuals

Height to 120cm; flowers July to October. Widespread and abundant in Orkney (23/28); easy to find.

Of the three Sow-thistles that occur in Orkney, this is the only perennial. It is a tall and showy Dandelion-like plant, often reaching well over a metre in height, and can usually be found in amongst the back-shore vegetation adjacent to cultivated land. Its creeping roots spread easily

8. Silverweed at South Bay, North Ronaldsay

7. Perennial Sow-thistle at South Wick, Papa Westray

through loose sand and shingle and its shiny green leaves boast fine spines which when cut, exude a milky juice. Reverend George Low (18th Century) referred to this plant as the *Tree sow-thistle*. Sows knew by natural instinct that the plant would increase the flow of their milk when they had farrowed but older legend connects the plant with the hare and it was known as *Hare's house* or *Hare's palace*.

8) Silverweed (*Potentilla anserina*)   Rose family

Moors, **Moorek** - *Bread and cheese, Bread and butter, Silver feather, Midsummer silver*

Height to 15cm; flowers June to August. Widespread and abundant in Orkney (27/28); easy to find.

Potentilla – 'little powerful one' – with its cheery five yellow petals and silver-green fern-like leaves can be found in a variety of habitats including shorelines, links, open grassy swards, rough ground and roadsides. It can be invasive, the long, thread-like, underground stolons break easily and disturbed ground such as farm gateways can be commandeered.

It is a perennial and a plant whose importance as a food source over the centuries and in different cultures should not be underestimated. The parsnip-flavoured roots can be boiled, roasted, eaten raw or ground into meal for bread and porridge. Pollen records indicate that it has been available to the earliest settlers throughout the northern hemisphere; in North America, Silverweed was cultivated in raised beds along the shore while in Gaelic culture it was known as one of the 'seven breads of the Gael'. In North Uist it was claimed that a man could sustain himself on Silverweed from a square of ground his own length. It was cultivated for its root long before the arrival of the potato and was once an important source of carbohydrate in coastal Scotland and upland Britain particularly when other foods were in short supply. In Somerset it is known as *Bread and cheese* or *Bread and butter*. The plant contains tannin, is strongly astringent and has the reputation of being an herbal cure-all used in the treatment of ulcers, stones, wounds of 'the privy parts', indigestion and the removal of freckles. Even the leaves have had their use; inserted in shoes, they kept feet cool. It is the leaves, silver with a felting of long fine hair, which give the plant its common name. The reference to 'silver' occurs in many parts of UK: in Oxfordshire it is known as *Silver feather* while in Ireland it is *Midsummer silver*.

9) *Oraches* (Atriplex spp.) Goosefoot family

Height to 70cm; flowers July to September. Widespread and abundant in Orkney (20/28); easy to find.

Oraches are quite the commonest of the seashore plants but specific identification may involve a fair degree of head scratching. Five different species occur on Orkney's shores: Spear-leaved (*A. prostrata*), Babington's (*A. glabriuscula*), Grass-leaved (*A. littoralis*), Common (*A. patula*) and Frosted (*A. laciniata*). They are all annuals and have

9. Orache at the Piers, Whitehall, Stronsay

the most inconspicuous of flowers. Far more obvious are the fleshy, triangular and greyish-green leaves which often display a red tinge. Archaeological evidence has shown that the plant has been part of the Scottish diet since prehistoric times; it can be cooked as you would spinach i.e. lightly boiled and buttered. Spear-leaved Orache is possibly the most abundant of the group and is found on sand and shingle beaches usually quite close to the strand line. Babington's Orache is also frequently met with; it has subtle differences including diamond-shaped bracteoles and is usually procumbent.

10) Sea Sandwort (*Honckenya peploides*)　　　　　Campion family
Sea chickweed

Height to 10cm; flowers May to August. Widespread and frequent in Orkney (16/28); fairly easy to find.

The most obvious feature of this fairly common seashore perennial is the form of its waxy, yellow-green, oval leaves which in sequences of four, sit on top of each other in geometric and hypnotic synchronicity. Looked at from above, the plants have a cacti-like appearance. Its star-shaped five-petalled white flowers are resoundingly inconspicuous – in marked contrast to the fat and round seed capsules which are such a feature in late summer as they turn from green to black. En masse the plants stretch like a thick and verdant carpet helping to bind the mobile sand as beach turns into dune. One of Orkney's early botanists, the venerable George Low, named this plant *Sea chickweed*.

10. Sea Sandwort at Bight of Lindy, Evie

Salt marshes

Salt marsh occurs on lowland grassland sites that are periodically flooded by the sea. This highly specialised habitat occurs on low energy coasts and the amount and frequency of covering by salt water determines which plants will be present. One of the most obvious features of salt marshes is the meandering creeks which intersect to allow water to drain in and out. For plants to survive and prosper they must be tolerant of wet and salty soils.

In Orkney, salt marshes are absent from the high energy coasts of South Ronaldsay, Hoy, Mainland, Rousay, Westray and North Ronaldsay. In the main this specialised habitat can be found around the sheltered bays and beaches of Scapa Flow, Sanday and on the northeast coast of Mainland between Gorseness in Rendall and Deerness.

The largest salt marshes with the greatest plant diversity include the Ouse in Firth, Swarsquoy and the Bay of Suckquoy in St Andrews, Waulkmill in Orphir, Cumminess in Stenness, the Ouse in Veantrow Bay on Shapinsay and the Sanday sites of Tor Ness and Quivals Creek, Cata Sand and Little Sea. All these sites are greater than 2.5 hectares.

Oyce of Herston, Widewall Bay, South Ronaldsay with Herston Chapel

Additionally, along the soft Orkney shores many smaller areas of salt marsh occur, some of them tiny, as for example along the shallow edges of the Peedie Sea in Kirkwall. Here, as is the case for many other Orkney sites, small grassland areas – often no bigger than a doormat– support typical salt marsh plants such as Scurvygrass and Sea Plantain.

This zone does not yield large numbers of wildflower species. The section refers to ten of them, only one of which, Glasswort, is restricted exclusively to salt marsh. The other eight species, Scurvygrass, Sea Plantain, Sea Arrowgrass, Annual Sea-blite, Saltmarsh Rush, Sea Milkwort, Sea Aster, Greater Sea-spurrey and Lesser Sea-spurrey, may be found also on cliff tops and cliff faces, where, in the latter, the drenching of sea spray mimics the tidal flooding and produces a vertical salt marsh.

1. Scurvygrass at the Peedie Sea, Kirkwall

1) Scurvygrass (*Cochlearia officinalis*)   Cabbage family

Height to 25cm; flowers April to July. Widespread and abundant in Orkney (28/28); easy to find.

An early bloomer, this perennial herb can be found in Orkney on salt marsh, sea cliffs, rocky shores and cliff top turf – in fact almost anywhere influenced by salt spray. Try looking for this plant away from the sea – it can be seen in full flower growing at the base of a wall near the Co-op on Pickaquoy Road, Kirkwall and can be found in the heart of the county, as far from the sea as is possible in Orkney. It can also be found growing on mountains in Scotland and northern England – on Ben Lawers in Perthshire it grows at 1155m. Recently it has become a roadside colonist along salted roads; in April and May the verges of the Caithness section of the A9 are parallel ribbons of white. With its shiny and glossy, deep green, kidney to heart-shaped leaves it is a very conspicuous plant and becomes even more obvious in seabird colonies where nutrient enrichment results in much larger leaves and plants. Less conspicuous than the leaves are the honey-scented flowers which range from the standard white to a delicate shade of violet. It is obvious that in Orkney there is a great variation in size, petal colour and leaf shape giving rise to many unconfirmed records of the subspecies known as *scotica*.

The plant has high vitamin C content and its antiscorbutic properties are widely known. In Faroe the leaves were employed in the treatment of nutritional disorders and in coastal England it was used as a folk remedy to counter scurvy long before the voyages of the 16th Century. In the mid-17th Century there was a fashion for a morning drink of Scurvygrass and it was commonly grown in the physic corner of

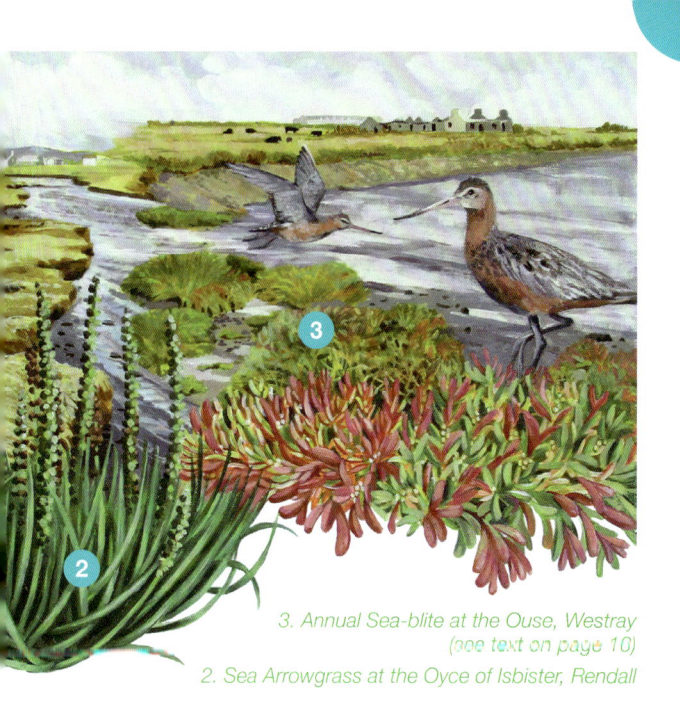

3. Annual Sea-blite at the Ouse, Westray
(see text on page 10)
2. Sea Arrowgrass at the Oyce of Isbister, Rendall

the garden. Writing of his Shetland experiences in the 18th Century Brand states 'They (the Shetlanders) have much Scurvygrass: God so ordering it in his wise Providence…that seeing the scurvy is the common disease of the country, they should have the remedy at hand'.

2) Sea Arrowgrass (*Triglochin maritimum*)   Arrowgrass family

Height to 40cm; flowers June to September. Widespread and abundant in Orkney (22/28); fairly easy to find.

There is something of a similarity between this species and the previous one, Sea Plantain. Both have an upright attitude and both, when mature have similar large, cylindrical, green and fleshy leaves. Generally the Sea Arrowgrass is taller. However, in Orkney, whereas Sea Plantain can be found in many different salt-influenced habitats, Sea Arrowgrass is much more particular and is virtually confined to the less-dynamic shore where big green clumps can often be found growing just above the high water mark. It is also very similar to Marsh Arrowgrass (page 58), a plant that may also be found on salt marsh but is more likely to be found in Orkney's wetlands. Sea Arrowgrass has unfurrowed leaves and oblong fruits, Marsh Arrowgrass has deeply furrowed leaves and arrow-shaped fruits.

In Britain, besides growing on salt marshes, Sea Arrowgrass may also be found on cliff edges that are doused with sea spray, along the banks of tidal rivers and inland over salt deposits, such as those in Cheshire. As with other halophytes (salt-loving plants), it may be found inland along salt-treated roads.

3) Annual Sea-blite (*Suaeda maritima*)   Goosefoot family

Height to 15cm; flowers July to September. Local and rare in Orkney (6/28); hard to find.

In Orkney, this annual can be found normally in the upper zone of very sheltered shores below the high water mark of spring tides. It is intolerant of wave action and grows close to the ground on a substrate mix of settled stones and mud. With half-cylindrical fleshy leaves of pink, purple, brown and green it may initially be mistaken for a seaweed. The flowers, in small clusters, are white and quite inconspicuous. Within the county it has been located in the splash zone on cliff tops while elsewhere in Britain it occurs on shell and shingle banks and in thinly vegetated brackish areas behind sea walls.

(see illustration on page 15)

4) Sea Plantain (*Plantago maritima*)   Plantain family

Height to 30cm; flowers June to August. Widespread and abundant in Orkney (26/28); easy to find.

The late Elaine Bullard, doyenne of Orkney botany, considered this perennial to have the most widespread distribution of any plant in the county. Generally it is found on coastal turf but it frequently grows well away from the coast and has been located in every parish. Its habitat preferences in Britain are broad and include salt marsh, coastal turf, rocks, cliff, coastal heath, shingle beaches, inland salt marshes and mountains. More recently, as with other salt-loving plants, it has taken to colonising inland road verges. It is a plant that can vary in size considerably; tiny examples, no bigger than a thumb nail can be found close to the sea where conditions are most severe. Elsewhere in more sheltered locations, plants can attain almost 30cm. The leaves are fleshy and quite cylindrical while the long flowering spikes support large-stamened greenish flowers. In Orkney, it was believed that sheep that grazed on Sea Plantain would fatten more quickly and have improved quality of meat.

5) Common Saltmarsh-grass (*Puccinellia maritima*)   Grass family

Height to 40cm; flowers June and July. Widespread and frequent in Orkney (19/28); fairly easy to find.

On Orkney's salt marshes this distinctive and vigorous grass can be dominant over large areas in the lower and middle parts of the marsh and in pans and depressions in the upper marsh. With shallow-rooted long runners it colonises bare coastal mud rapidly and it is only the drainage gullies which hinder the formation of a continuous sward. As the tides advance and recede, its leaves and stems act as filters which collect silt and debris, thus helping to raise the level of the marsh. As with other halophytes it has been observed inland as a colonist by salt-treated roads.

6) Saltmarsh Rush (*Juncus gerardii*)   Rush family

Height to 40cm; flowers June to July. Widespread and abundant in Orkney (24/28); easy to find.

This is the rush that you are most likely to find close to the sea. It forms clumps which can cluster and develop into fairly dense swathes on the higher parts of salt marshes or in turf above the high water mark. It may also be found around rock pools and even in cliff top turf if it receives liberal douches of salt spray. The flowers are dark brown, the stems are three-angled and stiffly erect and the dull green leaves are channelled and rounded.

4. Sea Plantain at Sandisand, Deerness

5. Common Saltmarsh-grass at Mill Burn, Waulkmill, Orphir

6. Saltmarsh Rush at Mill Burn, Waulkmill, Orphir

7. Sea Milkwort at Stove, Sanday

8. Lesser Sea-spurrey at Dead Sand, Stenness

7) Sea Milkwort (*Glaux maritima*)　　　　　　　　Primrose family

Height to 20cm; flowers June to August. Widespread and abundant in Orkney (24/28); easy to find.

Look closely at this dainty perennial plant which is related to pimpernels and primroses. It has no true petals; its pink flowers consist of five pink sepals. Beneath the star-shaped flower-heads are fleshy, strap-shaped leaves in pairs. It can be found in dense colonies on salt marshes but may also be seen flourishing on rocky and shingle shores, cliff tops, spray-drenched rock – in fact anywhere where there is moist saline soil. It is widespread around Britain's coasts and in Orkney, like Sea Plantain, is known from every parish. Another similarity with that species is that while Sea Plantain was believed to help fatten sheep more quickly, Sea Milkwort was believed to increase the yield from a cow.

8) Lesser Sea-spurrey (*Spergularia marina*)　　　Campion family

Length to 20cm; flowers June to September. Local and occasional in Orkney (10/25); not easy to find.

The Lesser Sea-spurrey is an annual though smaller but equally as pretty as its relative above. There are other differences. Essentially the two species flourish in the same maritime habitats. However, it may be that the Lesser Sea-spurrey prefers less exposed locations

9. Greater Sea-spurrey at Grandag, St Andrews

evidenced possibly by its remarkable expansion of range along inland roads from Cornwall to Sutherland with concentrations around Inverness-shire, Scotland's central belt, northeast England, the north Midlands, East Anglia and southeast England. Its five-petalled flowers are always deep pink and are no longer than the sepals while later in the season its ripe seeds are without a winged border. Like the Greater Sea-spurrey the leaves are short, pointed and fleshy.

9) Greater Sea-spurrey (*Spergularia media*)   Campion family

Length to 30cm; flowers June to September. Local and frequent in Orkney (15/28); fairly easy to find.

In Orkney, this pretty perennial appears to be more common than its slightly smaller and brighter annual relative, Lesser Sea-spurrey. The natural habitat for the Greater Sea-spurrey is strictly maritime and in the county it can be located not only on salt marshes but also on shingle strandlines and occasionally on cliffs and cliff tops. It is noted generally as occurring at lower elevations on salt marshes than Lesser Sea-spurrey. In Britain since 1970 it has been recorded on a few occasions as a colonist on roads treated in winter with salt. The five-petalled flowers are white or pink (paler than those of Lesser Sea-spurrey) and usually longer than the sepals; the leaves are short, pointed and fleshy. The ripe seeds show an obvious clear winged border unlike those of Lesser Sea-spurrey which are wingless.

10) Sea Aster (*Aster tripolium*)   Daisy family

Blue daisy, Summer's farewell

Height to 50cm; flowers July to September. Local and occasional in Orkney (6/28); not easy to find.

This, the '*blue daisy of the saltings*', is a short-lived perennial plant that is not confined solely to salt marshes; in Orkney it is known also from cliff locations, both the tops and the faces. However, there must be many salt spray drenched localities which remain out of sight and whose plants remain anonymous. As with other true salt marsh plants, inland salt-treated roads on mainland Britain have provided the right conditions for the Sea Aster to spread. It is very similar to the familiar garden species, Michaelmas Daisy. Both species have blue-rayed florets surrounding yellow discs but one crucial difference is that the Sea Aster, like many salt-tolerant plants, has fleshy spear-shaped leaves, while the landlubber Michaelmas Daisy has thin, fleshless leaves. Sea Asters thrive by the sea, Michaelmas Daisies are happiest away from it. In Elizabethan times, the Sea Aster was a popular garden plant whose roots helped heal wounds.

11) *Glassworts (*Salicornia* agg.)   Goosefoot family

Height to 5cm; flowers in August. Local and occasional in Orkney (7/28); hard to find.

These strange looking annual plants are marine succulents composed of fleshy segments. Their leaves are fused in opposite pairs to a brittle and jointed 'glass-like' stem and the plant's white flowers are

10. Sea Aster at the Ouse, Firth

the tiniest of tiny. There are many different species of Glasswort and botanists acknowledge that this genus, which can be found on a variety of coastal habitats including salt marsh, mud, sand and even in fields behind sea walls, is 'difficult'. *The Atlas of the British Flora* describes seven species, three of which are considered to be in Orkney – **Purple Glasswort** (*S. ramosissima*), **Common Glasswort** (*S. europaea*) and **Shiny Glasswort** (*S. nitens*). Within the county the Glassworts are confined to a few channels in a few salt marshes on Hoy, Sanday and in Orphir, St Andrews and Deerness. It may be that once they were more abundant and widespread but they are fragile species and susceptible to pollution and drainage.

It is a versatile plant and important both in the kitchen and in industry. An alternative name is Samphire (from *herbe de Saint-Pierre*) and traditionally it has been harvested throughout the world for human consumption. In Scotland, gathering for both commercial and domestic use has occurred around the Dornoch Firth while in eastern England the plant is frequently seen on fishmonger's slabs. Industrially the ashes of Glasswort (and kelp) were long used as a source of soda ash in glassmaking and soap making but with the advent of new technologies, its use declined in the 19th Century. However it has witnessed resurgence in the modern world with experimental fields in Saudi Arabia, Mexico and Eritrea aimed at the production of biodiesel and animal feedstuff on coastal land where conventional crops cannot be grown.

11. Glasswort at Toyness, Orphir

Dunes, links and dry grasslands

Orkney's sandy coasts are characterised by dune landscapes which protect the more mature and stable links and dry grasslands that have developed in the lee of the dunes. Sandy beaches are not numerous and account for approximately ten per cent of the county's coastline; indeed they are absent from some islands and parishes and rare around the more sheltered waters. Many of Orkney's most extensive sand systems are found around the perimeter of the county, where the coastal processes are more vigorous and energetic and there are numerous notable examples on the North Isles.

For centuries the sand that forms Orkney's dunes and links has been extracted in small volumes for local use. It is a valuable commodity and prized by both the agricultural and construction industries. Being rich in shell fragments and consequently having a high content of calcium, it is ideal for agricultural use as a substitute for imported lime. Additionally, as concrete has replaced stone as the prevailing building material, Orkney's sand resources have been targeted to supply sufficient to meet the current demands.

North Links, Burray with the Bu and Bu Sand

Undisturbed and intact dunes and links have an interesting and varied flora; they are also exceedingly rare. Dunes and links are extremely fragile environments and are very susceptible to inappropriate activities. Extraction of course takes its toll but damage can be caused by overgrazing and unsympathetic recreational activities. The fine sward which binds the sand together is easily damaged and once violated will degenerate quickly as wind-blow and infestation by coarse and opportunistic plants takes place.

This section refers to 26 species, and ranges from the all-important 'sand-binders' Marram, Lyme Grass and Sand Sedge that exist closest to the sea, via the more mature links and their stabilising plants such as Yarrow, Wild Pansy and Lady's Bedstraw to the permanent and cultivated 'machair-like' dry grasslands. Most of the plants within this chapter can be found at any of these sandy sites throughout the county but a few such as Lesser Meadow-rue, Sea Bindweed, Curved Sedge and Cowslip have a much more restricted distribution. The section also includes those opportunistic plants that readily invade areas of bare sand – plants such as Common Ragwort and Lesser Burdock.

1) Wild Pansy (*Viola tricolor*) Violet family

Heartsease, Kiss-me, Stepmothers, Herbe of the Trinity, Trinity violet, Three-faces-under-a-hood

Height to 10cm; flowers April to September. Widespread and frequent in Orkney (17/28); fairly easy to find.

In Orkney carpets of Wild Pansies can decorate mature and stable links such as those found in Sanday and Westray. Elsewhere this annual or perennial can be equally prolific on dry, cultivated and sandy soil. The flowering heads are usually purple with a central yellow patch but may be yellow with purple veins and the fairly inconspicuous leaves are sharply pointed. There can be few flowers that generate more affection than Pansies and it is easy to conjure human faces from the colours and open arrangements of the petals. Consequently it is a plant with numerous names and associations especially of love. In Shakespeare's *A Midsummer Night's Dream* Oberon squeezes the juice of *Viola tricolor* into Titania's eyes so that she falls in love with Bottom. We see also two side petals kissing within a hood formed by the upper and lower petals and it is from this picture that perhaps the name *Heartsease* derives – a kiss to give ease of the heart. Another look reveals three faces, the lower a girl with suitors at her side. The name *Stepmothers* is explained by the large rich lower petal (the Stepmother), above which are the two side petals (her own children), and the two upper, half-hidden petals (the neglected step-children). It was also the *'Herbe of the Trinity'* – three faces in a hood. See Field Pansy (page 96).

2) Sand Sedge (*Carex arenaria*) Sedge family
Metticks, Mettos

Height to 10cm; flowers June to July. Local and frequent in Orkney (14/28); fairly easy to find.

1. Wild Pansy at Tres Ness, Sanday
2. Sand Sedge at Sandside Bay, Graemsay
3. Lady's Bedstraw at Dingieshowie, Deerness

With its long and evenly-spaced lines of star-shaped clusters of leaves creeping across open sandy areas in far-reaching rows, Sand Sedge is one of the most recognisable of the Sedge family. Like Marram and Lyme Grass, it is a valuable plant in binding loose sand and preventing erosion; indeed in some fragile sandy areas this perennial is specifically planted for that purpose. The plant's value as a bygone herbal remedy for bronchitis, catarrh, arthritis and urinary problems and consequently its gathering may have exacerbated erosion in some parts of Britain, a similarity it shares with the large-scale removal of Marram for thatching and basketry in past centuries. In some parts of the Hebrides, the roots were woven into ropes to tether cattle and sheep.

3) Lady's Bedstraw (*Galium verum*)   Bedstraw family
Rennet plant, Cheese rening

Height to 50cm; flowers June to August. Widespread and frequent in Orkney (25/28); easy to find.

Cushions and pillows of Lady's Bedstraw can be found sprawling across Orkney's dunes and links – with their bunches of tiny golden-yellow flowers, dark green stems and leaves, they typify a sunny summer's day. This perennial herb is not only of great importance in folklore but also of great importance culturally. In the Scottish Highlands and Islands it was known as the *Rennet plant* or *Cheese rening* and used to curdle milk for cheese-making. It was also sought after as a source of red dye, the only native plant, other than lichens, from which red could be obtained. During the 16th and 17th Centuries great quantities were harvested in the Hebrides resulting in the destabilisation of whole dune systems. Concerned landlords prohibited collection, but such was the plant's worth that illegal gathering still continued.

Lady's Bedstraw has always been associated with the birth of Jesus. According to Medieval legend, the Virgin Mary lay on a bed of bracken and bedstraw. The bracken refused to acknowledge the arrival of the child and lost its flower; the bedstraw welcomed the child and golden-yellow flowers blossomed. Throughout northern Europe it has been gathered for bedding; its qualities include elasticity, softness, astringency (valuable in countering fleas) and smelling of honey when fresh and of hay when dry – it is rich in coumarin. It also coagulates blood and was a common styptic.

4) Marram (*Ammophila arenaria*) — Grass family

Height to 120cm; flowers July to August. Local and occasional in Orkney (10/28); fairly easy to find.

In Britain, Marram is more widespread and abundant than Lyme-grass. In Orkney the situation is reversed and Marram is considered to be declining as its habitat is lost due to a combination of activities including sand extraction, agricultural improvement and over-wintering of livestock. While Lyme-grass appears to prefer young dunes, Marram is concentrated on the old. With narrower and needle-like leaves and smaller all round flowering spikes, it is a finer and more delicate grass than its dune cousin.

In previous centuries it has been much harvested throughout Britain. During the 19th Century there was a thriving Marram weaving industry based along the southwest coast of Anglesey. Each family had its own dune and items such as mats for haystacks, cucumber frames, nets, cordage and even shoes were produced for distribution throughout Wales. In the Hebrides it was important for thatching roofs – the grass was cut in the autumn when it was at its strongest and laid in two distinct layers over a roof cover of Yellow Iris leaves. Additionally it was used for basketry and in particular for a certain style of coiled grain basket known in Gaelic as a *ciosan* and its versatility included the manufacture of horses' collars, cushions for ponies, pack saddles, hats and bags. Even its roots have been utilised: in the Hebrides as floor-scrubbers and in Orkney woven into loops for hanging caesies (baskets) over the backs of ponies. However, the wholesale removal of links plants created and exacerbated erosion in many coastal areas; at Culbin estate in Moray in 1694, during a violent storm, the dunes gave way and farms and a mansion were buried in 30 metre drifts.

5) Lyme-grass (*Leymus arenarius*) — Grass family

Height to 150cm; flowers June to August. Widespread and frequent in Orkney (20/28); easy to find.

Both Lyme-grass and Marram are perennials and instrumental in the early formation of dunes and links. They are grasses whose network of long underground roots trap and bind loose wind-blown sand. Lyme-grass is often the first of the grasses to colonise the shifting sands and is usually to be found on the younger dunes. It is tall and robust and clothes the yellow dunes in a sweep of blue-grey. In summer and en masse it appears as a swathe of pale wheat-like flower-heads moving and flowing with the wind. The leaves, broader than those of Marram, are flat and deeply-ribbed. It is also less strictly confined to dunes and links and occasionally is found growing in small, sandy deposits on shingle or rocky shores.

4. Marram at Bay of Skaill, Sandwick

5. Lyme Grass on Glims Holm

6. Grass of Parnassus at Doomy, Eday

6) Grass-of-Parnassus (*Parnassia palustris*)　　　　Saxifrage family

Height to 15cm; flowers July to October. Widespread and frequent in Orkney (23/28); fairly easy to find.

An alternative name, and thankfully one that is rarely used, *White buttercup*, scarcely does this perennial justice. Its flower has been described as 'stunningly beautiful, smelling faintly of honey' and the 16th Century Flemish botanist Mathias de l'Obel referred to it as 'the grass of the holy mountain of Apollo and the Muses'. It has dark green and shiny kidney-shaped leaves and glistening white five-petalled flowers which are delicately veined with green nectar guidelines. The seed capsules have more than a passing resemblance to an electric light bulb. In Orkney it occurs on all the main islands and in all parishes and can be found in many base-rich wet habitats; however it appears to have a particular preference for the damp patches to be found in links. It may be that there are two forms in Orkney: plants that occur in grassland and maritime heath are usually small and solitary, while those that occur in wetter conditions are generally larger and densely tufted. Historically, Grass-of-Parnassus has been used in the treatment of liver complaints and an infusion of leaves was considered to aid digestion.

7) Mouse-ear Hawkweed (*Pilosella officinarum*)　　　　Daisy family

Height to 15cm; flowers May to September. Local and occasional in Orkney (13/28); not easy to find.

As 'Dandelions' go, this perennial is surely one of the prettiest. Most of its relatives have gaudy and garish flower-heads of bright yellow. The

8. Cowslip at Aikerness, Evie

7. Mouse-ear Hawkweed at Sands of Wright, South Ronaldsay

disc of Mouse-ear Hawkweed is altogether more subtle – pale lemon-yellow flowers with individual petals streaked red on the undersides. The dark green oval leaves on creeping silvery stems are covered with white felt on the reverse while the top side is decorated with scattered and stiff, long white hairs. In Orkney, other than on links, it can be found in open dry areas often with rock nearby; however, it appears to be absent from suitable areas in the Outer North Isles. Medicinally it has been used as a treatment for jaundice and in folklore, hawks were believed to use the plant's juices to strengthen the eyesight of their young.

8) Cowslip (*Primula veris*) — Primrose family

Cowslop, Palsywort

Height to 25cm; flowers April to May. Local and rare in Orkney (4/28); hard to find.

Superficially it is similar to a Primrose (page 138), however whereas the Primrose is close to the ground, the Cowslip stands tall with upright, dark green and wrinkled leaves and many apricot-yellow flowers, spreading and drooping, on a slender pale stem. Its 'wild' distribution on links or grassy sea banks in Orkney is quite limited; small numbers of these splendid spring flowers only occur in Evie and on Egilsay, Sanday and Westray. Like other dune plants, it has suffered declines as its links habitats are removed or compromised by activities such as dumping and overwintering of livestock. However, near Davy's Brig in Firth, a roadside meadow was seeded with Cowslips in the mid-1990s – the modern spring result is hundreds of nodding heads adorning the verge of the A965.

It receives its common name from the perception that it springs up in meadows wherever a cow lifts its tail – hence *Cowslop*. Because of the plant's nodding manner it was considered to be a cure for palsy or paralysis and was blessed with the name *Palsywort*. The nodding flowers also suggest a bunch of keys – the badge of St Peter – and wherever St Peter dropped his keys, Cowslips grew.

9) Field Gentian (*Gentianella campestris*) Gentian family

Height to 15cm; flowers July to October. Local and occasional in Orkney (11/28); hard to find.

Gentians are named after Gentius, a king of Illyria who discovered that these herbs had tonic properties. The Field Gentian is an annual or biennial which can be found in a variety of open grassland habitats. It is rare in England and Ireland and many sites have been lost through overgrazing; however this delightful late flower becomes far more frequent in Scotland especially in the north. In Orkney it appears to have a preference for dry links that have been influenced by shell sand.

The tonic properties discovered by Gentius were utilised in Scotland

9. Field Gentian at Moclett, Papa Westray

to defeat kidney stones while in Shetland it was used to combat digestive disorders. Indeed the plant has a Shetland name, *Ridin girse*, and was fed to cows that appeared reluctant to come into season. Its stem springs vertically from a rosette of dark green oval leaves. The flowers are clustered in bell shapes with usually four blue-lilac petals. It is easily distinguished from its near-twin, the Autumn Gentian, by having two of the four calyx lobes (which sit just under the flower-head) larger than the other two.

10) **Autumn Gentian** (*Gentianella amarella*)   Gentian family
Felwort, Dead man's mittens

Height to 15cm; flowers late July to September. Local and occasional in Orkney (14/28); not easy to find.

Unsurprisingly it shares many similarities with its close relative the Field Gentian. Both are annuals or biennials and both prefer the well-drained soils that are found in links systems. Superficially both have comparable physical characteristics relating to their size and shape. However the Autumn Gentian that occurs in Orkney is *septentrionalis* which has off-white petals as opposed to the four blue-lilac petals of the Field Gentian. Closer observation reveals that the Autumn has four equal-sized calyx lobes (just under the flower-head). Its tonic properties were recognised in Orkney as a cure for jaundice while in Shetland it is known as *Dead man's mittens*, its 'half open buds are like livid fingernails protruding from the turf'. In Scotland it is less common than the Field Gentian.

10. Autumn Gentian at Nettle Knowe, Egilsay

11. Yellow Rattle at Maeness, Egilsay

11) Yellow Rattle (*Rhinanthus minor*)   Figwort family
Penny girse, Pennies, Gowk's siller, Money-in-the-purse

Height to 40cm; flowers May to August. Widespread and abundant in Orkney (25/28); easy to find.

In its autumn state, Yellow Rattle is more conspicuous than when flowering. As the summer vegetation dies down this annual's multitude of pale, papery and near-circular seed cases create conspicuous tracts among grasslands. In Shetland it is known as *Penny girse* or *Pennies*, while in southern Scotland its name is *Gowk's siller* (fool's silver). Like its cousins Red Bartsia and the Louseworts (page 176/177) it is partially parasitic on grasses and can be found, not solely in links, but in many semi-natural habitats with low fertility. It is an erect and slender annual with coarse-toothed leaves set in opposite pairs above which its lemon-yellow, two-lipped flowers flourish from leafy spikes. As the large seeds ripen they rattle within the case providing this widespread plant with many other descriptive appellations based on this late summer theme – *Money-in-the-purse* or *the-box* or *the-basket*. It is an extremely variable plant and has been divided into many subspecies which grow in distinctly different conditions. In Orkney three subspecies have been identified.

12) Common Twayblade (*Neottia ovata*)   Orchid family
Sweethearts, Adder's tongue

Height to 30cm; flowers June to September. Widespread and occasional in Orkney (16/28); not easy to find.

The plant is aptly named – the Common Twayblade has two blades

12. Common Twayblade at Sandside, Deerness

13. Yarrow at Grobust Links, Westray

– two large, ribbed, grey-green and opposite leaves. For the same reason it was christened *Sweethearts* in Somerset while the lip of the flower has given us its Wiltshire name *Adder's tongue*. Gerard in his *Herbal* of 1597 described each flower as 'resembling a gnat or a little gosling newly hatched' and recommended it as a healer of wounds. In Orkney it is often found in the older dunes but it can prosper also on some of the county's finer verges where this perennial's inconspicuous appearance may be its downfall when the mower approaches – it is an understated and subtle orchid lacking the colourful impact of Orkney's purple orchids. The tall flower spike may carry up to 20 inconspicuous yellowish-green flowers.

13) Yarrow (*Achillea millefolium*)   Daisy family

Meal-and-folly, Melancholy, Dog feenkle – *Meely follies, Tea flooer, Dog flooer*

Height to 30cm; flowers June to November. Widespread and abundant in Orkney (26/28); easy to find.

This, one of the most widespread plants in Orkney and Britain, is found in all types of grassland habitats ranging from lawns to montane communities but is especially common on coastal sand dunes and dry grasslands. In actuality it is only absent from areas where the soil is either lacking in nutrients, is strongly acidic or permanently waterlogged. The plant is strongly aromatic with feathery and delicate, fern-like green leaves. The flowering heads are a dense mass of white, or pink or purple flowers.

Yarrow is a plant steeped in tradition and folklore; it has long been regarded as a remedy for wounds made by iron weapons – hence its generic Latin name which refers to Achilles, the Greek hero of the Trojan War. Throughout Scotland this perennial has the reputation as an herbal cure-all. In Orkney it was common practice to prepare digestive tea from the plant's flowers and leaves; the resulting brew was supposed to help depression and melancholy. Elsewhere in Scotland it was used to staunch bleeding and dry up wounds or even to treat haemorrhaging in childbirth and, mixed with milk, to arrest nosebleeds. From other northern hemisphere cultures we find that it was chewed as a general cure-all in Faroe; in Wales it was pounded and applied to the body to destroy parasites and by burning the leaves and stems, the Okanagon-Colville Indians in North America waged war against mosquitoes. Yarrow contains sesquiterpenes which is the basis for commercially available insect repellents. It is also one of the herbs of St John and in much of Europe was hung up in houses to avert illness.

14) **Lesser Burdock** (*Arctium minus*) Daisy family
Sticky buttons

Height to 130cm; flowers June to October. Local and occasional in Orkney (8/28); hard to find.

In Britain this tall perennial can be found in a variety of habitats including woodlands, scrub, hedgerows, roadsides, railway banks, rough pastures, sand dunes and waste ground. It is well distributed around the country and flourishes everywhere except in the most mountainous and boggy areas. In Orkney it is anything but widespread and markedly less catholic in its habitat choice, limiting itself to links and sandy soils in a handful of localities. The leaves are dull green, large and rough while the flower-heads consist of clusters of thistle-like purple and red florets. The bracts below the florets are hooked and will cling to anything – it is not unknown for small birds to become entangled and trapped by them. The stems and leaves are edible but beware – Gerard's *Herbal* informs us that consuming it 'increases seed and stirs up lust'. The plant has diuretic properties and not only is it an astringent but also the root was used for the relief of kidney stones and the removal of skin blemishes.

In Queensferry, West Lothian, the Burry Man is completely clothed in Burdock burrs and walks the streets every second Friday in August and has done so since at least 1687. The meaning of this tradition remains clouded but he may represent the pagan spirit of vegetation and fertility, an obvious close relative of the Green Man. Another possibility is that he tours the town, and as he does so, the burrs collect evil spirits. This tradition now only survives in Queensferry but history records other Burry Men from the east coast fishing towns of Buckie and Fraserburgh.

15) Red Bartsia (*Odontites vernus*) — Figwort family
Cock's comb

Height to 20cm; flowers June to August. Widespread but infrequent in Orkney (22/28); not easy to find.

This erect, slender and slightly downy annual is partially parasitic on the roots of grasses – a characteristic it shares with its close relative, Yellow Rattle. The long leafy flower spikes have pinkish-purple flowers and the small, toothed leaves are pointed. The whole plant seems to be tinged with red. In general the plant prefers to grow on soils of low fertility and can often be found on trampled grasslands, tracks and even seashores. In Orkney, it appears to be more common in soils with a high sand content. Red Bartsia was once regarded as offering a cure for toothache and this helps explain the first part of its botanical name, *odons* being Greek for tooth.

14. Lesser Burdock at Melberry, Hoy

15. Red Bartsia at South Links, Burray

16) Common Ragwort (*Senecio jacobaea*)   Daisy family
Kemp, *Die flooer* – *Ragweed, Stinking Willie*

Height to 100cm; flowers June to October. Widespread and frequent in Orkney (19/28); easy to find.

This tall and colourful daisy has few admirers. Since it is toxic to cattle, horses, pigs and chickens, it has the dubious accolade of being a notifiable weed under the Control of Weeds Act (1959) and Ragwort Control Act (2003) and as such subject to statutory control. It can be prolific and is especially adept at colonising areas of open dry grassland which has been overgrazed or neglected. Degraded dunes are especially favoured, the more so if they are infested with rabbits. The bright yellow, daisy-like flower-heads form a loose starry umbel at the head of the stem and the dark green and vaguely glossy leaves are heavily dissected.

In parts of Europe, Common Ragwort is revered and known as the *Herba Sancti Jacobi* (herb of St James); his feast day is 25th July when the plant is in full bloom. There is no reverence in Scotland where it is known as *Stinking Willie* – this is a direct reference to William, Duke of Cumberland who is held responsible for introducing Common Ragwort into the country during the Culloden campaign, by way of seeds in horse fodder. In folklore, Common Ragwort was used for locomotion; Irish faeries and witches and those too of the Highlands and Islands, used these sticks of *Ragweed* to cross the narrow seas from island to island. It is all there in Robert Burns' poem *'Address to the Devil'*:

> Let Warlocks grim, an' wither'd Hags
> Tell how wi' you on ragweed nags,
> They skim the muirs an' dizzy crags
> Wi' wicked speed.

16. Common Ragwort at the Links of Scockness, Rousay
17. Red Clover at Warebeth, Stromness
18. Hardheads at No 4, Burray (see text on page 38)

Common Ragwort does have some merits though – not only is it a source of yellow dye and a rodenticide but also its stems were used in the Outer Hebrides for baskets. It is highly attractive for many insects; during both the day and the night a procession of 'mini-beasts' can be found intoxicated on its flower-heads.

17) **Red Clover** (*Trifolium pratense*) Pea family
Curly doddy – *Bee bread, Honeystalks, Sugar plums*

Height to 20cm; flowers May to September. Widespread and abundant in Orkney (26/28); easy to find.

With its round, purple-veined and pink-red flower-heads scattered across grassland, this perennial is one of our most familiar flowers. The oval leaves are in threes (hence *trifolium*) and are grey-green often with a white crescent-shaped spot across them. Red Clover grows on a wide range of grasslands and has a definite liking for the dry conditions associated with links. However, it does thrive on both old and new pastures throughout Orkney and Britain and is only absent from the most acidic soils. The flowers are great sources of nectar and bumblebees appear to prefer Red Clover to White Clover. Many of its local names reflect its sweetness; in Kent it is known as *Bee bread*, in Somerset as *Honeystalks* and in Buckinghamshire as *Sugar plums*. The Orkney name *Curly doddy* appears purely descriptive – a curly tuft. Red Clover has long been recognised as a valuable fodder crop and its worth spawned the expression 'living in clover'. In Northern England the leaves were used as a charm against witches.

18) Hardheads (*Centaurea nigra*) Daisy family
Knapweed, Bull thistle, Chimney sweep, Drumsticks, Ironweed

Height to 50cm; flowers June to September. Local and frequent in Orkney (13/28); not easy to find.

Most of its names are explained by the hard knobbly heads on which the purple florets are set and the similarity with thistles is obvious. It is tall and slender with roughly hairy stems and leaves which are spear-shaped. In size, shape and colour the flower-heads are thistle-like; however, unlike thistles it is prickle-free. In Orkney it is not everywhere but where it does occur, most usually on dry and sandy pastures, it is often abundant. It tends to be a late bloomer and since it prefers similar habitat requirements to the Great Yellow Bumblebee, the nectar-rich flowers are sought out by bees as the first cold airs of autumn touch the county. As a vulnerary it has been used for wounds, ruptures, bruises, sores, scab and sore throats and its juice has been used for ink and to dye linen bright blue. As with a few other plants, the heads have been used to foretell the future of love. Having been picked, girls place the florets inside their blouse; after an hour they look at it again hoping that the florets will have blossomed as a sign that love will come their way. (see illustration on page 37)

19) White Clover (*Trifolium repens*) Pea family
Smero, **Smuiro**, **Kippacks** – *Dutch clover*

Height to 20cm; flowers May to September. Widespread and abundant in Orkney (27/28); easy to find.

There is hardly an area in Britain where this perennial does not grow. If anything it is more abundant and widespread in Britain and Orkney

19. White Clover at Scapa, St Ola

than its sibling Red Clover and it is only the wettest and most acidic ground on which it does not occur. Just like its sibling, it appears to prefer the drier conditions afforded by dry grasslands and links but is often found in shorter turf and is clearly scarcer in taller grasslands. However, its success as a fodder crop is based on its ability to tolerate a wide range of situations which it does so with ease. Wherever it does grow, it creates a colourful and sweet-smelling patchwork attractive to grazing animals and insects, especially hive bees. The globular heads are white and the leaves, often with a white spot, are rounder than those of Red Clover. The White Clover features on the badge of Clan Sinclair and in the ancient Welsh romances of *The Mabinogion*, the goddess Olwen, daughter of the chief of the giants, left a track of White Clover wherever she walked. The name *Dutch clover* reminds us that Britain borrowed its cultivation from the Low Countries.

20) Bugloss (*Anchusa arvensis*) Borage family

Height to 30cm; flowering June to September. Widespread and occasional in Orkney (15/28); hard to find.

There are few plants that feel as rough as a piece of sandpaper – Bugloss is one of them. The wavy-edged leaves are dark green, pointed, covered with a multitude of short bristles and have swollen bases. The flower tube has a distinctive bend half way down and the flowers, which are set in a compact spray, are small, bright and of a piercing blue. It was once far more common and found not only in links but also in sandy cultivated fields. With agricultural intensification and an increased use of herbicides, Bugloss has become much scarcer.

20. Bugloss at Rackwick, Westray

21. Common Bird's-foot-trefoil at Bay Creekland, Hoy

21) Common Bird's-foot-trefoil (*Lotus corniculatus*)   Pea family

Cocks and hens**, **Smero – *Lady's boots, Grand*mother's slippers, Lamb's toes, Crowfeet, Dead-man's fingers, Old woman's toe-nails, Hop o' my thumb, Bacon and eggs

Height to 20cm; flowers May to September. Widespread and abundant in Orkney (27/28); easy to find.

Its abundance in Britain is reflected by its multitude of names – through-out the length and breadth of the United Kingdom this very familiar perennial has been blessed with at least 70 local names. Some names relate to the flowers and some to the seed pods which turn black and resemble claws. The flowers look like shoes (*Lady's boots, Grandmother's slippers*) and the pods may be mammal's claws, bird's claws, thumbs, fingers, toes or feet (*Lamb's toes, Crowfeet, Dead-man's fingers, Old woman's toe-nails*). The seed pods are also the fingers of the godchild of the Queen of the Faeries, Tom Thumb (*Hop o' my thumb*). Mostly the flowers are deep yellow but among them on the same plant can be found blooms of orange and red; this colour combination is the provider of its *Bacon and eggs* appellation.

It occurs in a wide variety of different grasslands from sand dunes to mountains and is absent from only the most acid of soils. It thrives in a well-drained and calcium-rich soil hence its preference for links, but it is also a poor competitor and as such needs the right amount of grazing. The plant has been used as a source of yellow dye and in South Uist an infusion was used to treat styes. It has always been considered an excellent fodder crop for livestock and an equally important food plant for the Common Blue butterfly.

22. Curved Sedge at North Links, Burray
23. Bulbous Buttercup at Sand of Rothiesholm, Stronsay

22) Curved Sedge (*Carex maritima*) Sedge family

Height to 10cm; flowers May to June. Local and rare in Orkney (7/28); hard to find.

This small and relatively inconspicuous perennial is an Orkney speciality growing in wet and sandy places by the sea often near freshwater. The stems are stiff and curved and the flowering heads are of similar size and appearance to rabbit droppings.

Classed as an Arctic-alpine plant, it is abundant along the whole of the northern coast of Europe, Asia and America and grows in the southern hemisphere around the Straits of Magellan. It also occurs in the Alps, Rockies and Andes. During the 20th Century this sedge has suffered a considerable decline due to the construction of coastal leisure facilities such as car parks, seaside bungalows, camping sites and golf courses. Paradoxically however, once re-established on a golf course, the sedge may find the conditions very congenial. Some of the largest British colonies, estimated at over 300,000 plants, occurred at St Andrews golf course among intermittently flooded turf; it would appear that they have succumbed to changes in management, drainage and turf removal. In Britain it has been lost from England and is confined now to Scotland's northern and eastern coasts.

23) Bulbous Buttercup (*Ranunculus bulbosus*)   Buttercup family

Height to 20cm; flowers April to June. Local and occasional in Orkney (10/28); hard to find.

The buttercup of the dune is a neat and creeping perennial. In Britain it can be found in meadows and grassy places but is absent from intensively farmed fertile grassland and from strongly acidic soils. In Orkney it appears to be rather more selective and since it has a liking for calcium-rich soil, it is most often found on links. Like all members of its family, Bulbous Buttercup has the typical butter-yellow flower-head with five petals. However Bulbous Buttercup has two very distinctive features which make identification quite easy. Firstly, the sepals (underneath the flower-head) are turned down and secondly it has a bulbous tuber, in shape like a tiny onion, just below the surface.

Buttercups of all species are renowned for their 'biting qualities' and have long been used in medicine for producing blisters. The substance that produces the blisters is anemenol and buttercups were used specifically to combat bubonic plague. In rural Scotland, a widespread tradition was that of rubbing cows' udders with May Day buttercups to ensure a productive yield of milk.

24) Selfheal (*Prunella vulgaris*) Dead-nettle family
Hook-seal

Height to 15cm; flowers June to September. Widespread and abundant in Orkney (26/28); easy to find.

One of the most widely distributed plants in Britain and Orkney, Selfheal is a generalist occurring in all manner of grasslands particularly those associated with moist fertile soils and especially old pastures. In Orkney this perennial may even be found growing alongside *Primula scotica* in coastal grassland. The oval leaves are stalked and widest at the base; the flower-head is cylindrical with purple flowers – very occasionally the flowers may be white.

Historically it has been used as a remedy for sore throats and a cure for wounds; its Latin name *Prunella* is derived from *Braune*, the German for Quinsy (inflammation of the tonsils). In the Highlands it was used to remove obstructions of the liver, spleen and kidneys and in Colonsay was harvested and stored to treat winter chest complaints.

25) Sea Bindweed (*Calystegia soldanella*)   Bindweed family

Sprawling to 50cm; flowers June to August. Local and rare in Orkney (1/28); hard to find.

Exclusively found on sand dunes and shingle beaches, this trailing perennial with kidney-shaped leaves and a pink trumpet, slashed-with-white, is more common in the southern half of Britain. Indeed Orkney's small colony of Sea Bindweed, located on South Ronaldsay, represents the most northerly location in Britain; the nearest plants to Orkney are on South Uist (300km west), Rum (300km southwest) and Montrose (250km south). It is a relatively new addition to the Orkney botanical list having been first 'discovered' as recently as 1963. Legend suggests that Bonnie Prince Charlie celebrated his landfall on Eriskay in 1745 by planting the seeds of Sea Bindweed – hence its Gaelic name, *flur a phrionnsa* (Prince's flower).

26) Lesser Meadow-rue (*Thalictrum minus*)   Buttercup family

Height to 50cm; flowers June to August. Local and rare in Orkney (6/28); hard to find.

Slender, wiry and uncommon, this perennial is confined almost entirely to a few links in the county – two of the most easily accessible are Eastside on South Ronaldsay and Dingieshowe in Deerness. In Britain it is more catholic in its choice of locations but always needs base-rich conditions, consequently it may be found on limestone cliffs, slopes and grasslands and on rocky edges by rivers and lochs. The Latin meaning of its name is 'green shoot' which describes it appropriately since the flowers are without petals but have green sepals and conspicuous long stamens and yellow anthers. The leaves are very dainty and fern-like in structure. Medicinally it was used by women in Skye and Mull – an infusion, which included Fairy Flax, was used to treat suppressed periods.

24. Selfheal at Birsay Links, Birsay
25. Sea Bindweed at Newark Bay, South Ronaldsay
26. Lesser Meadow-rue at Newark Bay, South Ronaldsay

Lowland freshwater – lochs, burns, marshes and wet grasslands

Orkney's lowlands are peppered with wetland areas that include lochs, burns, marshes and grasslands. It has been calculated (Berry, 1985) that within Orkney there are 131 burns and 48 standing freshwater bodies. There are lochs of all sizes (except on Graemsay) – from the largest (Harray, Stenness and Boardhouse), through medium-sized lochs such as Bosquoy and Sabiston (all in the West Mainland), to small ones such as Eves Loch (Deerness) and Trolla Vatn (North Ronaldsay) and to the smallest which are generally unnamed. Draining into and out of these lochs are Orkney's burns and ditches. In general, and in a national context, these watercourses are small; indeed previous literature has made reference to there being no rivers in Orkney. However we might argue the case and suggest that the mighty tumbling burns of Rackwick on Hoy and Woodwick in Evie are equal to any rivers elsewhere, although there are no significant

Bride's Loch, North Ronaldsay looking west to Viggay

watercourses in Eday, Egilsay, Papa Stronsay, Papa Westray, Sanday or Wyre.

This chapter includes 35 lowland species all of which require their roots to be in moisture of varying amounts. Many of the wildflowers that feature in this section are almost totally aquatic or emergent, with not only the roots in water but also much of the rest of the plant. These may be found either in the lochs, along water margins or in marshes; such examples include Mare's-tail, the Water-crowfoots, Water Mint and Bogbean. At the other end of the scale are those wildflowers that are more likely to be found on wet grasslands, and will flourish without having their legs in the water; such examples include Sneezewort, Butterbur, Marsh Thistle and Lady's Smock.

Many wetland sites have been lost due to developments and changes in agricultural practices. Some of the more obvious examples include the Loch of Burwick on South Ronaldsay and Craig Loch on Westray. Both of them have been subjected to inappropriate management in recent times and both of them have lost valuable wetland flora. Thankfully many of the wetland sites now receive long overdue protection in the form of international, national or local designations and more enlightened management.

1. Marsh Marigold at Loch of Swannay, Birsay

2. Ragged Robin on Swona

1) Marsh Marigold (*Caltha palustris*) Buttercup family

Yellow gowan – *Golden kingcup, Kingcup, Soldier's buttons*

Height to 40cm; flowers March to July. Widespread and abundant in Orkney (26/28); easy to find.

As welcome as Primroses, the Marsh Marigold is in flower early in the year while the ground is still cold after winter. In Orkney it prefers non-acidic conditions and flourishes alongside burns, lochs and ditches. The leaves are kidney-shaped and often quite large; when floating in water they can appear like lily-pads. The flower-heads are buttercup-yellow and have no true petals – the flower is composed of five yellow sepals and many yellow stamens.

This common perennial produces a yellow dye and can also be used as an ingredient in rennet for curdling milk – both of these properties were readily used in Scotland. The plant is also edible; among the Native North Americans, the Abenaki of Quebec in Canada harvest the leaves and stems. In addition, the buds of Marsh Marigold can be pickled in lieu of capers.

2) Ragged Robin (*Lychnis flos-cuculi*) Campion family

Meadow pink, Cock's comb

Height to 50cm; flowers May to August. Widespread and abundant in Orkney (26/28); easy to find.

In the height of summer some damp meadows are flushed pink; they are meadows awash with Ragged Robins swaying with the summer breezes. Appropriately, in Devon and Somerset, Ragged Robin is known as the *Meadow pink* and in Lanarkshire, its divided petals are the reason for it being called *Cock's comb*. It is a perennial with slightly

3. Water Mint at the Loch of Harray, Harray

hairy and rough spear-shaped leaves and pink flower-heads that are composed of five petals each of them dissected into four lobes – the effect is, unsurprisingly, one of raggedness. Ragged Robin likes to have wet feet and occurs in damp habitats that include grassland, rush pasture, fens, ditches, loch edges and even damp woodland. Like some other wetland plants it has experienced declines in some areas of Britain due to drainage.

3) Water Mint (*Mentha aquatica*) — Dead-nettle family

Height to 60cm; flowers July to October. Widespread and abundant in Orkney (24/28); easy to find.

In the height of summer shallow wetlands are perfumed with the damp fragrance of Water Mint. Its scent is not as sharp as Garden Mint but when crushed underfoot, the bouquet is quite over-powering. Gerard wrote that 'the smell….it rejoiceth the heart of man'. It can be found in marshes and wet pastures or by ditches, ponds and burns throughout most of lowland Britain – it is only in the Highlands of Scotland where it becomes scarce. The mauve flower-heads are rounded and set at regularly-spaced intervals while the toothed, oval leaves sit in opposite pairs along the stem. In some parts of Scotland, the leaves were utilised in cooking while in the Outer Hebrides, a poultice of Goldenrod and Water Mint helped cure Athlete's Foot.

4) Meadowsweet (*Filipendula ulmaria*) — Rose family

Yule girse – *Goatsbeard, Blacknin' girse*

Height to 100cm; flowers June to August. Widespread and abundant in Orkney (24/28); easy to find.

In the height of summer, wet lowland areas, valleys, the edges of lochs, the sides of burns and ditches and marshes are bedecked with swathes of foamy, creamy-white Meadowsweet flowers. In Orkney it can be found countywide although in some of the Outer North Isles it is less abundant and even absent. Permanently waterlogged ground is shunned and grazing is not tolerated. It is a tall plant with pointed oval leaves edged with teeth; the undersides of the leaf are downy. The flowers are small but packed densely to form a loose umbel. It is equally eye-catching in winter when the leaves of the dying plant turn silver.

Archaeological finds in Fife and Rum indicate that the herb was used to flavour mead, an association endorsed by its Scandinavian label which means 'beer grass'. The old apothecary's name for this perennial was *Goatsbeard* the source of which relates to its pungent, sweet and overpowering smell. Medicinally it has the same properties as aspirin and was used to combat headaches and fevers; it is also an astringent and diuretic. In Ireland bunches were used for scouring milk churns and in Shetland it is known as the *Blacknin' girse* from which black dye is obtained. In some parts of Scotland Meadowsweet was strewn over floors as a sweet-smelling carpet and occasionally put to use as thatching material. The Orkney name is *Yule girse* and appears to have no Christmas connotations – yule is a smack – and children were on the receiving end.

5) Great Willowherb (*Epilobium hirsutum*) Willowherb family

Codlins and cream, Currant dumpling, Gooseberry pudding, Plum pudding, Milner flower

Height to 150cm; flowers July and August. Local and rare in Orkney (6/28); hard to find.

It would appear that this tall and handsome perennial, has been introduced to Orkney. Certainly its distribution is thin along the eastern coast of Scotland north of Dundee but there are native stands a few miles away in northern Caithness. Thriving in wet and fertile soil, its favoured haunts are marshes, ditches and the edges of lochs.

4. Meadowsweet along Wideford Burn, St Ola

The flowers are purple-pink and the leaves are lance-shaped and set opposite each other on a round and downy stem. Many of its local names are linked to fruit probably due to the flower colours. Throughout much of Britain it is commonly known as *Codlins and cream* (Codlins are cooking apples) and it is called *Currant dumpling* in Northumberland, *Gooseberry pudding* in Sussex and *Plum pudding* in Cheshire. As in other counties it can be abundant near mills and in Lancashire it was known as the Milner flower, the flower of the miller.

There is a form with soft apple-blossom pink flowers that apparently originated on London bomb sites; it can now be found in some of Orkney's burns and ditches.

6) Lady's Smock (*Cardamine pratensis*) — Cabbage family

Cuckooflower, Milking maids

Height to 30cm; flowers April to July. Widespread and abundant in Orkney (26/28); easy to find.

After the dark days of winter Lady's Smock, like the Marsh Marigold, is a welcome early bloom. It is common on damp verges where it provides a ribbon of colour or in marshes, ditches and damp pastures where on a spring day its four-petalled flowers of lilac are scattered like stars in the firmament. In among the lilac flowers are less numerous ones of rose-pink and white. Its lower leaves are large and kidney-shaped like those of Water-cress (a very close relative) while its upper leaves are narrow

This perennial has many local names most of them relating to milkmaids and smocks, cuckoos and virgins. It is a spring flower, coming out with the first calls of the Cuckoo. The *Lady's smock* refers to the smock of the Virgin Mary, a relic supposedly found in the cave at Bethlehem. It has been little-utilised in medicine but in Scotland it has been gathered as a salad and as a cure for epileptic fits.

5. Great Willowherb at the Brig o' Brodgar, Stenness

6. Lady's Smock at St Andrew's Mill, St Andrews

7. Marsh Willowherb at Sabiston Mill, Birsay

8. Marsh Pennywort at Tor Ness Light, Hoy

7) Marsh Willowherb (*Epilobium palustre*)   Willowherb family

Height to 50cm; flowers July to August. Widespread and abundant in Orkney (26/28); easy to find.

This common perennial prefers acidic sites and can be found in bogs, marshes, ditches, flushes, on the sides of lochs and burns and in agriculturfens. Like all of the Willowherb family it possesses leaves that are arranged in opposite pairs. The leaves of Marsh Willowherb are without stalks, pointed, thin and narrow, being no more than a centimetre wide. The flowers are small and have four notched petals; usually they are pale pink but occasionally lilac or white.

8) Marsh Pennywort (*Hydrocotyle vulgaris*)   Carrot family

White rot *– Farthing rot, Penny rot, Shilling rot, Fairy tables*

Sprawling stems may reach 20cm; flowers June to August. Widespread and abundant in Orkney (26/28); easy to find.

The white flowers of Marsh Pennywort are so small and insignificant that they are nigh on invisible, indeed, they are often absent. This mat-forming perennial is all leaf and stem and can be found in a wide range of damp or wet habitats that include both acidic and calcium-rich conditions. The leaves are circular, have shallow teeth and are held like parasols on stems and can be as big as British pre-decimalisation pennies. It's difficult to believe that Marsh Pennywort is in the same family as some of our most recognisable members of the Carrot family such as Hogweed, Cow Parsley and Wild Angelica.

Historically it has been blamed for causing liver fluke infestations in sheep in the same way that other plants of poor pastures, such as Lousewort and Butterwort, have also been blamed. This widespread

9. Bogbean at Grugar, Egilsay

belief is the basis for its Orkney name *White rot* and for similar names such as *Farthing rot* in Norfolk, *Penny rot* in Shropshire and *Shilling rot* in Ayrshire. Away from the monetary theme, in Cheshire it was known as *Fairy tables*.

9) Bogbean (*Menyanthes trifoliata*)   Bogbean family
Crawshoe

Height to 30cm; flowers June to July. Widespread and frequent in Orkney (18/28); easy to find.

Few plants can have had such significance to such a wide range of peoples in the northern hemisphere as Bogbean. As a food, the roots were ground into flour by Laplanders and Native North Americans in Alaska. As a stimulant, its roots were chewed in the Outer Hebrides while elsewhere in Scotland made into tobacco. As a medicine, it was esteemed as a cure-all and used to treat digestive ailments, headaches, migraine, ague and rheumatism. Known as *Gulsa girse* in Shetland it treated jaundice and in Germany it was known as fever clover. Its bruised leaves were applied to the sores of scrofula and in brewing it was a sought after bittering agent in England and Scotland.

Bogbean grows in bogs, swamps and fens and in the shallow waters at the edge of lochs. With its ability to trap sediments, it can be responsible for drying out areas of open water. In his *Herbal*, Gerard described this 'beauty of the black moorland waters' as follows: 'toward the tip of the stalk standeth a bush of feather-like flowers of a white colour dasht with a wash of light carnation'. The flowers have five lobes, star-shaped and fringed with stiff white hairs. The long-stalked, grey-green, oval leaves are in threes and stand proud of the water.

13. Soft Rush at the Mill, Mill Bay, Eday
14. Sneezewort at Quoys, Graemsay

13) Soft Rush (*Juncus effusus*) Rush family
Axes girse

Height to 100cm; flowers June to August. Widespread and abundant in Orkney (22/28); easy to find.

In Orkney there are ten true rushes, i.e. members of the *Juncus* genus. Generally they are upright and tufted and grow in damp locations. One of the commonest and tallest is Soft Rush which forms thick clumps in wet fields, ditches, marshes, the edges of lochs and open heaths and moors. There is a Shetland saying 'keep wide a da floss' (Soft Rush) which is meant to help travellers find a safe route through the moorlands. More specifically this perennial appears to thrive in overgrazed and badly drained boggy fields. Its stem is green, leafless and smooth while the brown flower-head tends to flower in a loose, open fashion.

It has been one of Orkney's most important plants almost up to the present day. For centuries the pith of rushes furnished the all-important wick for the cruisie lamp which, in turn, provided most Orkney crofts with their sole source of light. The task of peeling and revealing the pith, a job for dexterous fingers, was often allocated to children. Further afield, the early sprouting shoots were eaten raw by the Snoqualmie people of Washington State, North America.

14) Sneezewort (*Achillea ptarmica*) Daisy family

Height to 50cm; flowers July to August. Widespread and frequent in Orkney (20/28); easy to find.

Its closest relative is Yarrow, a plant that thrives in dry conditions. In contrast, Sneezewort differs by preferring sites that are far damper such as marshes, flushes, wet heaths, wet meadows and rush pastures. Sometimes the plants are attacked by a gall which reduces this perennial to a ground rosette of leaves. The flower-head

15. Marsh Ragwort at the Loch of St Tredwell, Papa Westray

is composed of four-petalled, button-like flowers which are a less-than-brilliant white (some books refer to them as dingy) while the thin and pointed leaves are finely and sharply toothed.

Historically it has had two major uses: the leaves were chewed to counter toothache and the flowers were dried to be made into snuff. The species name *ptarmica* comes from the Greek word *ptairo* which means sneeze and Gerard in his *Herbal* considered that its smell was enough to make one sneeze. In Orkney it was gathered to make a tea to aid digestion.

15) **Marsh Ragwort** (*Senecio aquaticus*) — Daisy family

Tirso – Ragweed, Stinking Willie, Herba Sancti Jacobi

Height to 60cm; flowers July to August. Widespread and abundant in Orkney (22/28); easy to find.

In Orkney, Marsh Ragwort is more widespread and abundant than Common Ragwort (page 36); in Britain it is the reverse. The two species have distinct habitat preferences: Marsh Ragwort, a biennial, flourishes in wet meadows, rush pastures, marshes and ditches while Common Ragwort is typically a plant of dry and sandy soils such as those found in dunes and links. Physically the two species are quite different: while both species have yellow flowers, those of Common Ragwort form a loose starry umbel at the head of the stem while those of Marsh Ragwort are loosely-branched and spreading. The leaves differ significantly too: those of Common Ragwort are dark green, vaguely glossy and heavily dissected, while those of Marsh Ragwort are much larger and have oval end-lobes.

The two species hybridise to produce *Senecio* x *ostenfeldii*, conceivably now the most common of Ragworts in Orkney.

You can find the Common Ragwort story on page 36.

16) Common Marsh-bedstraw (*Galium palustre*)   Bedstraw family

Sprawling stems may reach 50cm; flowers May and June. Widespread and abundant in Orkney (25/28); easy to find.

This slender and rather insignificant perennial grows in a creeping manner wherever it is wet including ditches, ponds, marshes and meadows. Like many of the bedstraws, the four-petalled flowers are white and tiny (often no more than 3mm across). The leaves may be ten times the size of the flowers and are set in whorls around the stem. A magnifying glass will reveal the backward pointing prickles on the leaf edges.

17) Water-cress (*Rorippa nasturtium-aquaticum*)   Cabbage family
Well-girse

Height to 60cm; flowers May to October. Widespread and frequent in Orkney (15/28); fairly easy to find.

For centuries, Water-cress has been considered a very valuable herb. It is a perennial and found beside or in moderately nutrient-rich freshwater burns and ditches or around the edges of lochs. It can even be found in wells hence the Scottish name *Well-girse*. The stems float in the water and the erect shoots with small white flowers are set above the dark green hairless leaves which remain green throughout the winter.

It is less widely used as a potherb than previously, probably because of concerns that liver fluke may enter the digestive system. On Colonsay it was made into a broth known as *Brot biolarach* and throughout the Highlands it was used along with Lady's Smock to alleviate fevers. It had a slightly different use in the Hebrides where during the 19th Century women considered it a remedy for childlessness.

16. Common Marsh-bedstraw at Sean, Sandwick
17. Water-cress along the Lingro burn, St Ola
18. Yellow Iris at Boloquoy Mill, Sanday

18) Yellow Iris (Iris pseudacorus) — Iris family
Yellow lily, **Segs** – *Yellow Flag, Queen-of-the-marshes, Queen-of-the-meadows*

Height to 120cm; flowers May to July. Widespread and abundant in Orkney (26/28); easy to find.

In the early days of April the first clumps of sword-shaped leaves stand proud like fakirs' beds in all of Orkney's damp and low-lying country. By June time these leaves are a metre high and chrome-yellow tipped buds, the colour of Whooper Swan's beaks, soon unfurl chrome-yellow petals. Come late autumn, the salt-laden gales have blackened the swords and the statuesque beauty of this perennial has shrivelled.

Iris is Greek for rainbow and symbolised life and resurrection and as an apotropaic averted evil. It is the source of the fleur-de-lys badge of French royalty and by the 19th Century had risen to become a plant of poetry. It is also a versatile plant and has been put to a wide variety of practical and medical uses. The rhizomes and seeds produce a strong black dye for ink while in the Highlands and the Western Isles, the leaves were used for thatching and basketry. Coopers found a use for the dried leaves as gap fillers between the staves of barrels. Medicinally it featured as an astringent, a powerful cathartic, a treatment for ulcers in the Outer Hebrides while in Orkney, and quoted in Spence's *Flora Orcadensis*, it appears that the juice from the roots was sucked up through the nose as a cure for toothache. Equally dramatic was its use on Mull where the rhizomes were crushed with Daisies and a teaspoonful of juice poured into each nostril, prompting a copious flow of mucus and saliva. The seeds were roasted to provide 'coffee' and ground to provide 'snuff'. Not so long ago, children in Orkney made 'seggy boats' from the leaves and there was a belief among those that made the boats, that chewing the leaf would render one dumb. Remains of Yellow Iris have been found in the ancient middens of Orkney's Skara Brae.

19. Lesser Spearwort at Stanger Head, Flotta
20. Marsh Arrowgrass at the Loch of Ness, Papa Westray

19) Lesser Spearwort (*Ranunculus flammula*) Buttercup family

Goosetongue, Snake's tongue

Height to 20cm; flowers May to September. Widespread and abundant in Orkney (26/28); easy to find.

As with the Marsh Marigold, Lesser Spearwort prefers to keep its feet in water or at the very least damp earth. It is a perennial of wet habitats such as ponds, marshes, lochsides or ditches and particularly favours areas with seasonal water fluctuations. Like other members of the buttercup family in Orkney it has a small round butter-yellow flower-head composed of five petals. However its leaves are quite unlike those of the other buttercups making identification simple. The simple spear-shapes provide us with its Scottish name *Goosetongue* and its Berwickshire name *Snake's tongue*.

Although poisonous, its root was pounded and then applied to the skin in a limpet shell to encourage blistering in the battle to extract disease and plague sores; this practice was widespread in the Scottish Highlands and Islands. On Colonsay it was used as a curdling plant. Gerard called the plant *Banewoort* because 'it is dangerous and deadly for sheepe; and if they feede of the same it inflameth their livers, blistereth their guts and entrailes'- be warned!

20) Marsh Arrowgrass (*Triglochin palustris*) Arrowgrass family

Height to 30cm; flowers June to August. Widespread and abundant in Orkney (23/28); not easy to find.

There are just two species of Arrowgrass in Britain, Sea and Marsh.

21. Marsh Cudweed at The Bu, Wyre

They are perennials and it is possible to find both species occurring in the same locality. However, despite the fact that Marsh Arrowgrass can occur in salt marshes by the sea, it is much more likely to be met with in wet meadows, rush pastures and fens. Marsh Arrowgrass is more slender than Sea Arrowgrass (page 15) and is more grass-like than its fleshier-leaved sibling. In addition Marsh Arrowgrass has deeply furrowed leaves and arrow-shaped fruits while Sea Arrowgrass has unfurrowed leaves and oblong fruits.

Both species are highly nutritious; the strong belief in Orkney was that sheep and cattle would fatten more quickly and have improved quality of meat if they grazed on Arrowgrass.

21) Marsh Cudweed (*Gnaphalium uliginosum*)   Daisy family

Clodweed

Height to 5cm; flowers July to August. Widespread and frequent in Orkney (19/28); fairly easy to find.

Possibly the most obvious feature of this damp-loving annual is its woolly leaves (although some books actually refer to them as cottony). Both sides of the leaf are woolly but the upper side is less so and appears greener. The yellowish-brown flowers are in a crowded cluster and the topmost leaves oversee the flower-heads almost appearing like long petals.

Though called Marsh Cudweed, it is probably more characteristic of muddy ground that is prone to waterlogging in winter. It is particularly fond of trampled field entrances and the edges of summer-dry ponds that have been poached by cattle. In Buckinghamshire this attribute is reflected in its name *Clodweed*. A possible origin of the more familiar name Cudweed is that the plant, according to Mascal's *Government of Cattle* (1662), bruised with a little fat, was put into the mouths of cattle which had lost their cud.

22) **Marsh Thistle** (*Cirsium palustre*) Daisy family

Height to 150cm; flowers July to August. Widespread and abundant in Orkney (25/28); easy to find.

This is the most graceful and stately of the thistles that occur in Orkney. It is a biennial, growing from seed in year one and flowering and dying in year two. During the winter, the basal rosette of leaves is like exquisite and symmetrical filigree. Damp sites are its preference and it may be found in marshes, wet meadows, rushy pastures and flushes. Many plants are a metre in a height and occasionally some may be substantially more than that. The stems are hairy and teeming with spines and the dark green leaves are often flushed with purple. The flower-heads occur in crowded clusters; normally the florets are dark mauve, however occasionally they can be white.

22. Marsh Thistle at Stembister, St Andrews

23) Butterbur (*Petasites hybridus*)   Daisy family
Umbrella leaves, Bog rhubarb

Height to 40cm, leaves up to 50cm wide; flowers March to May.
Local and occasional in Orkney (5/28); fairly easy to find.

The most obvious feature of this perennial herb is the large size of its leaf; in Yorkshire it is known as *Umbrella leaves* and in Somerset as *Bog rhubarb*. Gerard described it as being 'bigge and large inough to keepe a man's head from raine, and from the heate of the sunne'. In fact the plant's scientific name derives from *petasos* which was a broad-brimmed sun hat worn by the ancient Greeks and, modified with wings, was the preferred headgear for Hermes, the messenger god. The flower arrives long before the leaf and during early spring the pink-purple stems which are covered with strap-shaped bracts push upwards through damp ground before unfurling into a spike of numerous grey and pink flowers.

Throughout Britain it can be found on moist and fertile soils in wet meadows, marshes, along roadsides and even in woodland. Orkney is no different and there is even an extensive patch in the woodland at Gyre in Orphir but it is believed that the plant rather than being native was introduced into the county. This may account for the plant's frequent occurrence in the vicinity of graveyards.

Historically, the leaves were used for wrapping butter and medicinally the dried roots, which contain petasine, were taken against fevers especially the plague; in Germany, Butterbur is known as *Pestwurz* or *Pestilenzeurz*. Petasine is also considered to counter migraine and hayfever.

23. Butterbur at the Doocot, Hall of Rendall, Rendall

24. Monkeyflowers along the Burn of Heddle, Stenness

24) *Monkeyflowers (Mimulus* agg.) Figwort family

Height to 40cm; flowers July to September. Local and occasional in Orkney (10/28); fairly easy to find.

Monkeyflowers originate in the Americas; Native North Americans and early travellers used it as a salt substitute to flavour wild game. It appears that the first plants to reach Europe came from the Aleutian Islands off the western coast of Alaska in the 18th Century. The family includes Monkeyflower, Coppery Monkeyflower, Musk and Blood-drop-emlets and a very complex assortment of hybrids. By 1812, English gardens were resplendent with the family's colourful blossoms and escaped plants were first noted during 1824 in South Wales. In the following 100 years members of the genus became widely naturalised throughout Britain especially on marshy ground, along the edges of watercourses and on river shingle. Colonisation was made easier with the great increase in mileage of Britain's canal system.

In Orkney the most common species are **Monkeyflower** (*Mimulus guttatus*) and **Blood-drop-emlets** (*Mimulus luteus*). Both are perennials and both have yellow flower-heads but Monkeyflower has small red spots in its throat while Blood-drop-emlets has large red or purple blotches. Coppery Monkeyflower, with its coppery-orange flowers, occurs sparingly. It is believed to have been introduced in 1903 but Magnus Spence's *Flora Orcadensis* (1914) makes no mention. Monkeyflowers are thoroughly naturalised in Orkney and although looking quite at home along burns and ditches, they are absent from many parts of the county. Apparently during part of the 20th Century, it was common practice for a couple who were moving to a new parish to take a handful of roots to naturalise in their new surroundings.

25. Marsh Cinquefoil at Mill Dam of Rango, Sandwick
26. Early Marsh-orchid at Como, Rendall

25) Marsh Cinquefoil (*Potentilla palustris*) Rose family
Bog-strawberry

Height to 40cm; flowers May to July. Very widespread and abundant in Orkney (24/28); easy to find.

In Orkney's permanently damp and marshy areas, especially those where the soils are poor and slightly acidic, the perennial Marsh Cinquefoil is very common. It seems to be particularly fond of abandoned peat cuttings or the margins of lochs where its vigorous growth can help dry out soggy ground. It is a handsome plant with the 'cinquefoil' referring to its arrangement of five strongly-toothed leaflets. The flowers have five narrow purple petals and five purplish sepals, longer and wider than the petals. The fruits are strawberry-like and in the Isle of Man it is known as the *Bog-strawberry*. In the Highlands and Islands of Scotland its roots were used for tanning leather and nets.

26) Early Marsh-orchid (*Dactylorhiza incarnata*) Orchid family
Dead man's liver

Height to 15cm; flowers May to July. Widespread and frequent in Orkney (15/28); easy to find.

Debatably, this perennial is less striking than its cousin the Northern Marsh-orchid; it is also less common. The Early Marsh has reddish flesh-coloured flowers on a narrow and quite cylindrical flower spike; petal colour is most probably responsible for its Orkney name *Dead man's liver*, and for other colloquial names such as *Dead man's finger* and *Dead man's hand*. The yellow-green leaves, which are usually unspotted and strongly keeled, appear quite upright and taper to a narrow and hooded tip. Its preference is for damp, lime-rich soils in meadows and marshes. Plants with white flowers are occasionally met with.

Identification of Orchids can be quite difficult since this group is still undergoing the process of evolution. Consequently there are many subspecies and many hybrids, which are often identified by their large size.

27) Amphibious Bistort (*Persicaria amphibia*) Dock family
Yallowin' girse

Trailing stems to 100cm; flowers July to September. Widespread and frequent in Orkney (15/28); fairly easy to find.

This perennial has two distinct forms – an aquatic form and a terrestrial form. Both have a tight and dense cluster of pink flowers and lance shaped leaves – those of the open-water form are usually hairless while those of the land form are hairy. Sometimes the leaves of both forms may be blotched with black. Lochs, ponds, canals and slow flowing rivers are preferred by the aquatic form and arable ground by the dry form. It is generally believed that the plant of the open water appears to flower more freely. In Shetland's Fair Isle, it was known as *Yallowin' girse* from which a yellow dye was extracted.

28) Mare's-tail (*Hippuris vulgaris*) Mare's-tail family
Trowie-spindle – *Old man's beard, Faeries' spindles*

Height to 40cm; flowers June to July. Widespread and frequent in Orkney (19/28); easy to find.

Given its looks, it is hardly surprising that this perennial, which flourishes in small lochs and ditches, has long been associated with the devil, and with fairies and goblins. At one time it was believed to be a female Horsetail (*Equisetum* spp.) – the name Mare's-tail is the result. It occurs in two growth forms – firstly there are the erect 'bottle brush' shoots which are round and spongy and have whorls of strap-shaped leaves and secondly there are the submerged plants which have long flaccid stems and translucent leaves. The flowers which only occur in the axils (the upper angle between a leaf and the stem) of the emergent plant are tiny, green and petal-less.

29) Northern Marsh-orchid (*Dactylorhiza purpurella*) Orchid family

Adam – Long purples

Height to 25cm; flowers June and July. Widespread and abundant in Orkney (27/28); easy to find.

During the height of the summer, Northern Marsh-orchids are scattered liberally across Orkney's wet meadows, marshes, flushes, loch edges, road verges and even lawns. Against a background of vibrant green grasses and sedges, the equally vibrant and deep purple of this orchid's flower-heads makes for a dramatic and colourful show. The leaves are generally unspotted but if there are any spots, they are confined to the tip. They are popular flowers; with a recent increase in rural housing, many wet meadows in the county's countryside have become lawns and it is not uncommon to see islands of orchids spared by the caring lawnmower.

From the appearance of the paired subterranean tubers, the Greeks named the plant *Orchis*, meaning 'testicle' and for centuries and across many cultures Orchids have been a prime source of aphrodisiac food and love potions. Their venereal heritage has influenced aspects of folklore, art, medicine and food. In eastern Scotland, the dried tubers were carried as love talismans and Shakespeare's *Hamlet* refers to the *Long purples* which were symbolically included in the garlands of the drowned Ophelia. Robert Turner (*Botonologia: the British Physician*, 1664) remarked that enough Orchids grew in Cobham Park, Kent to pleasure all the seamen's wives in Rochester.

27. Amphibious Bistort at the Loch of Ouse, Deerness
28. Mare's-tail at the Loch of Ouse, Deerness
29. Northern Marsh-orchid at the Mill, Stronsay

30

30) *Water-crowfoots*   Buttercup family

Spreading to 40cm; flowering May to July. Generally the family is far more widespread in England than in Scotland.

These '*white buttercups of the water*', which can be annuals or perennials, grow in shallow water or on mud in marshes, ponds and ditches. There are four different species of Water-crowfoot in Orkney and they are not the easiest of plants to identify due to possible hybridisation. They are all very similar in that they have white flowers composed of five petals, the bases of which are yellow. Some of them have finely divided leaves known as capillary leaves which are submerged and others have broad leaves known as laminar leaves which float; some of them have a combination of both types of leaf.

Brackish Water-crowfoot (*Ranunculus baudotii*)

Local and occasional in Orkney (12/28); not easy to find.

Found in open brackish water near the sea; has both capillary and laminar leaves.

Common Water-crowfoot (*Ranunculus aquatilis*)

Widespread and occasional in Orkney (16/28); not easy to find.

Found in shallow eutrophic water in marshes, ponds and ditches; has both capillary and laminar leaves.

Ivy-leaved Water-crowfoot (*Ranunculus hederaceus*)

Local and rare in Orkney (0/20); hard to find.

Found in wet places in cultivated land, often on the cattle-poached edges of ponds, ditches and burns and in wet gateways; has no capillary leaves. In Orkney it is only found on Papa Westray and South Ronaldsay.

Thread-leaved Water-crowfoot (*Ranunculus trichophyllus*)

Local and occasional in Orkney (14/28); not easy to find.

Found in still or slow-moving eutrophic water; has no laminar leaves

30. Brackish Water-crowfoot at the Noup, Westray

31. Greater Bird's-foot Trefoil at Newhouse, Shapinsay

31) Greater Bird's-foot-trefoil (*Lotus pedunculatus*) Pea family

Height to 60cm; flowers June to August. Local and occasional in Orkney (10/28); hard to find.

Superficially Greater Bird's-foot-trefoil is very like the much more widespread and familiar Common Bird's-foot-trefoil (page 40). However there are a number of obvious differences which make separation fairly straightforward. In general Greater Bird's-foot-trefoil has a preference for damp ground and can be found in rushy pastures, wet meadows, marshes and ditches. It is a tall, bushy and hairy perennial with hollow stems and yellow flowers. Common Bird's-foot-trefoil favours much drier ground, such as links or coastal grassland, has solid stems and is usually quite hairless. Additionally the flowers of Greater Bird's-foot-trefoil are a clear banana-yellow whereas those of Common Bird's-foot-trefoil, although yellow, often have orange and red tinges to their petals. One other significant difference is that Greater Bird's-foot-trefoil flowers a good month later.

In Orkney, some believe it to have been introduced since earlier botanists made no mention of it; alternatively, because of its similarity to Common Bird's-foot-trefoil, it may simply have been overlooked. Records indicate that the plant has spread quite rapidly across the county since the 1960s but it appears that it is still absent from many of the northern isles.

32) Brooklime (*Veronica beccabunga*) Figwort family

Height to 40cm; flowers May to August. Local and occasional in Orkney (12/28); not easy to find.

In Orkney, this handsome wetland perennial is most likely to be found in wet ditches, slow-moving and shallow burns and on the margins of lochs. It is a recognised poor competitor alongside taller plants and thrives best in open situations. It has blue, four-petalled flowers

32. Brooklime along the Crantit burn, St Ola

typical of many plants in the Speedwell clan e.g. Field Speedwell (page 107), Germander Speedwell (page 107), and Heath Speedwell (page 165). Brooklime's flowers however are quite distinctive in that the flower stems, on which there may be a dozen flowers, grow from the axils of both of the paired and opposite leaves.

Along with Water-cress, which is often found growing in similar locations, Brooklime was considered to be a salad plant throughout much of northern Europe. Not without other uses, its chief claim for inclusion in the medicine cabinet was due to its recommendation as a cure for scurvy. John Pechey in *The Compleat Herbal of Physical Plants* (1694) conjures up the following: 'To cure the scurvy: take of the juice of Brook-lime, Water-cresses and Scurvy-grass, each half a pint; of the Juice of Oranges, four ounces; fine Sugar, two pounds; make a Syrup over a gentle fire: take one spoonful in your Beer every time you drink'.

*Horsetails (Equisetum spp.)   Horsetail family
Lithy girs

These primitive looking perennials are closely related to ferns. Possibly the most obvious feature of this family is the jointed stem which is leafless, ridged, hollow and rough; in fact so rough that the stem of one species (Dutch Rush) has been employed by cabinet makers and flute makers as a substitute for sand paper. The joints are covered by toothed sheaths. In Orkney there are six species and they tend to grow in places that are usually damp. The commonest of them are Marsh Horsetail and Water Horsetail which feature in this wetland section, Field Horsetail which is included in the *Arable fields, waysides and disturbed ground* section and Wood Horsetail which appears in the *Wild woods and dales* chapter. The other two, Dutch

Rush (*Equisetum hyemale*) and Shady Horsetail (*Equisetum pratense*) are rare with the former restricted to Hoy and the latter to one site on Rousay.

By crushing and then soaking the whole plant for 24 hours in hot water, the resulting mix is an effective organic fungicide which can combat mildew. Native North Americans utilised the juice of Horsetails as a weedkiller and an insecticide.

33) Marsh Horsetail (*Equisetum palustre*)

Height to 60cm; flowering spores ripe May to July. Widespread and abundant in Orkney (24/28); easy to find.

Found in marshes and wet meadows, it has whorls of branches whose sheaths are green with black teeth. The sheaths on the main stem sit loosely against the stem and are black with broad white edges; the stem itself has six to ten ridges.

34) Water Horsetail (*Equisetum fluviatile*)

Height to 100cm; flowering spores ripe June to July. Widespread and abundant in Orkney (22/28); easy to find.

This is the most aquatic of the Horsetails and is found in a variety of watery habitats from ditches to lochs, both big and small. It usually lacks branches and appears as a tall single stem often forming dense stands. Although having up to thirty ridges, the ridges are obscure and the stem looks and feels smooth. The green sheaths sit tightly against the stem and the central hollow is larger than in any other horsetail, filling up to four-fifths of the stem.

33. Marsh Horsetail along the Mill Burn, Stromness

34. Water Horsetail along the Mill Burn, Stromness

35) Meadow Buttercup (*Ranunculus acris*)   Buttercup family

Butter and cheese, Butter flowers, Butterchurn, Gold cup, Crazy, Crazy weed

Height to 70cm; flowers April to June. Widespread and abundant in Orkney (27/28); easy to find.

This is the tallest and largest of Britain's buttercups and very occasionally may stand a metre high. It is typically a plant of damp meadows and pastures and though tolerant of many soil types, thrives on rich soil and shuns dry and acid conditions. The leaves are finely dissected and have three, four or five lobes; the five-petalled flowers are golden-yellow.

Throughout Britain buttercups have been blessed with a wealth of local names. Many of them relate to the colour of the petals so that we have *Butter and cheese* in Somerset, *Butter flowers* in Derbyshire, *Butterchurn* in Warwickshire and *Gold cup* in Cornwall. Other names emphasise its poisonous reputation so that we have *Crazy* in Devon and *Crazy weed* in Buckinghamshire. Gerard suggests that if the root 'be hanged in a linen cloth about the necke of him that is lunatic in the wane of the moon, then he shall forthwith be cured'. More on buttercups can be found under Bulbous Buttercup (page 41) and Creeping Buttercup (page 98).

35. Meadow Buttercup at Kirbist, Egilsay

Sea cliffs, coastal grasslands and coastal heaths

The hard rock faces of Orkney's cliffs are subjected to regular and frequent drenching from salt-laden spray; the plants that exist in this extreme environment have to be salt-tolerant. This zone is effectively a vertical salt marsh and consequently many of the plants that occur are those that may be found typically on a salt marsh or sand and shingle shore – Scurvygrass, Sea Plantain, Sea Campion and Sea Mayweed. There are also a couple of special cliff plants, Sea Spleenwort which is usually located in caves or cliff recesses and Roseroot which is an impressive sight along some of Hoy's west coast.

On the cliff top, conditions can be equally harsh and the broken scree-fields, grasslands and heaths that occur on some of Orkney's most exposed cliffs are made up of more salt-tolerant plants which are invariably stunted and wind-clipped. Grasslands here are composed of Thrift and plantains such as Buck's-horn and Sea while slightly

Vat of Kirbuster, Stronsay – background Burgh Head

further inland can be found a sward that yields Spring Squill, Common Dog-violet, Eyebright and even Scottish Primrose.

On sheltered sea banks and in coastal valleys, tall and at times lush 'dales' vegetation can be found, often marked by large swathes of Red Campion (see *Wild woods and dales* chapter). At many coastal sites, most markedly on the west coasts of Orkney, the grassland gives way to a special type of heathland known as coastal heath which prospers on the thin soils which overlie Old Red Sandstone rocks. This habitat's main characteristic is that it includes plants from the grassland and heathland so that in among the heathy Ling, Crowberry and Devil's-bit Scabious are species such as Spring Squill, Carnation Sedge, Glaucous Sedge and Sea Plantain.

Orkney is well blessed with sea cliffs that support these two important habitats. They are fragile habitats and have been at risk in the recent past from agricultural pressures most notably an increase in grazing and fertilisation. Some of Orkney's finest examples are now protected through national and international designations and other sites are being brought back into prime condition via targeted management thanks to agri-environment schemes. The county's premier sites include North Hill on Papa Westray, the West Westray coast, Quendal, Brings and Faraclett on Rousay, the Stromness heaths on West Mainland and the western side of Hoy.

1. Sea Spleenwort at Glims Holm

1) Sea Spleenwort (*Asplenium marinum*)   Fern family

Height to 30cm; flowering sori are ripe between June and October. Widespread and occasional in Orkney (15/28); not easy to find.

Around the British coast, this evergreen perennial fern inhabits crevices and shallow caves. It is almost entirely confined to cliffs that are exposed to sea spray and can only exist in a frost-free environment, consequently inland records are exceptional. The fronds are divided into simple oval segments which are bright green, shiny, quite leathery and have a red-brown stalk.

Formerly used for spleen disorders, the plant's reputed virtue is no doubt due to the lobular spleen-like shape of the leaf.

2) Thrift (*Armeria maritima*)   Sea-lavender family

Arby – *Sea pink, Cushions, Lady's pincushion*

Height to 15cm; flowers April to August. Widespread and abundant in Orkney (25/28); easy to find.

Sea cliffs covered by carpets of this perennial's candy-pink heads are characteristic of Orkney's coasts during the summer. On a bright sunny day swathes of 'pinks' are a striking foreground to a deep blue ocean, an azure blue sky and bright green coastal grasslands. It is primarily a plant of the coast and flourishes in the poorest of salt-soaked soils on cliffs, stabilised shingle and salt marsh but elsewhere in Britain it may be found on mountain ledges, and alongside roads that have been treated with salt. It shuns competition and observers consider that it flowers best after a stormy winter has dealt harshly with any 'opposition'.

The flower-heads are round and composed of clusters of flowers

2. Thrift at Mousetter, Copinsay

3. Buck's-horn Plantain at Whey Geo, Westray

which vary in colour from deep pink to white. The leaves are narrow and numerous and form quite substantial cushions; hence the colloquial names.

In Orkney, its roots, which are considered to be reviving and nourishing, were sliced and boiled in milk and used as a remedy for tuberculosis. Its pliable stems have been used in basketry and the dried flowers often feature in arrangements. Those of us who can remember three penny (3d) pieces may also recall that the punning emblem of that coin was Thrift.

3) Buck's-horn Plantain (*Plantago coronopus*)   Plantain family

Height to 10cm; flowers May to July. Widespread and abundant in Orkney (26/28); easy to find.

In very exposed conditions the circular rosettes of leaves are often strikingly conspicuous on bare earth or in short grassland near the coast. They are the tiny spokes of a tiny cartwheel and those plants closest to the harshest of the elements are the most hairy and take on a sheen of silver. This biennial is the only Plantain in which the leaves are divided into toothed leaflets; plants in less exposed locations are bigger and more upright and the antler-like leaves resemble the horns of a buck. The flowers are yellow-brown and sit in short greenish spikes on top of an unfurrowed stalk. Its distribution in Orkney and Britain is chiefly coastal but in the south and southeast of England it ventures quite far inland and as with some other halophytes, it is increasing beside salt-treated roads.

Plantains were valued as healing herbs chiefly because of their ability to withstand trampling. Sympathetically this would mean that they could remedy bruising, crushing, tearing, burns and sores.

4) Scots Lovage (*Ligusticum scoticum*)   Carrot family
Scots parsley

Height to 60cm; flowers July to August. Widespread and frequent in Orkney (17/28); fairly easy to find.

Scotland is its British stronghold and this perennial can be found the length of the Scottish coastline from Kirkcudbright in the west to Berwickshire in the east. In England it occurs sparingly in Northumberland, an extension of Scotland's east coast monopoly. Cold and wet conditions are necessary for seed germination and as such it is almost exclusively coastal and found on sea cliffs, shingle beaches and mature sand dunes. In Orkney it can be seen growing between the concrete blocks of the Churchill barriers. It is a robust plant and seeds can survive long periods of immersion in the sea.

The greenish-white flowers sit in dense umbels on top of stout, purple stems. The fresh leaves are dark green and shiny and the plant has the scent of celery. In Scotland it has been regarded as a culinary herb, a vegetable (known as Scots parsley), an antidote for scurvy and a tobacco substitute. In Alaska it was considered a winter vegetable and its leaves were preserved in seal oil.

A last word from Martin Martin during his journey through the Hebrides in the late 17th Century indicates the plant's importance: '*Shunnis* (Scots Lovage) is a plant highly valued by the natives who eat it raw, and also boiled with fish, flesh and milk. It is used as a sovereign remedy to cure the sheep of the cough. The root taken during fasting expels wind'.

5) Kidney Vetch (*Anthyllis vulneraria*)   Pea family
Lady's fingers, Lady's slippers, Butter-fingers, Yellow crow's foot

Height to 50cm; flowers May to September. Widespread and frequent in Orkney (21/28); easy to find.

In Orkney there are considered to be two subspecies of this perennial.

Both of them have soft yellow flowers, often with hints of red or purple, and green leaves that are covered with silky and silvery hairs. The subspecies *lapponica* is more silvery and has a large terminal leaflet; the other subspecies *vulneraria* is decidedly less silky and has a terminal leaflet the same size as the plant's other leaves. While it is most frequently encountered around the county's coasts either on cliff faces or in the coastal grassland, it also occurs in old quarries and on gritty and stony turf. Some of the most extensive and impressive displays occur on the cliffs of Birsay.

Kidney Vetch is equally well-known as *Lady's fingers* and in addition it shares many vernacular names with its near relative Common Bird's-foot-trefoil. Footwear, digits and feet feature frequently. Its species name indicates its esteem as a wound herb throughout Europe. It is an ancient remedy for eruptions of the skin, slow-healing wounds, cuts and bruises.

6) Common Dog-violet (*Viola riviniana*)   Violet family

Height to 15cm; flowers April to July. Widespread and abundant in Orkney (26/28); easy to find.

The appearance of these blue-violet flowers in April is as welcome as any of Orkney's iconic spring blooms. Throughout Britain this popular perennial can be found in a range of habitats that include deciduous woodland, hedgerows, meadows, sea cliffs, heaths and mountains.

It is probably of more frequent occurrence on the hill or near the sea. The long-stalked and heart-shaped leaves are very obvious and recognisable in the short spring sward and occasionally the massed ranks of dark flowers include one or two white ones. It is a violet without scent – hence the term Dog, meaning inferior.

4. Scots Lovage at Cumla Geo, Banks, South Ronaldsay.
5. Kidney Vetch at Marwick, Birsay.
6. Common Dog-violet at Bacon Tub, St Andrews

*7. Scottish Primrose
at Inga Ness, Yesnaby, Sandwick*

7) Scottish Primrose (*Primula scotica*)　　　　　　Primrose family

Height to 10cm; flowers April to August. Local and occasional in Orkney (12/28); not easy to find.

There is probably nothing left to say about this tiny perennial whose world distribution is limited to northern Scotland – all the superlatives have been used up many times. To call it a jewel is no exaggeration; it is a miniature, crafted with precise perfection.

In Orkney its favourite habitat is coastal grassland – the strip of green that is found on the cliff top close to the sea. In its other Scottish strongholds, Caithness and Sutherland, it is known to occur on machair and links. However, whatever the habitat it is rarely more than five hundred metres from the sea or above one hundred metres. It has two flowering periods within the summer. The pale green rosettes of untoothed oval leaves are surprisingly conspicuous against the short turf and the purple-magenta five-petalled flower, with a yellow eye, sits on the top of a stout stem.

It requires very specific growing conditions, hence its restricted world distribution. During the last one hundred years, it has been lost from many of its former sites in the county including Orphir, Sanday, Shapinsay, Stenness and St Andrews. Nowadays it is limited to Papa Westray, Westray, Rousay, South Walls and the parishes of Stromness and Sandwick but even in those strongholds it has experienced declines. Many of its locations are amenable to cultivation and subsequent losses have resulted. Additionally the Scottish Primrose is not a robust competitor and will struggle if the grazing regime is not to its liking.

9. Cat's-ear at Stephen's Gate, Eday

8. Wild Thyme at Maovi, Shapinsay

8) Wild Thyme (*Thymus polytrichus*)
Tae girse   Dead-nettle family

Straggling stems up to 7cm long; flowers May to August. Widespread and frequent in Orkney (21/28); easy to find.

This prostrate and mat-forming perennial herb prefers sunny places in short turf. In Orkney its favoured locations include rock outcrops and species-rich heath both of which can be found in abundance near sea cliffs; observation indicates that it is a frequent companion of *Primula scotica*. The plant's distribution in Orkney is more western than eastern, a similarity it shares with the rest of Britain. The leaves are oval and often quite woolly, as are the stems, while the rounded cluster of flowers comes in shades of pink, reddish-purple and very occasionally white.

Wild Thyme is aromatic and there can be few finer descriptions than in Rudyard Kipling's poem *Sussex* which includes the line 'thyme that smells like dawn in Paradise'. In the Highlands the tea brewed from it had the power to prevent nightmares; its smell gave courage and strength. In Shetland it remains known as *Tae girse* but it is doubtful whether anyone still gathers the leaves as ingredients for an herbal tobacco. Along with Lady's Bedstraw, Wild Thyme provided the Virgin Mary with an aromatic mattress.

9) Cat's-ear (*Hypochaeris radicata*)   Daisy family

Height to 25cm; flowers May to September. Widespread and abundant in Orkney (25/28); easy to find.

Cat's-ear is another Dandelion-type plant that deserves closer scrutiny. It is a perennial that favours steep and well-drained heathy and grassy banks not solely by the sea but also in meadows, links and roadside verges. Its main requirement is a growing medium that is free-draining and – blessed with that – it frequently appears in lawns. Waterlogged soils are shunned.

The tall and slender stem is leafless and grows from a basal rosette of lance-shaped, rough, bristly and wavy-toothed leaves which are between 5cm and 10cm long. The flowers are bright yellow and the collar (or involucre) is bell-shaped and narrows quickly to the stalk. The massed nodding flower-heads are a welcome addition to Orkney's late summer and early autumn wildflower displays.

10) **Autumnal Hawkbit** (*Leontodon autumnalis*)   Daisy family

Height to 25cm; flowers June to October. Widespread and abundant in Orkney (26/28); easy to find.

Along with Cat's-ear, another Dandelion-type perennial plant is commonly found among coastal grasslands. Autumnal Hawkbit is superficially very similar to Cat's-ear in that both have the typical yellow Dandelion-like flower-heads. However, a closer examination will reveal a few quite obvious differences especially with regard to the leaves – those of the Autumnal Hawkbit are hairless; those of the Cat's-ear are bristly. Furthermore, the leaves of the Autumnal Hawkbit are deeply toothed with narrow and pointed lobes; the leaves of the Cat's-ear are wavy-toothed. Lastly, the leaves of the Autumnal Hawkbit have a prominent vein; on those of the Cat's-ear it

10. Autumnal Hawkbit at North Hill, Papa Westray

is indistinct. Finally, any further doubt may be dispelled by looking at the collar (or involucre) – that of the Autumnal Hawkbit tapers to the stem while that of the Cat's-ear narrows rapidly.

11) Roseroot (*Sedum rosea*) Stonecrop family
Midsummer men – *Snowdon rose*

Height to 30cm; flowers May to August. Local and occasional in Orkney (7/28); hard to find.

In Orkney, although this perennial occurs sporadically on inland cliffs especially on Hoy, it is chiefly a plant of the sea cliff. Elsewhere in Britain it occurs with much more frequency inland and is a feature of the high mountains of Scotland, England, Wales and Ireland. Indeed in North Wales it is known as the *Snowdon rose*. Its common name derives from its smell; Gerard wrote that the cut stock gives out a delicious smell 'like the damaske rose'. The Orkney name refers to the plant's upright stance and period of flowering. On the island of Skye, Roseroot was used as a purge for calves and in Alaska the Inupiat Inuit resorted to fermented rhizomes in times of famine.

On top of its tough, woody, grey stock that grows out of crevices in the rock are orange-yellow four-petalled flowers clustered in flat-topped heads. The leaves are thick, stiff, oval and succulent and often completely obscure the stem. It is a striking plant and has become a favourite in gardens.

11. Roseroot at the Brough of the Berry, Hoy

12. Spring Squill at White Fowl Nevi, Deerness
13. Sea Ivory at Head of Geo, Wyre

12) Spring Squill (*Scilla verna*)   Lily family

Swine's beads *– Sea onion*

Height to 10cm; flowers April to June. Widespread and abundant in Orkney (25/28); easy to find.

For a short period in May and June coastal grasslands in Orkney shimmer with a soft and hazy violet-blue. Such can be the intensity of this unexpected and surprising blue glow across the green sward that you may catch yourself rubbing your eyes in disbelief. The leaves are grass-like, narrow, fleshy and often curly and appear before the six-petalled sky-blue flowers. Very occasionally white flowers are met with. In its autumn, those leaves turn yellow and the flower-heads turn into papery capsules brimming with seeds of jet-black, the source of its Orkney name *Swine's beads*. It is the only truly wild plant in the county that is also a bulb; it is the bulb that no doubt accounts for its Manx name *Sea onion*.

In Europe Spring Squill can be found along the western seaboard from Portugal to Faroe via Spain, France, the United Kingdom and Norway. In Orkney it occurs on almost every coast and as with other areas that have pronounced oceanic climates, it can grow well inland too.

13) Sea Ivory (*Ramalina siliquosa*)   Lichen

Height to 10cm. Widespread and abundant in Orkney; very easy to find.

Throughout coastal Orkney, and also frequently inland where the

14 Eyebright at Roseness, Holm

influence of the sea remains strong, rocks, dykes, trees, gravestones and even fence posts may be adorned with this striking and conspicuous lichen. Indeed, where it is abundant, the density of growth may completely mask the surface upon which it is growing; forests of Sea Ivory are stunningly decorative and add a whole new dimension to the ordinary.

It is a shrubby and tufted lichen, either yellow-grey or blue-green grey. It is hard, brittle and dry to the touch. The strap-shaped leaves often have granular wrinkles and warts and the frequently seen spore-producing discs sit on very short stalks.

14) Eyebright (*Euphrasia officinalis* agg.) — Figwort family

Brighteye

Height to 12cm; flowers June to September. Widespread and abundant in Orkney (24/28); easy to find.

There are few groups of plants that occur in Orkney that are as complex as the Eyebrights. Even on a short summer's walk one cannot fail to notice the variability in plant and flower size of the various species and subspecies of these parasitic annuals; within that short summer walk you may encounter the tiniest specimens barely two centimetres high with minute flowers to match, yet a few steps further on there may be individuals ankle-high and flowers as large as a fingernail. In Britain there may be as many as twenty species all favouring a variety of natural habitats. In Orkney it is probable that there are ten different species, the most frequent being *Euphrasia arctica, Euphrasia foulaensis, Euphrasia micrantha* and *Euphrasia confusa*. It is the first of that list of four which is the Eyebright that one is most likely to encounter on coastal cliffs. The green stems are often tinged with purple as can the leaves which are fleshy, oval and sharp-toothed. The white bell-shaped, two-lipped flowers are suffused with purple or violet and feature an open yellow throat.

Eyebright has been traditionally important in the treatment of eye ailments. In the Middle Ages it was renowned for brightening the eyes and in Milton's Paradise Lost, the Archangel anointed Adam's eyes until he could see death and the miserable future of mankind. In Scotland Eyebright was infused in milk and applied by feather. Elsewhere the juice was dropped into eyes to ease inflammation. It appears to have had a reputation as an herbal cure-all; not only was it used to clear sinuses but in the Outer Hebrides an infusion of Eyebright was considered a calming beverage.

15) **Mountain Everlasting** (*Antennaria dioica*)   Daisy family

Cat's foot, Cat's paws, Pussy toes, Scottish edelweiss

Height to 10cm; flowers May to July. Widespread and occasional in Orkney (19/28); not easy to find.

Gerard described the *Scottish edelweiss* as 'the cotton weede of the hills and stonie mountains…so exceeding white and hoarie, that one would thinke it be a plant made of wool'. The male and female flower umbels, which grow in small clusters, are on separate plants and it would seem that Gerard is referring solely to the male since the female's petals are rose-pink. A leafy and white woolly stem is trimmed with alternate leaves; it rises from the centre of a rosette of leaves which, like those of the stem, are green above and woolly and white below. It is a perennial that favours well-drained, dry grasslands and heaths and is quite likely to be found growing in association with Wild Thyme.

In Somerset it is known as *Cat's foot*, in Cumbria as *Cat's paw* and in parts of the United States as *Pussy toes* – it is the arrangement of flowers which prompts the feline connection. It is also an everlasting or an imperishable '*immortelle*' and in bygone times constituted a main element of dried winter bouquets.

16) Alpine Meadow-rue (*Thalictrum alpinum*)   Buttercup family

Height to 8cm; flowers June and July. Local and occasional in Orkney (10/28); not easy to find.

If ever you are crawling about on your hands and knees among damp and heathy grassland or flushes that are found near the coast, you may be fortunate to find one of Orkney's subtle gems, Alpine Meadow-rue. Normally it is a plant of the mountains but in the far north of its range it may be found at much lower altitudes and in northern Scotland and Orkney it grows almost at sea level. It is a tiny and delicate perennial whose fern-like leaves on a wiry and thread-like stem, are far more obvious than the drooping petal-less flowers; it is the yellow anthers and purplish stamens that give the flower what colour it has.

15. Mountain Everlasting at Little Lobust, Rousay
16. Alpine Meadow-rue at the Breck, Orphir

17) Crowberry (*Empetrum nigrum*)   Crowberry family
***Heather berry**, Wireling*

Height to 25cm; flowers April to June, fruits June to September. Widespread and abundant in Orkney (25/28); easy to find.

The Yorkshire name is *Wireling* – a succinct description of this tough and wiry-stemmed, evergreen relative of heather. Across Britain it is a shrub of the uplands, far more abundant in Scotland than in Wales or England. In Orkney it can be found on acid soils countywide but appears to prosper on the heaths that are close to the sea. The leaves are glossy green and linear with rolled back margins which make the underside impossible to see. The flowers are tiny and composed of six minute and separate pink sepals. The female plant bears the berries which turn from green to black.

For centuries in Orkney, Crowberry was high on the list of useful and indispensable plants. Archaeological excavations at Skara Brae unearthed small pieces of rope twisted from the stems of this shrub. From 'ropes' it is a fairly small step to 'baskets' and for maybe 5000 years Crowberry was integral to the manufacture of *cubbies*, *luppies*, *skep* and *kaisies*, all of them woven containers of different types and capable of performing different functions. It provided a purplish dye and another of its merits was that it was edible – hence its Orkney name *Heather berry*. However, the small black berries make for poor eating so that extremely large gatherings are needed to make jam or jelly. In the raw state, the fruits are gritty, with stones bigger than flesh, and tasting of turpentine.

18) Goldenrod (*Solidago virgaurea*)   Daisy family

Height to 70cm; flowers July to September. Local and occasional in Orkney (10/28); not easy to find.

In Britain, Goldenrod occurs in both lowlands and uplands and frequents woodlands, hedgerows, heaths, sea cliffs, rocky burns, dales, mountains and tundra. It has obviously fewer options in Orkney,

17. Crowberry at Tafts, Rousay.
18. Goldenrod at Fillets, Graemsay
19. Carnation Sedge at Inyama Hellia, Birsay

but even here can be found from sea level to the summits of the hills of Hoy by way of coastal cliffs, ledges, dales, burns and heath. There is a similarity to Common Ragwort in appearance but Goldenrod is an imposing and erect plant of deep greens and bright yellows. The stalked leaves are toothed and lance-shaped while the discs and rays of the numerous florets within the flower-head are chrome-yellow.

Historically it was highly prized as a healing herb for wounds and undoubtedly saved the lives of many involved in sword fights or stabbings. Its value was reflected in its price – during Elizabethan times an ounce of Goldenrod cost half-a-crown, the equivalent of a fortnight's pay for a house servant. Its Latin name comes from the verb *solidare*, to make things whole.

19) Carnation Sedge (*Carex panicea*)   Sedge family

Pink-leaved sedge

Height to 20cm; flowers May to June, fruits June to September. Widespread and abundant in Orkney (26/28); easy to find.

Carnation Sedge is almost as widespread in Britain and Orkney as Glaucous Sedge. However, it would appear that this perennial, with extensive creeping rhizomes, is possibly more tolerant of acid conditions. Just like Glaucous Sedge though it can be found in a wide range of damp or wet habitats including wet meadows, heaths, flushes, mires and salt marshes. Its physical differences from Glaucous Sedge are fairly clear in the leaf colour and structure. The leaf is unveined, glaucous on both sides and terminates in a three-sided tip, which is as easy to feel as it is easy to see. It also has close fitting white or pinkish sheaths which possibly accounts for Magnus Spence referring to it as the *Pink-leaved Sedge*. In addition, it has a sparser flowering head with a single male spike and one to three female spikes.

20) Devil's-bit Scabious (*Succisa pratensis*) Teasel family
Blue bonnets, *Blue buttons*, *Blue heads*, *Blue kiss*.

Height to 80cm; flowers June to October. Widespread and abundant in Orkney (25/28); easy to find.

One of the most conspicuous of Orkney's late summer flowers, Devil's-bit Scabious is known from just about everywhere in the county except Sule Skerry. It enjoys moist and slightly acidic soils and although it is frequently encountered amongst cliff top heath, it is also profuse on inland heaths, in rough grassland and in mires but it is predictably scarce in sandy areas. The rounded flower-heads are generally in shades of purple, violet, mauve and blue but occasionally white or pink may be met with. Colloquial names referring to the colour of the flower-heads are widespread nationally. It is a hairy perennial with elliptical, untoothed leaves which often have dark blotches.

The plant has a very short root-stock as though part of it has been bitten off. The story goes that the Devil was envious of the plant's ability and virtue and bit the root to destroy it or render it less effective. In medieval times it was the apothecaries' plant for the scab or scabies but in later years it was considered an herbal cure-all especially for scrofula and toothache.

21) Glaucous Sedge (*Carex flacca*) Sedge family
Carnation grass

Height 20cm; flowers May to June, fruits June to September. Widespread and abundant in Orkney (27/28); easy to find.

In coastal grasslands, the shortest turf is usually found nearest the sea and salt spray and it is here where competition is less intense, that the pale leaves of the perennials Glaucous Sedge and Carnation Sedge stand out most clearly. Both species are very alike and can be found in very similar ground conditions. However an observant eye and hand can differentiate them readily with practice. Glaucous Sedge is so named because the underside of the leaf is glaucous and contrasts with the dull green of the upperside. The leaf, unlike that of Carnation Sedge, is veined to the tip and the flowering head is usually made up of one to three male spikes above one to five female spikes.

Throughout Britain, it is found commonly in wet habitats such as flushes, meadows, fens, bogs and even salt marshes. Much the same can be said of its distribution in Orkney where it is frequent in damp species-rich heaths and fens and additionally, is invariably found in close proximity to *Primula scotica*.

22) **Common Sorrel** (*Rumex acetosa*) — Dock family

Soorick, **Souricks** – *Sour dock*, *Sour leaves*, *Sour grass*, *Sour sauce*, *Sour suds*

Height to 70cm; flowers May to June. Widespread and abundant in Orkney (27/28); easy to find.

For members of the Dock family it is always going to be an uphill struggle to win favour. However over the centuries Common Sorrel has been able to gain some well-deserved points. It is an abundant perennial and may be found not only in grasslands near the coast but also in less maritime localities such as roadside verges and even in some of Orkney's woodlands. The inflorescence is made up of loose whorls of reddish flowers while the shiny leaves are arrow-shaped with backward pointing lobes.

It is the leaves for which this plant is held in high regard. They have a sharp and refreshing flavour and have been used over the centuries as a salad vegetable, as a flavouring ingredient for ale and as a sauce to accompany fish.

20. Devil's-bit Scabious at Carlin Geo, Stronsay

21. Glaucous Sedge at North Campi Geo, Head of Work, St Ola

22. Common Sorrel at North Taing, Auskerry

Arable fields, waysides and disturbed ground

This chapter has developed into something of 'catch all' section; within it are a variety of habitats, none of them natural, all of them man-made. Among the habitats included are arable farmland, waysides and disturbed ground, and of course within this broad category there may be a high degree of overlap. This being the case, some of the wildflowers that are described and illustrated in this chapter are widespread and quite ubiquitous in their distribution – Daisy and Dandelion immediately spring to mind; both species may be found in almost any location.

Some of Orkney's most abundant and widespread wildflowers can be found in these various man-made habitats. The disturbed ground around building developments, whether domestic or industrial, is often an ideal site for half a dozen of the county's most common wildflowers to colonise; the list is likely to include Creeping and Spear Thistles, Prickly Sow-thistle, Hogweed, Groundsel, Pineappleweed and Broad-leaved Dock. All these plants need to see is a spade; within six months what was flower-less newly-turned soil has become dense thickets of some of Orkney's least fragile flowers.

By contrast this chapter also contains some of the county's

Above Flotta kirk and Kirk Bay, Flotta

disappearing flowers. Arable farmland and pasture is a broad category but one which contains many of the wildflowers that are described and illustrated in this chapter. With changes in agricultural practices some of what were Orkney's most familiar arable wildflowers have become increasingly scarce over the last fifty years. Field Pansy, Sun Spurge, Corn Spurrey, Corn Marigold and a selection of Fumitories flourished on Orkney crofts throughout the parishes and islands. So common was Corn Spurrey that it was looked upon as a staple food in times of famine. Nowadays the discovery of a field of Corn Marigolds sets botanists' pulses racing.

Wayside verges vary greatly in quality and composition. Some of the best are those on shallow peat and the resulting array of flowers bears favourable comparison to the best displays that can be found on the hill ground. Other verges, particularly those that have received fertiliser from neighbouring fields, are of poorer quality and can be choked with Hogweed and dockens. However, three colourful favourites can be found scrambling exuberantly along fences – the purple Bush Vetch, the blue Tufted Vetch and the bright yellow Meadow Vetchling.

Near some of Orkney's older houses, the verge may contain some of the flowers that have crossed the garden border. It can be quite commonplace to see Rhubarb and Sweet Cicely growing alongside each other – at the dining table, the latter sweetened the former. Nearby there may be stands of Tansy, another dessert provider, and Sweet Rocket.

1. Daisy at Heath house, Stenness

1) Daisy (*Bellis perennis*)   Daisy family

Mimmy-feeblick*, *Cockalowrie – *Day's eye, Eye of the day, Silver pennies, Kokkeluri*.

Height to 6cm; flowers March to October. Widespread and abundant in Orkney (27/28); easy to find.

This very familiar and common perennial, though a tough little plant, dislikes too much competition. Heavily grazed or trampled grassland which for some of the year has also been relatively wet appears to be its favourite situation. It is less common in natural habitats but may be found along the edges of burns, lochs and slacks. The leaves are clustered into a rosette from which arises a single slightly hairy stem. The lone flower-head is composed of a yellow central disc surrounded by white petals tipped with crimson. There is a widely held perception that spring has truly arrived when one foot is able to cover seven flowering Daisies.

Medicinally, Daisies have been used widely as an herbal cure-all and in Orkney they were a component of the 'miracle drink' (the beverage that was hailed as a cure for Axes, see page xviii). The young leaves and buds may be eaten raw, and the buds may be pickled in vinegar as a substitute for capers.

2) Spear Thistle (*Cirsium vulgare*)   Daisy family

Height to 125cm; flowers July to October. Widespread and abundant in Orkney (27/28); easy to find.

Often quite tall and always with a stately bearing, this very abundant

3. Creeping Thistle at Bomo, Eday

2. Spear Thistle at Rerwick Head, St Andrews

perennial is possibly the 'Scotch Thistle' and certainly bears the closest resemblance to those thistles seen on early coins. Despite these grand affinities though, it is considered by the authorities to be a noxious weed and subject to control by landowners. It occurs in a wide variety of habitats, the common denominator often seems to be disturbed ground. The leaves have several deep points armed with spines and look quite murderous, while the slightly cottony stems are adorned with similar sharp barbs. The flowers are usually pink-purple but are fairly frequently white. Elaine Bullard believed that a persistent strain of white-flowered plants occurs on the Brough of Birsay.

3) Creeping Thistle (*Cirsium arvense*)   Daisy family

Height to 100cm; flowers June to September. Widespread and abundant in Orkney (27/28); easy to find.

There is a theory that Scotland adopted the thistle as its symbol because of its resemblance to the schiltron. Creeping Thistles are often found as tall, dense and impenetrable obstacles armed with blades; the schiltron was a massed rank of spears employed by the Scottish army and used so effectively at the Battle of Bannockburn in 1314. However, these noble thoughts count for nought, since it is considered to be a serious weed and landowners are obliged to eradicate it.

Disturbed ground and overgrazed pastures are the likeliest places to find this invasive perennial and it can regenerate prolifically from rhizome fragments – the roots are very persistent and may descend and spread to 50cm. The flower-heads are usually mauve but white flowers are not uncommon. The stems lack spines but the wavy and toothed edges of the leaves are armed with strong and slender points.

4) Dandelion (*Taraxacum officinale* agg.) Daisy family
Dog flooer – *Piss-a-bed, Pissimire, Fairy clocks, Clock flower, Time teller* and *Shepherd's clock*

Height to 30cm; flowers March to September. Widespread and abundant in Orkney (27/28); very easy to find.

There are few wildflowers that are as well-known as the Dandelion, but there is more to this humble perennial than meets the eye. It's hard to believe that more than 230 micro-species of this one species have been identified in Britain. In Orkney 19 micro-species have been catalogued, surely only a small number of the micro-species that are truly here. However, two of these micro-species have been found nowhere else in the world, and one – *Taraxacum orcadense* – has even been named after our county, following its discovery in Mainland and on Cava.

During April and May the Orkney countryside is bright with the golden yellow discs that suddenly materialise. The spear-shaped leaves which emerge from a rosette are lobed and toothed and the stems, which exude a milky latex, are smooth and hollow. The gold discs range from 2cm to 6cm and are composed of up to 200 florets. Of course it is the leaves' teeth which give us the name Dandelion from the French '*dent de lion*', and the fruiting head colloquial names such as *Fairy clocks, Clock flower, Time teller* and *Shepherd's clock*.

Dandelions have given of themselves in a multitude of ways. As an edible food, the leaves can be eaten cooked or raw and the roots may be dried, roasted or ground and converted into 'coffee'. Medicinally, Dandelions once were widely used as a diuretic and for urinary disorders, hence the names, *Piss-a-bed* and *Pissimire*. In addition, it was regarded as quinine substitute and used to treat sore throats, chests and stomachs. Even the milky sap was considered to hold healing properties for those with alcohol induced hangovers.

4. Dandelion at Senness, North Ronaldsay
5. Smooth Sow-thistle on Pier rd, St Margaret's Hope, South Ronaldsay

5) Smooth Sow-thistle (Sonchus oleraceus) — Daisy family
Dog thistle – *Milkweed, Milky dickle, Hare's lettuce, Hare's house, Hare's palace, Rabbit's meat, Rabbit's victuals*

Height to 150cm; flowers June to August. Widespread and frequent in Orkney (15/28); fairly easy to find.

Of the three Orkney Sow-thistles this annual is the least savage of the triad, indeed its leaves lack the spines that the other two Sow-thistles are armed with. The leaves of the Smooth Sow-thistle are non-glossy and have a grey-green colouration. They have shallow teeth and the ends of the leaves terminate in a broad triangle. Like the Prickly Sow-thistle, the flower-heads cluster in a loose umbel but whereas those of the 'Prickly' are golden-yellow, those of the 'Smooth' are pale yellow. It can be found in all sorts of disturbed ground but seems to be more frequent in coastal habitats and less frequent in upland than 'Prickly'.

6) Prickly Sow-thistle (Sonchus asper) — Daisy family
Milkweed, Milky dickle, Hare's lettuce, Hare's house, Rabbit's meat, Rabbit's victuals, Swinies

Height to 150cm; flowers June to August. Widespread and abundant in Orkney (25/28); easy to find.

There is no getting away from the fact that this annual is a fearsome looking plant. The leaves, the colour of boiled green cabbage, are glossy, crisped, deeply toothed and bear stiff and barbarous spines. The base of the leaf clasping the stem is rounded and the deep golden-yellow flowers are in a loose umbel. It tolerates damper soils than its close relative Smooth Sow-thistle, is intolerant of grazing and is also more likely to be found in uplands.

As with other Sow-thistles it is closely linked with rabbits, hares, sows and milk.

6. Prickly Sow-thistle at Burnside, Flotta

7. Corn Spurrey at Hawn, Wyre

7) **Corn Spurrey** (*Spergula arvensis*) Campion family
Ruithy girs

Height to 15cm; flowers July to September. Widespread and occasional in Orkney (22/28); not easy to find.

Often where it does occur, it grows in great abundance and it is not uncommon to see whole arable fields covered. It is an annual that can flourish in open and recently disturbed ground such as ploughed fields especially where the soils are light. Despite its generally fragile appearance it is a plant with a robust and important history. There is evidence of its use as human food during Roman times and there is also speculation that in Orkney it may have been a key food source during the Neolithic period. We know for a fact that Corn Spurrey has been grown as a fodder crop in Britain for centuries and in times of poor crop yields and shortages, its seeds were mixed with the crop grain and ground for flour. When not feeding humans it was more usually given as feed to hens.

The leaves appear dusty and are thin, blunt and furrowed below. They are thread-like and arranged in conspicuous whorls. Brittle stems support tiny, white, five-petalled flower-heads which are often turned down almost bestowing a shyness to this delicate and now declining plant.

8) **Field Pansy** (*Viola arvensis*) Violet family
Kiss-me, Stepmothers, Herbe of the Trinity, Trinity violet, Three-faces-under-a-hood.

Height to 15cm; flowers April to September. Local and rare in Orkney (3/28); hard to find.

As with the Wild Pansy of the links, the Field Pansy is a plant that flourishes on light, well-drained soils. In William Turner's *the Names*

8. Field Pansy at Brodgar, Stenness
9. Field Forget-me-not above Mill Burn, Orphir

of Herbes (1548), he wrote that 'it groweth oft among the corn' and although declining in Orkney, this annual can still be found in intensively cultivated arable fields or persisting on field margins and banks that are not affected by weedkiller. The Field Pansy differs from the Wild Pansy by having much larger leaves and creamy-yellow flowers whose petals are much shorter than the sepals.

Pansies are steeped in associations of love principally because of the face-like patterns that appear on the petals and seem to be kissing. Some of these associations have already been described for the Wild Pansy (page 24) as have some of the many names for this winsome plant. The word Pansy is derived from the French for thought, *pensée*, and was in use in England by 1500.

9) Field Forget-me-not (*Myosotis arvensis*)   Borage family

Field scorpion-grass, *Scorpion grass*, *Snake grass*

Height to 15cm; flowers April to September. Widespread and abundant in Orkney (22/28); easy to find.

Whereas many forget-me-nots occur in damp or very damp places, Field Forget-me-not is an annual plant that prefers to keep its feet dry. Additionally it is very much a plant of cultivation but may also be found on dry waste places and sandy links. In its early history, it was known as *Scorpion grass* since the young, tightly-coiled flower-head gradually unfurls and so bears more than a passing resemblance to a scorpion's tail or serpent – in Yorkshire it bore the name *Snake-grass*. It is generally a short and softly hairy plant with its lower leaves stalked and forming a conspicuous rosette. The flowers are uniformly grey-blue.

See Tufted Forget-me-not and Water Forget-me-not, pages 52/53.

10) Creeping Buttercup (*Ranunculus repens*)　　　Buttercup family

Creeping stems may reach to 50cm; flowers May to August. Widespread and abundant in Orkney (27/28); easy to find.

Like many of the wildflowers in this section, this particular buttercup is tolerant of many situations. However, it is most at home in wet or damp disturbed habitats and where the soil is rich such as wet meadows and farm gateways. Creeping Buttercup is a very common and familiar perennial and at times may be considered to be a pestilential weed especially when encountered in the garden.

While most buttercup flower-heads are very similar to look at making identification of different species problematic, the leaves generally provide much more help. Those of the Creeping Buttercup are hairy and have three lobes, the middle one of which has a noticeable stem. Additionally, the flower stem is grooved and of course it may also be distinguished from other buttercups by its creeping habit.

Buttercups have had a variety of medicinal uses in Scotland including the combat of bubonic plague.

11) Lesser Trefoil (*Trifolium dubium*)　　　Pea family

Height to 10cm; flowers May to October. Local and occasional in Orkney (13/28); not easy to find.

This miniature clover maintains a low profile in hay meadows, waysides, waste places, lawns, open rocky situations and is equally likely to be found in dry or damp conditions. The globe-like flower-heads, composed of up to 25 flowers, sit on a single stem and are lemon-yellow; the leaves are almost hairless. There are two very similar species with which it can be confused: Hop Trefoil (*Trifolium campestre*) which has sparsely hairy leaves, is generally bigger and

10. Creeping Buttercup at St Margaret's Hope recycling centre, South Ronaldsay

has more flowers on its flower-head and Black Medick (*Medicago lupulina*) which has a tiny, pointed tip to its leaves.

Some writers believe that Lesser Trefoil is the Irish shamrock; shamrock is the anglicised version of '*seamrog*' meaning 'little clover'. The flower's reputation and subsequent immortality derives from the legend of St Patrick and his reference to it in his explanation of the Holy Trinity. St Patrick's Day is March 17th, a day when spring may begin, and when lucky charms, such as the Trefoil, may provide protection against sorcery.

12) Field Horsetail (*Equisetum arvense*)　　　　　　Horsetail family

Height to 80cm; spores ripe March to June. Widespread and abundant in Orkney (24/28); easy to find.

Most of Orkney's horsetails like to feel damp around their roots; two already included in the book are Water Horsetail (page 70) and Marsh Horsetail (page 70) and they can be found in the Lowland Freshwater section. Field Horsetail does not have such wet requirements. It is much more tolerant of drier conditions than other members of the family and this feature, combined with vigorous growth and resistance to herbicides, means that this perennial can be found in a variety of locations such as paths, roadsides, quarries and gardens.

It has two different types of stem. Pinkish-brown fertile stems with a 'cone' appear early in the year. As this 'cone' ripens, sterile stems that are green and many-grooved, appear with whorls of branches spreading from the stem joints. A cross section of the green stem reveals a central hollow which is less than half the diameter of the whole.

11. Lesser Trefoil at Sutherland, Flotta

12. Field Horsetail at the Shop, Eday

13. Colt's-foot at Loth, Sanday
14. Common Hemp-nettle at Dale, Harray
15. Stinging Nettle at Skogar, Birsay

13) Colt's-foot (Tussilago farfara) Daisy family
Tishalago – *Foal foot, Sow foot, Calves' foot, Horse hoof, Hoofs, Son before father*

Height to 25cm; flowers March and April. Widespread and abundant in Orkney (25/28); easy to find.

This perennial is usually the first of the year to produce a conspicuous flower in Orkney. The sunny-yellow heads on the distinctive scaly stems brighten up March and April but in favoured southerly situations will bloom in the depths of February. It appears to prefer hard bare places such as can be found on verges or on the shore at the base of cliffs but it may also be found in flushes. The Orkney name, *Tishalago*, and the Scots name *Dishilago* are both very similar to the Latin. However its common name refers to the shape of the leaves and elsewhere in Britain it has various similar names associated with the leaf shape.

Throughout Scotland, Colt's-foot has been used extensively as a cure for coughs, consumption, sprains, and as a tobacco and tea substitute. Its leaves have even been transformed into beer, jelly, syrup and wine. In Orkney, Magnus Spence in his *Flora Orcadensis* reports that a sweetened decoction of flowers was drunk as a cure for colds and dried leaves were smoked to cure coughs and bronchitis. Indeed it was considered to be the apothecary's best herb for lungs. One of its most notable features is that the flower is visible much earlier than the leaf giving rise to another of its names, *Son before father***.**

14) Common Hemp-nettle (Galeopsis tetrahit)   Dead-nettle family

Height to 60cm; flowers July to September. Widespread and abundant in Orkney (20/28); easy to find.

The Common Hemp-nettle is entirely lacking in any downy attributes; it is a coarse plant, both to look at and to touch. The stems are branched and bristly and covered in sticky hairs. The flowers are usually pink with purple markings on the lower lip but white flowers are not uncommon.

It appears to prefer damper soils to either the Red Dead-nettle or the Northern Dead-nettle and in Britain may be found in woodland clearings, fens, riverbanks and wet heaths. However, in Orkney, this annual is most likely to be encountered in areas of cultivation where it has a reputation of being a robust colonist that is both resilient and resistant to eradication attempts.

15) **Stinging Nettle** (*Urtica dioica*) Nettle family

Height to 150m; flowers May to September. Widespread and abundant in Orkney (27/28); easy to find.

Most of us will give little regard to this very familiar perennial and yet it has been until recently one of the most utilised plants throughout the world. Like many of the plants in this section it has the ability to travel the globe wherever man sets foot and wherever he has disturbed the ground. Its uses are manifold. As a food, Nettles have been valued for their nutritious properties and were cultivated as a vegetable, similar to Kale or Spinach, that could survive frosts. As a food for stock they were widely used; we know that in places as separate as Hungary and the Outer Hebrides they were harvested for fodder and in Orkney for fattening and improving the condition of pigs. Along with Marsh Marigolds they were used in rennet for curdling milk especially in the Western Isles of Scotland. As a medicine it has had an impressive range of applications from halting nosebleeds on Gigha, coughs in the Outer Hebrides, rheumatism in Orkney and Fife to childbirth remedies in South America and New Guinea. The Fife remedy whereby the affected area of rheumatism was thrashed with Nettles was not for the faint-hearted.

Nettles were also grown and harvested for making into cloth. Throughout Europe sheets, table cloths and clothing were manufactured and during the First World War Germany processed a staggering 2500 tonnes of raw plant material per year, much of it targeted for the production of uniforms. It was extremely labour intensive since 40kg of Nettles was necessary for a single shirt. Its role in the British war effort was less significant but Nettles were used for dyeing camouflage nets. Historically the stem fibres have been used to make twine and rope and this use is documented by the Nitinaht of Vancouver Island.

Given its stinging abilities, there can be few people who are unaware of its appearance. It is a coarsely hairy plant whose stem and triangular leaves are covered with stinging hairs. The inflorescence is cream-coloured and droops like catkins.

16) Shepherd's-purse (*Capsella bursa-pastoris*)   Cabbage family

Height to 20cm; flowers all year. Widespread and abundant in Orkney (24/28); easy to find.

Although this annual is considered to be a plant of disturbed ground and cultivated fields, it is probably best known as a plant of the pavement. It appears able to flourish in the soil-filled gaps between paving slabs. It is named from its purse-shaped seed heads; a tiny purse could only belong to a poor man, such as a shepherd. Yet despite this apparent lack of worth, its seeds are made into bread by the Apache in North America and in Shetland have been fed to poultry. The form of the seed head makes for easy identification; the

16. Shepherd's-purse at the Kirk, Graemsay
17. Red Dead-nettle at Fossil and Vintage Centre, Burray
18. Northern Dead-nettle at Fossil and Vintage Centre Burray

heart-shaped or purse-shaped triangle stands on its point at the head of a long and slender stalk. The main stem is erect and rises from a rosette of leaves which can be very variable in appearance. The clasping leaves on the stem have arrow-shaped lobes and the flower-head is a cluster of small and white, four-petalled flowers.

17) Red Dead-nettle (*Lamium purpureum*)   Dead-nettle family

Height to 20cm; flowers March to October. Widespread and abundant in Orkney (22/28); easy to find.

Despite a similarity in leaf shape to the Stinging Nettle, it's a blessing to know that the dead-nettles will leave your skin unscathed. One of the most obvious differences between dead-nettles and true nettles is that the former have square hollow stems and the latter have round solid ones. There are four members of the dead-nettle family in Orkney and the Red Dead-nettle, an annual, is possibly the commonest. Invariably it is described as a 'weed of cultivation' but possibly more charitably it should be known as a colonist of disturbed and fertile soils. It is a downy plant with a stem that is branched from the base. The toothed leaves are purple-green and the flowers pink with a hint of purple. It is not uncommon to find it in flower throughout the winter in Orkney.

18) Northern Dead-nettle (*Lamium confertum*)   Dead-nettle family

Height to 20cm; flowers April to August. Widespread and frequent in Orkney (18/28); easy to find.

Superficially the Northern Dead-nettle is similar to the Red Dead-nettle, with which it often grows alongside in Orkney. However, the upper leaves of the Red Dead-nettle are longer than they are wide, while those of the Northern Dead-nettle are wider than they are long. In the Northern Dead-nettle the sharp points of the calyx are as long or longer than the pink petal tubes while those of the Red Dead-nettle are not. It is a plant of the north and is almost entirely restricted to coastal Scotland and the Isle of Man where it appears to prefer light soils.

19) Hybrid Woundwort (*Stachys* x *ambigua*)   Dead-nettle family
Lamb's lugs

Height to 100cm; flowers May to August. Widespread and abundant in Orkney (23/28); easy to find.

There are four Woundworts in Orkney – Hedge (*Stachys sylvatica*), Marsh (*Stachys palustris*), the mixture of both (Hybrid Woundwort) and Field (*Stachys arvensis*). The uncommon Hedge Woundwort can be found in plantations, the equally uncommon Field Woundwort grows in cultivated ground, the more common Marsh Woundwort grows in fens and ditches, and the hybrid can be found widely on either rough or cultivated ground and often on roadsides. They are all tall perennials and very similar to look at but Hybrid Woundwort seems to have more in common with Marsh Woundwort: both are bristly and both have pinkish-purple flowers. The difference is that the upper leaves of Marsh Woundwort lack stalks, while those of Hybrid Woundwort have short stalks. It may be too that the flowers of Hybrid Woundwort are more purple. Hedge Woundwort, which is extremely rare in the county, has flowers of beetroot-red and is decidedly pungent.

It is probable that the Woundworts were brought into Orkney by Norse settlers. The plants contain a volatile oil with antiseptic properties and as vulneraries were especially useful in stemming the flow of blood.

20) Charlock (*Sinapis arvensis*)   Cabbage family
Bresso, **Runcho** – *Wild kale, Wild mustard, Wild turnip, Bazzocks, Kinkle, Skellocks, Corn cail*

Height to 80cm; flowers April to July. Widespread and frequent in Orkney (19/28); fairly easy to find.

19. Hybrid Woundwort at Breckaskaill, Westray
20. Charlock at St Ninians kirk, Deerness
21. Sun Spurge at Strathborg, Sandwick

Generally, in Britain, Charlock is known as a plant of cultivated and waste ground, railways and tips. In fact previously it was not uncommon to see fields of young wheat yellow with Charlock. However, it appears that this annual is easily controlled by herbicides and consequently is less frequent now in such situations. It has been a notable plant in the past; not only has it served as a pot herb, more importantly it has been utilised as a famine food. We know that in Orkney during the late 19th Century and in the three month period prior to harvest-time when grain was predictably scarce, the seeds of Charlock were gathered to make a life-saving *reuthie* bread.

Overall, Charlock is rough and hairy with lower leaves that are large, very bristly, toothed, stalked and lyre-shaped. Many members of this family are quite similar but the four-petalled, yellow flowers of Charlock are distinguished by having sepals that spread to 90 degrees.

21) Sun Spurge (*Euphorbia helioscopia*) Spurge family

Warty girse*, *Wartiwort – *Deil's churnstaff*

Height to 35cm; flowers April to October. Local and occasional in Orkney (10/28); hard to find.

All the members of the Spurge family have milky juice and it would appear a certain toxicity. The milk is acrid and contact with the skin can cause irritation and inflammation. Sun Spurge has been used in Orkney as a cure for warts and, in the form of a poultice, a cure for gout. In the 18th Century, George Low referred to it as *Wartiwort* but it is also known by the name *Warty girse*. Gerard says of it that the juice or milk 'cureth all roughness of the skinne, mangines, leprie, scurffe, and running scabs'. Typically this is an annual of lighter and well-drained soils and frequently found in cultivated ground with root and leaf crops and also occurs on waste ground and roadsides. Its single erect stem is hairless and the leaves are blunt and oval-shaped. The flowers, which sit in an open umbel, are yellow green.

22) Sweet Rocket (*Hesperis matronalis*) — Cabbage family

Dame's-violet, Night-scented gilliflower, Mother-of-the-evening.

Height to 100cm; flowers May to July. Local and frequent in Orkney (10/28); fairly easy to find.

History tells us that this plant of southern Europe and western Asia was introduced into Britain and known as a garden plant since 1375. Having escaped from gardens in the early 19th Century, this tall and untidy plant is found in hedgerows, woods, roadside verges and waste ground wherever the soil is slightly moist. In Orkney this perennial or biennial is likely to be found near habitation or where garden refuse has been dumped.

The stems are leafy and become woody with age while the hairy leaves are spear-shaped and possess stalks and teeth. The four-petalled flowers are in clusters, come in shades of white and violet and are heavily fragrant. This fragrance is most noticeable in the evening, a fact reflected by its colloquial names and its Latin name, *Hesperis*, which refers to the Evening Star.

*Speedwells (*Veronica* spp.) — Figwort family

There are at least 13 different species of Speedwell in Orkney most of which have flowers of various shades of blue. The collective name possibly refers to their healing properties, apparently especially good for healing wounds. Speedwells, which are frequently seen along the

22. Sweet Rocket on Pier road, St Margaret's Hope, South Ronaldsay
23. Germander Speedwell at the Kirk, North Ronaldsay
24. Field Speedwell at the Keelies allotments, Kirkwall

In Orkney, *Chocksy*, like Hogweed, is most commonly met with on paths and verges. Its tall and spreading nature often means that footpaths become overgrown and difficult to negotiate. Superficially the two species are fairly similar both of them being tall white-flowered umbellifers, however Cow Parsley is a finer and more delicate plant and invariably flowers well in advance of Hogweed. The hollow stems are furrowed and the leaves are finely dissected, almost lace-like, and contribute to one of its oft-used other names, *Queen Anne's lace*.

Some other country names are not so complimentary: perhaps the reason being that many similar-looking wildflowers, such as Hemlock, had harmful and deadly properties. It is a plant of 'lace and moonlight' and in days gone by had strong connections with the devil.

30) Groundsel (*Senecio vulgaris*) — Daisy family

Height to 30cm; flowers all year round. Widespread and abundant in Orkney (25/28); easy to find.

Groundsel can be found in almost any patch of cultivated ground in Britain and also in some semi-natural habitats such as coastal cliffs and sand dunes. The plants are more or less upright and consist of weak stems and irregular branches on which are widely-spaced leaves which are sometimes cottony and divided into toothed lobes. The flower-heads are in dense clusters, looking like small yellow shaving brushes and the bracts which surround the flower-head are often tipped black. When seeding, each head develops many seeds with a covering of fine white hairs; this has given the plant its generic name *Senecio* from the Latin *'old man'*.

The medical profession has utilised Groundsel for the treatment of rheumatism, bone pain and to regularise menstruation. In the veterinary world, this unprepossessing annual has been used in the treatment of swellings on horses and as a cure for 'staggers'.

30. Groundsel at Kirkwall marina, Kirkwall

31. Bush Vetch at Greenwall, Holm
32. Meadow Vetchling above the Pier, Wyre

31) Bush Vetch (*Vicia sepium*)　　　　　　Pea family
Moose-pea

Height to 60cm; flowers April to September. Widespread and abundant in Orkney (24/28); easy to find.

Bush Vetch and Tufted Vetch are perennials and likely to be seen in similar localities; rough pastures and roadside verges are popular and both are unable to tolerate well-grazed grasslands. Their flowering periods overlap although Bush Vetch may start earlier and finish later. The flowers of Bush Vetch are much less numerous than those of Tufted Vetch and commonly are in clusters of two or three. The petals are brownish mauve, duller than Tufted Vetch's vibrant deep blue. Like the flowers, the oval leaflets of Bush Vetch are fewer, widest at the leaf base and lack the silvery quality that characterises those of Tufted Vetch.

32) Meadow Vetchling (*Lathyrus pratensis*　　　　Pea family
Dog's peas, Fudsho

Height to 100cm; flowers May to August. Widespread and abundant in Orkney (27/28); easy to find.

Meadow Vetchling favours rough pastures and roadside verges where it scrambles and climbs. It is a bushy plant and gives the appearance of being permanently tangled; besides scrambling over other plants, it scrambles over itself. With the power of capturing atmospheric nitrogen to enrich the soil, Meadow Vetchling, along with other vetches, is looked upon as desirable in agricultural circles.

The bright lemon-yellow flowers of Meadow Vetchling are a common sight throughout Orkney in mid-summer. The cluster of flowers is

33. Fumitory at Kail Yard, Burray

atop a stalk, invariably much longer than the leaves. The stems of Meadow Vetchling are angled and each leaf has a pair of lance-shaped leaflets.

33) *Fumitories* (Fumaria spp.) — Fumitory family

Height to 50cm; flowers May to October.

Six of the ten species of Fumitory that occur in Britain grow in Orkney. The name derives from the Latin *fumus* meaning smoke and as it sprawls across the soil it certainly has a smoky appearance. Medicinally Fumitories have been used for liver complaints, jaundice and scurvy but pity the poor children who were prescribed to drink the juice to expel worms. All of the species have delicate fern-like foliage and long, tubular flowers that come in shades of white, pink or purple. Most appear to prefer light soils and are frequently found in arable fields, often among crops.

Common Fumitory *(Fumaria officinalis)*

Widespread and frequent in Orkney (21/28); easy to find.

Considered to be the commonest Fumitory in Orkney, it occurs on light soils and has small bright pink flowers and tiny sepals. The fruits are distinctive being flat-topped and upward pointing.

Common Ramping-fumitory *(Fumaria muralis)*

Widespread and frequent in Orkney (16/28); fairly easy to find.

Tending to favour slightly heavier soils than the other Fumitories, this one has flowers that are often dark rose-pink.

Purple Ramping-fumitory *(Fumaria purpurea)*

Widespread and frequent in Orkney (16/28); fairly easy to find.

Throughout Britain, this scrambling annual is found in relatively few localities; Orkney appears to be Britain's stronghold. The flower colour is pink or purplish-pink, although, confusingly, white when young.

34) Tufted Vetch (*Vicia cracca*)   Pea family

Height to 100cm; flowers June to August. Widespread and abundant in Orkney (25/28); easy to find.

This scrambling and climbing perennial with branched tendrils is typically found along the margins of fields, in rough pastures and on roadside verges. It can frequently be found draped around other plants and fence netting and may also occur in hay meadows. The leaves are composed of numerous paired leaflets, sometimes as many as a dozen. Similarly abundant are the deep blue flowers with as many as thirty individuals creating a ladder of blossom.

In the 19th Century, Tufted Vetch was valued as a fodder plant and a bovine aphrodisiac - the held belief was that a cow that ate well on this plant was more receptive to the bull's advances.

35) Broad-leaved Dock (*Rumex obtusifolius*)   Dock family
Bulwand, Bulmint

Height to 100cm; flowers May to October. Very widespread and abundant in Orkney (25/28); easy to find.

Docks are perceived as pests; their infestations degrade good grazing land. However, there was a time when this very common perennial was held in higher regard. In Orkney, docks were cut at harvest time; the stems were soaked in seawater to make them more pliable and fashioned into '*fursaclews*', which were traps for trout and '*huvies*' which were baskets that were used at sea to hold fish. Occasionally

34. Tufted Vetch at Mirkady, Deerness

35. Broad-leaved Dock at Burgar Hill, Evie

36. Tansy at Bankburn, Happy Valley, Stenness

the stems were woven into doormats known as *'flackies'*. The leaves were also used to wrap cheese and butter and a strong dye was obtained from the roots. Docks had curative properties as well. Probably the most well-known is as an antidote for Nettle stings. The leaves were boiled for pigs in the Borders and the seeds for poultry in Shetland.

It is a tall and robust perennial with large oval and blunt leaves which have shallow lobes at their base. The flowers are insignificant and lie in whorls above each other on the stem. The seed covers are triangular and whiskery and it is normal to find at least one of them possessing a large wart.

36) Tansy (*Tanacetum vulgare*) Daisy family

Height to 100cm; flowers July to September. Local and occasional in Orkney (13/28); not easy to find.

It is difficult to believe how useful and essential this highly aromatic perennial was considered to be, given that in contemporary Britain we utilise it but little. Its name is derived from an appellation for herb-flavoured omelettes and its connection with eggs is apparent in the tradition of eating an innard-cleansing meal at Easter time of Tansy with fried eggs. It was considered to be an herb of fertility and its status is summed up by Culpepper, 'let those women that desire children love this herb, tis their best companion, their husband excepted'. Boiled in beer or bruised and laid on the navel, it was also believed to prevent miscarriages. Its qualities as a repellent range from keeping bluebottles away from meat, earthworms from dead bodies, headlice and scabies from live bodies and in Sanday, children would scatter it under the corn stacks to keep out mice. Tansy is a handsome and striking plant. The leaves are feathery and fern-like and the flower-head is made up of numerous golden-yellow, rayless buttons. In Orkney it is frequently found near habitation and along verges.

37. Pineappleweed at Clumly, Sandwick
38. Bitter-cress at St Michael's kirk, Harray
39. Common Chickweed at Start Point, Sanday

37) Pineappleweed (*Matricaria discoidea*)   Daisy family

Pineapple mayweed

Height to 15cm; flowers June and July. Widespread and abundant in Orkney (26/28); easy to find.

This common annual possesses a surprising history. It originates from North America and northeast Asia and has spread to the four corners of the world. In Britain, as a medicinal herb with antiseptic properties, it appears to have been cultivated in the late 18th Century and was recorded in the wild in 1871. Since then it has earned the title of one of the fastest spreading plants of the 20th Century aided by tyres and footwear. However, its arrival in Orkney followed a different route and the belief is that it arrived with poultry food from North America in 1930. Now it can be found virtually Orkney-wide growing on trampled ground and tracks especially near field gateways, in arable fields and among cracks in town pavements.

Smelling as it does of pineapples and chamomile, it is an extremely aromatic plant, whose aroma is heightened if the leaves and flower-heads are crushed. The flower-head is yellow, conical, hollow and without petals and the leaves are numerous, short and fine pointed.

38) *Bitter-cresses* (*Cardamine* spp.)   Cabbage family

There are three members of the genus *Cardamine* in Orkney. The most obvious, the lilac-coloured Lady's Smock, features in the *Lowland freshwater* chapter. The other two members, Wavy Bitter-cress and Hairy Bitter-cress, are less noticeable and look alike. Both species are found on pavements, gritty paths, car parks, rock outcrops, by burns and in disturbed fertile ground; however Hairy Bitter-cress often prefers to grow in drier locations. Their physical characteristics include the following shared traits: their leaves consist of two or three pairs of leaflets with a single leaflet at the end and their flowers are white, four-petalled and in loose clusters; both have a peppery taste. Their colloquial name relates to the explosive character of their seed heads.

The differences are small and are described below.

Wavy Bitter-cress (*Cardamine flexuosa*)   Cabbage family

Poppers

Height to 15cm; flowers March to September. Local and widespread in Orkney (11/28); fairly easy to find.

The stems of this perennial are normally hairless and angular, the basal leaves are sparse and the flowers have six stamens.

Hairy Bitter-cress (*Cardamine hirsuta*)   Cabbage family

Poppers

Height to 15cm; flowers April to August. Local and widespread in Orkney (12/28); fairly easy to find.

The stems of this annual are normally hairy and straight, the basal leaves are abundant and the flowers have four stamens.

39) **Common Chickweed** (*Stellaria media*)   Campion family

Arvo

Height to 20cm; flowers all year, but mainly spring and autumn. Widespread and abundant in Orkney (27/28); easy to find.

This sprawling annual adds a rich verdant green to the colourscape. Its favoured growing sites are areas of nitrogen-rich disturbed ground; consequently it can be prolific on seabird cliffs and in gull colonies. The mass of rich green leaves are the plant's most obvious feature;

they are oval with a point at the tip and exhibit a strong central vein. By contrast the star-shaped flower-heads are unassuming being small and white with five petals so deeply notched they create the appearance of ten. Common Chickweed is a fine vegetable, both cooked and raw, and at one time its seeds were mixed with corn to feed poultry. Medicinally it was a remedy for chilblains and rashes while in Orkney a poultice of bruised leaves was applied to inflammations.

40) Greater Plantain (*Plantago major*)　　　　　　　Plantain family
Rat's tail, Healing blade, Englishman's foot

Height to 15cm; flowers May to September. Widespread and abundant in Orkney (27/28); easy to find.

It is surprising to discover how valued this perennial is in different parts of the Northern Hemisphere. This reputation stems from the resilience and toughness it demonstrates in the face of traffic whether human, livestock or motorised. *The Doctrine of Signatures* would tell us that a plant, capable of withstanding the heaviest of pounding, would remedy bruising, crushing and tearing. Native North Americans referred to it as the *Englishman's foot* – wherever he went Greater Plantain marked his progress.

Mostly it is found on trampled paths and tracks, field edges, gateways and roadsides. The distinctive rosette of leaves can lie almost flat thereby escaping the depredations caused by mowing or grazing. The leaves are many-veined, broad and oval; above them on a long

41. Ribwort Plantain at Ness boatyard, Stromness

40. Greater Plantain at Kettletoft, Sanday

stalk, rises the *Rat's tail*, a spike that is packed with tiny pale yellow and brown flowers.

41) Ribwort Plantain (*Plantago lanceolata*)   Plantain family
Ribgrass, Soldiers, Fighting cocks, Johnsmas flooer

Height to 25c; flowers April to August. Very widespread and abundant in Orkney (27/28); easy to find.

One of the commonest plants in Europe, this perennial's abundance is mirrored in Orkney where it occurs throughout the county and in Britain where it has been recorded from all but 68 squares of the 2852 10-km squares. It has a tendency to be a wildflower of cultivation but can flourish in a wide variety of habitats. As with most plantains, the flowers are inconspicuous – they are brown with prominent yellow anthers and are packed on to a short black head which sits upon a deeply-furrowed stalk. The slightly-toothed leaves are lance-shaped and have four or five strong parallel veins from tip to short stem.

It is a familiar plant of childhood; there can be few of us who have not played Soldiers or Fighting Cocks whereby the heads are struck against each other. Recipes recommend it for coughs and as a tonic, while in Shetland, known as the *Johnsmas flooer,* it was invaluable in predicting romance – new anthers on a flower-head picked 24 hours previously meant marriage was in the offing.

42) Common Mouse-ear (*Cerastium fontanum*)   Campion family

Height to 15cm; flowers April to September. Widespread and abundant in Orkney (27/28); easy to find.

Of all Orkney's wildflowers, Common Mouse-ear seems to have secured the title for being the most prosaic. Despite scouring all available botanical reference works, it is hard to find that nugget of information that will forever bring this plant to mind. Then again, maybe it is this very prosaic quality which means it will be remembered.

Throughout Britain and Orkney, this perennial occurs in cultivated ground and in what many people consider to be waste ground; however, it can be found almost anywhere. It is a low plant with runners and erect flowering shoots. The stems and leaves are considerably hairy, like a mouse's ear, while the flower-heads are composed of five deeply-cut white petals and the sepals have silvery margins.

42. Common Mouse-ear at Hackland, Rendall

Plantation woodlands

There are two oft-repeated and hackneyed misconceptions that authors and publishers of guide books about Orkney would do well to avoid, that either, a) there are no trees in Orkney or b) trees do not grow well in Orkney. There are plenty and they flourish.

The combination of salt and wind which must be a constant in the Orkney air is not an ideal ingredient for trees; but there are trees, and plenty of them, and they do grow. Dr William Traill in 1868 recounts that the Prince of Orange, when returning to Orkney from Iceland and Faroe a few years before, was relieved to see such 'a well-wooded country'. If it was then, it must surely be even more now. There was a period in the late 19th Century and early 20th Century when Orkney's grand houses decided to plant. In the space of a few years the estates of Balfour in Shapinsay, Trumland in Rousay, Carrick in Eday, Binscarth in Firth, Woodwick in Evie, Swanbister, Gyre and Smoogro in Orphir, Melsetter in Hoy and Berstane in St Ola were merry with tree planting and the folk of now should be grateful for their perseverance. Their foresight and determination has left us with a lasting wooded permanence which has added to Orkney's landscape and biodiversity; the county's largest woodland is Balfour amounting to just over 10 hectares.

Many of these manufactured woodlands are of the same vintage. The boom in the late 19th Century was an isolated phenomenon and tree

Binscarth wood, Firth with Binscarth Burn

planting remained rooted in that turn of the century craze until the Second World War. During the war years naval ratings commenced planting at the Sutherland plantation on Flotta and in the late 1940s and early 1950s, the 'Dig for Victory' and national self-sufficiency ethos was instrumental in the establishment and trialling of coniferous plantations at a number of sites on Hoy (Wee Fea, Lyrawa, White Glen, Hoy Forest and Hoy Lodge). In turn these conifer plantations represented another isolated tree-planting phenomenon – the resulting inspiration-less monoculture has never really been accepted as part of the Orkney tapestry.

Since 1998 however, and with grant-aided scheme incentives, 228 deciduous woodland plantations amounting to 127ha, have been created. Many of the plantations are composed almost entirely of trees with either an Orkney or northern Scotland provenance. The manicured woodlands of the 19th Century featuring strong representations from Sycamore and Wych Elm have been replaced by altogether more naturalistic layouts where Orkney's native trees, Downy Birch, Hazel, Aspen, Rowan and Willows are to the fore.

Many of the Victorian woodlands are heavy with Snowdrops, Hybrid Bluebells, Pink Purslane and Salmonberry. Some of them are ornate with introduced ferns and species such as Wood Anemone, Daffodil, Monk's Hood, Dog's Mercury and Ground-ivy. The newer plantations are likely to develop a much different ground flora more akin to Dales vegetation.

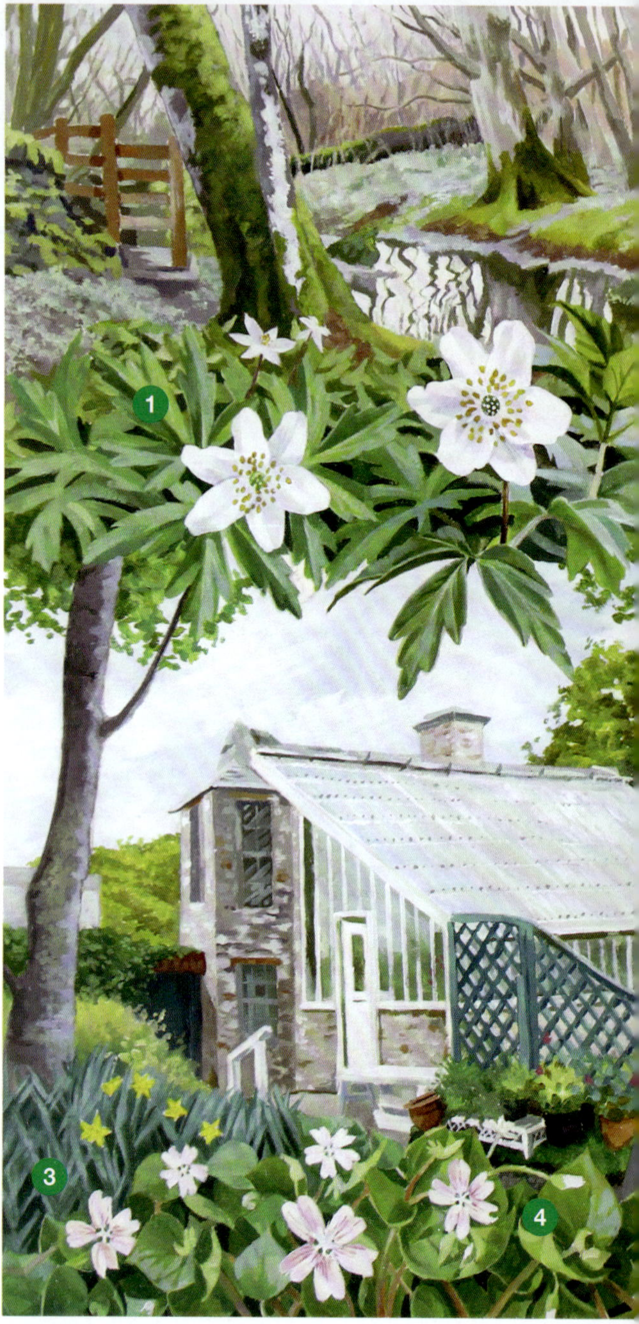
1
3
4

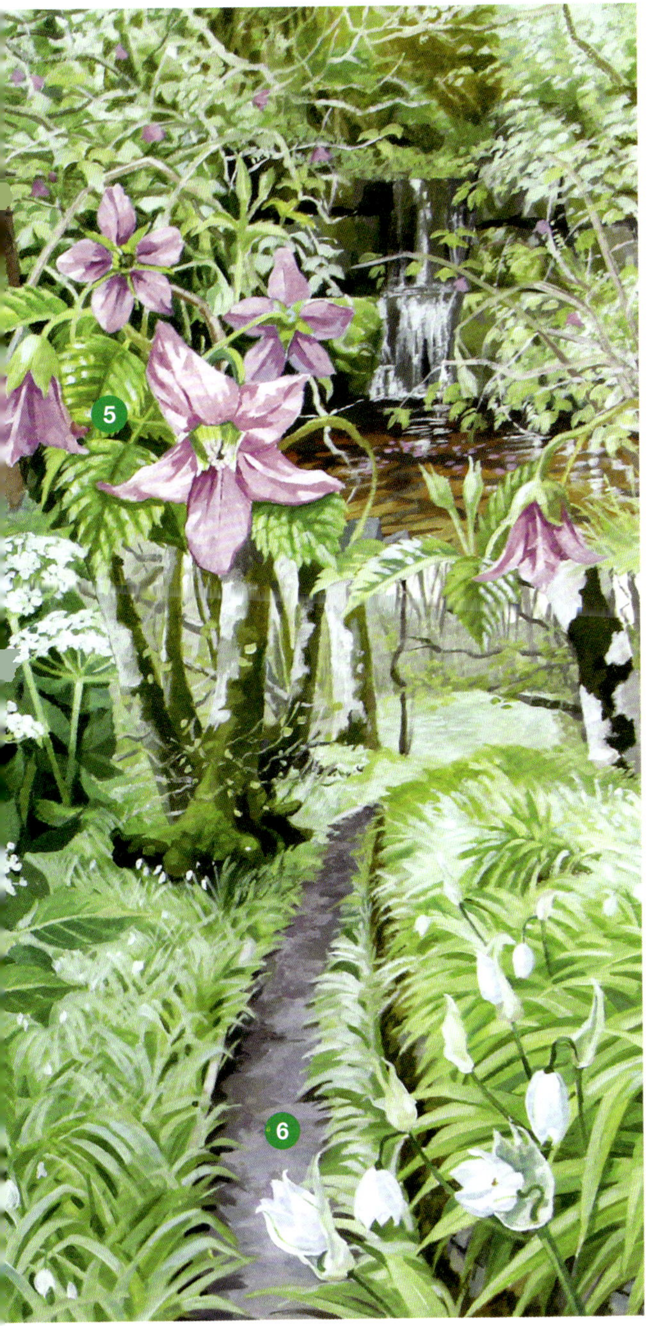
5
6

128

129

7) Lesser Celandine (*Ranunculus ficaria*) Buttercup family
Pilewort

Height to 20cm; flowers March to May. Widespread and abundant in Orkney (26/28); easy to find.

For many people the first flowering Lesser Celandine of the year is as noteworthy as the first Cuckoo. The sight of this perennial's bright, chrome-yellow flowers sparkling along the side of a ditch or banking is guaranteed to cheer. As the cold earth warms, its flowering is another significant milestone en route to summer. Generally it prefers damp soils and consequently is most at home in woodlands, hedges, meadows and on burn sides. The vivid flower-head is made up of eight to twelve narrow petals and usually three oval sepals while the glossy green leaves, which lie in rosettes, are on long stalks and are the shape of spades. It is also one of the earliest plants to die back – by June it is often impossible to see where Lesser Celandines might have been.

Medicinally it appears to have been used for centuries in the treatment of piles, hence the colloquial name *Pilewort*. *The Doctrine of Signatures* has great influence: given that the plant's bulbils resemble haemorrhoids, it was only right that it should be used as a treatment. This belief was pan-European and in Orkney a decoction was used to bathe piles. Research indicates that its value medicinally has been known and utilised since Mesolithic times given that a site in Oronsay contained charred tubers and bulbils. In the western isles of Scotland, the root, which resembles the udder and teats of a cow, was hung in the byre to guarantee good milk yields.

8) Snowdrop (*Galanthus nivalis*) Lily family
Snow-piercer, Flower of hope, Fair maid of February

Height to 20cm; flowers January to March. Widespread but infrequent in Orkney; not easy to find.

Like many of our woodland plants, the Snowdrop is welcomed as a sign that the earth has turned and the soil is warming. The *Snow-piercer* may often be seen pushing its head through the snow or earth and maybe it is the first floral indicator that winter will turn into spring. This bulb is as important to our hopes as the first Swallow hence another of its names the *Flower of hope*. Essentially it is a southern European species which flourishes in shady and damp woodlands. Whether it was introduced into Britain is a matter of conjecture but it was known in cultivation during Elizabethan times and was first recorded in the wild by 1778. Typically in much of Britain it is considered to be a plant of churchyards, old religious foundations, ruined abbeys and priories. Since the flowers had a strong association with Candlemas, the feast of Purification, many such sites were planted heavily – with each passing year the displays become more splendid. One of its vernacular names the *Fair maid of February* is connected to the Feast of Purification whereby village girls in the West Country would gather and wear Snowdrops to signify purity.

Galanthophilia is the ardent love of the Snowdrop and Galanthophiles have developed about 700 cultivated varieties from the twenty or so wild Snowdrop species that are found in Europe. A few different varieties can be found growing in Orkney where it has become naturalised in our woodlands. The nodding heads are milky-white with three spreading sepals protecting the much smaller three green-tipped petals. The strap-shaped leaves are bluish-green.

9) Ground-ivy (*Glechoma hederacea*) Dead-nettle family
Alehoof

Height to 20cm; flowers March to May. Local and occasional in Orkney (10/28); hard to find.

Throughout Britain, this creeping perennial may be found on fertile soils, carpeting woodland and hedgerows; gardeners may justifiably describe it as vigorous and tiresome. In some parts of England it has invaded deer-grazed woodlands and taken the place of more *bona fide* woodland flora. In Orkney, it is generally regarded as an introduced plant and earlier county botanists consider it to be a garden escape and also to have been deliberately planted in some situations. Its leaves are kidney-shaped, toothed and softly hairy; the lowest leaves are often darker. The two-lipped flowers are pale violet or occasionally pink and in whorls.

The older name *Alehoof* refers to its importance in brewing where, before the use of hops, Ground-ivy was the chief agent of bittering. It was utilised also as a general cleansing herb while in parts of Scotland it was a remedy with honey for coughs and consumption. In Shropshire kitchens its leaves were used as a stuffing for pork. The plant's all round properties ensured it would accompany the first settlers to New England.

10) Polypody (*Polypodium vulgare*) Fern family

Height to 40cm; spores ripen July to August. Local and occasional in Orkney (13/28); not easy to find.

Many members of the fern family flourish in damp and shady conditions. A few shy away from that habit and thrive in exposed locations where soils are thin or even non-existent. Polypody is one of the latter and in Orkney it may be found on dykes, storm beaches and on outcrops of rock which include the highest hills on Hoy. It may also be found growing as an epiphyte in the wild wood on the branches of Rowans and in plantations on the branches of Sycamores and Wych Elm.

The matted rootstock of this evergreen perennial has many (*poly*) foot-like (*pod*) divisions hence its name. Indeed Elaine Bullard has described the feet as being 'as hairy as the feet of hobbits'. The fronds may vary in size from a few centimetres to 40 and each frond is adorned with numerous spear-shaped lobes which grow smaller as they reach the tip. In past times it has featured in homely remedies specifically for the treatment of whooping cough.

Pages 128/129 *7. Lesser Celandine at Gyre wood, Orphir*
 8. Snowdrop at Trumland wood, Rousay
 9. Ground-ivy at the Willows, Kirkwall
 10. Polypody at Binscarth wood, Firth

11) Hybrid Bluebell
(*Hyacinthoides hispanica* x *H. non-scripta*)　　　　Lily family

Height to 40cm; flowers April to June. Widespread and occasional in Orkney (5/28); not easy to find.

There are three recognised types of Bluebell that occur in Britain. Firstly there is the true native Bluebell that grows in woodlands and hedgerows throughout much of Britain (though not Orkney) and which has a toehold in Caithness. Secondly there is the Spanish Bluebell which was introduced into British gardens in 1683 but is absent from much of northern Britain; and thirdly, there is the fertile hybrid of the two which arises spontaneously where the native ranges of the parents meet. It is the last named bulb that grows in Orkney and which can best be seen in woodlands such as Woodwick in Evie and Balfour on Shapinsay where its range of colours include blue, white, pink and lilac. It appears to be a recent addition to Orkney since the county's earlier botanists make no mention of it.

Like the Lesser Celandine, it is a welcome herald of spring and as such is venerated as a wildflower that symbolises generation and sexual power. With attributes as these it is little wonder that it figures prominently in literature and poetry from the pens of Shakespeare, Keats, Tennyson and Hopkins. In William Turner's *The Names of Herbes* (1568) he mentioned that boys in Northumberland 'scrape the root of the herb and glue their arrows and books with that slime'.

12) Opposite-leaved Golden-saxifrage
(*Chrysoplenium oppositifolium*)　　　　Saxifrage family

Creeping Jenny, Buttered eggs

Height to 10cm; flowers April to July. Local and rare in Orkney (5/28); hard to find.

Individually these relatively tiny perennials with greasy green leaves and yellow flower-heads can easily be overlooked given their preference to be in damp and shady places. Elaine Bullard considered them to be frequently found under the stems of tall wetland plants; in such situations they can be barely noticeable. However they are also frequently found on open ground in damp woodlands and when seen *en masse* they can be as vivid a carpet of yellow as Marsh Marigolds. In Orkney they are most usually found either alongside or close to some of the burns that run through Mainland plantations; some of the most extensive mats of this saxifrage can be found in Binscarth Wood, Firth and among Wideford Burn's trees in St Ola.

Medicinally it has been utilised to address melancholy and in the kitchen as a salad – in the Vosges it is esteemed as *'cresson de roche'* – rock cress. The leaves are opposite and rounded and the flowers are in golden-yellow umbels.

11. Hybrid Bluebell at Woodwick, Evie
12. Opposite-leaved Golden-saxifrage at Binscarth wood, Firth

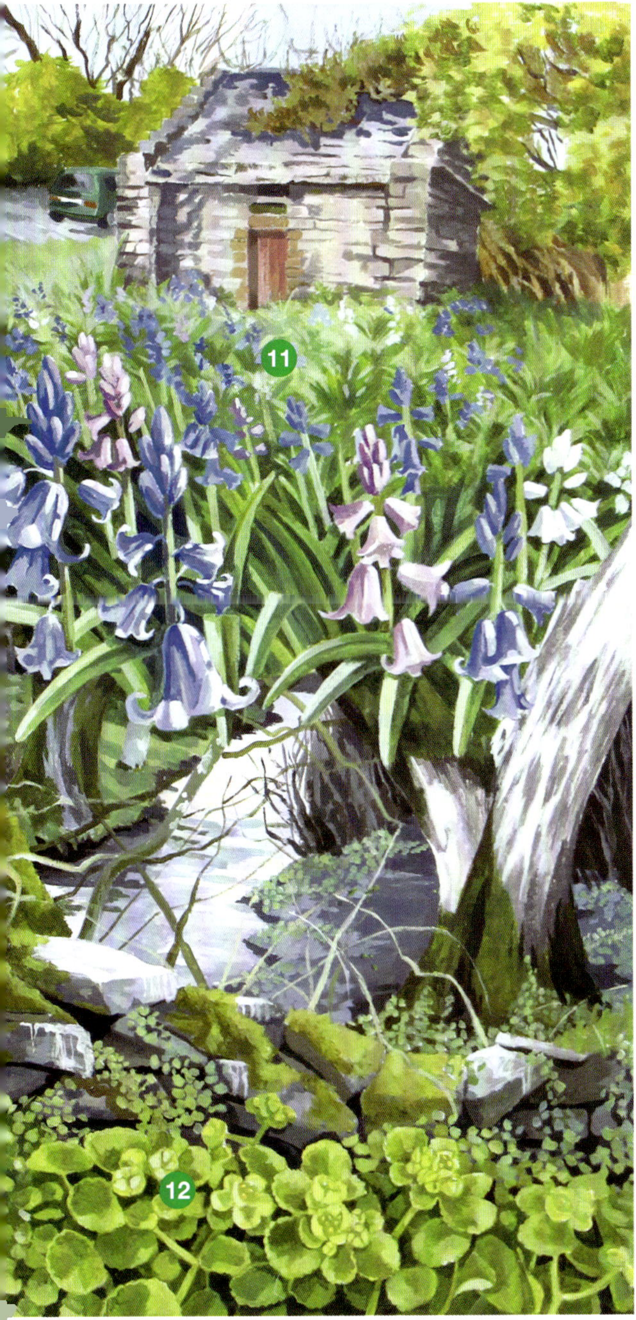
11
12

Wild woods and dales

In the present day Orkney's wild wood is quite limited in extent. The iconic woodland at Berriedale on Hoy is far and away Orkney's most extensive area of wild wood and possesses all of Orkney's native tree species. It is generally considered to be Britain's most northerly natural woodland; however there are some who would disagree and in turn put forward the credentials of another Hoy woodland, the Burn of Quoys. In recent years, following the fire of 1984 the fragility of Hoy's woodland resource has been clearly highlighted. From its ashes there arose a widespread desire to perpetuate Hoy's vulnerable woodland assets. Consequently, planting on Hoy using trees of local provenance was pursued with great enthusiasm to enhance already existing, but small, pockets of native woodland at for example the Burn of the Sale.

The desire to maintain ample supplies of true Orkney trees has been boosted by the various grant-aided woodland schemes. Throughout the Mainland of Orkney, tree planting in the last fifteen years has had an upturn in its fortunes and many of the 'new' plantations are burgeoning with Orkney native trees such as Rowan, Downy Birch, Hazel, Aspen and Willows of at least four different species. The future and security of Orkney's tree stock looks assured.

Berriedale, Hoy – background Ward Hill

Within the established wild woods is a rich and unique ground flora. In Berriedale for instance one can find Roses, Honeysuckle and scarce plants such as Wood Sage. However, these typical woodland plants can also be found in areas that are currently lacking trees; in Orkney these special places of 'treeless woodland' are known as 'dales'. Due to their sheltered nature and the fact that grazing animals found them difficult to penetrate, it is believed that Orkney's dales are where the old native woodland persisted. In general terms a dale consists of a hill valley that is drained by a burn. Some of these dales have rock outcrops and many have wet flushes and calcium-loving wildflowers.

Dales have a western and southern distribution in Orkney; they also tend to occur in the 'hill'. Consequently, they do not exist on a number of islands including North Ronaldsay, Sanday, Stronsay and Shapinsay and are found only sparingly on Eday, Papa Westray and Westray. They are though more common on Rousay, South Ronaldsay and in the East Mainland and numerous on Hoy and in the West Mainland. However, typical 'dales' vegetation is also met with among the steep ungrazed sea banks and geos at the coast.

136

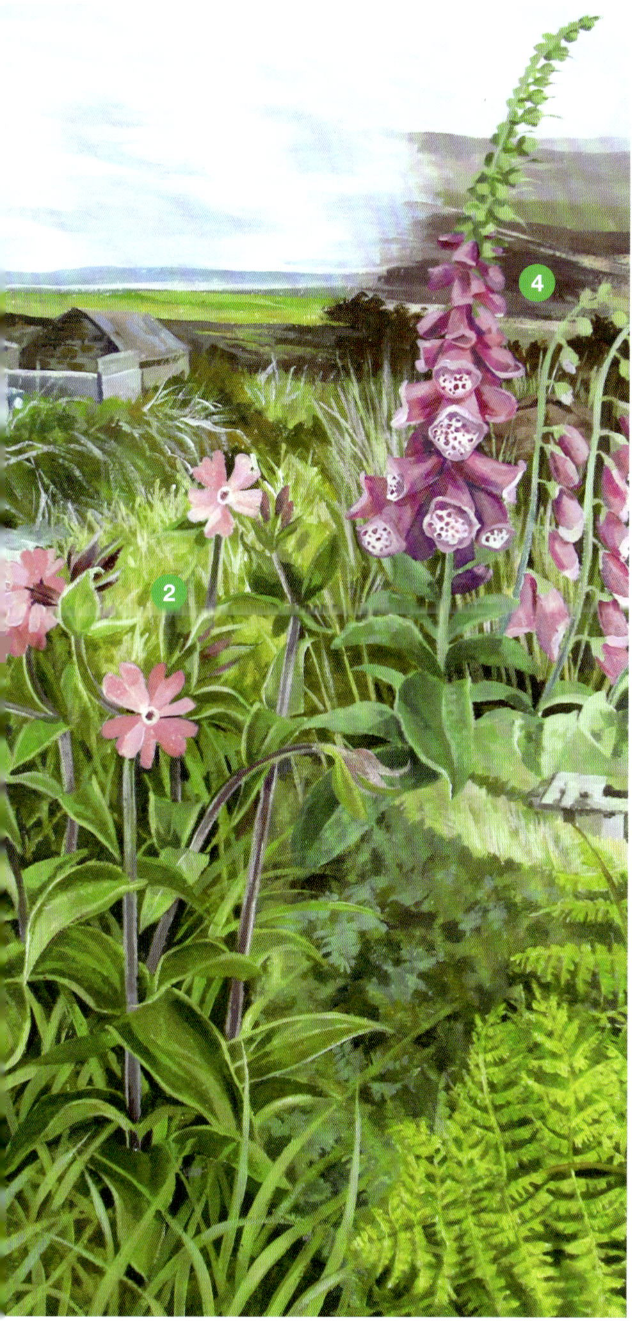
4
2

1) Primrose (*Primula vulgaris*) — Primrose family

May flooer

Height to 20cm; flowers March to May. Widespread and abundant in Orkney (24/28); easy to find.

The 'first rose of the year' is another one of those signal wildflowers, like Snowdrops and Lesser Celandines, whose appearance reminds us that lengthening daylight and warmer air are facts and not just the hoped-for-wishes of winter. Easter decorations in churches invariably include Primrose blossoms. Very occasionally, flowers are seen in February, but normally it is towards the middle of March before we see them lighting up south-facing dales, banks and verges both inland and at the sea. Throughout much of Britain, Primroses are most numerous in the shade of woodland, hedges and north-facing banks – they are not lovers of hot sun. Orkney's cooler temperatures seem particularly to their liking where they thrive in open situations. Textbooks indicate that the sticky seeds are usually dispersed by ants; ants in Orkney are nowhere near common and it may be that other agents are involved.

Those wheel-shaped flowers, with five petals the colour of moonlight, have honey-guides and centres a deeper yellow. Oddly, individual Primroses may be either 'pin-eyed' with stigma above the anthers or 'thrum-eyed' with stigma below the anthers. The flower-heads are carried singly on woolly stalks which rise from a rosette of oval, wrinkly and crinkled leaves. In the Outer Hebrides, the leaves were used to heal abscesses, while the flowers gave relief to sore throats.

2) Red Campion (*Silene dioica*) — Campion family

Height to 80cm; flowers May to November. Widespread and abundant in Orkney (25/28); easy to find.

One of this wildflower's most agreeable attributes is that its colour can be with us for at least eight, and occasionally nine months of the year. It is either a biennial or a perennial and flowering plants *en masse* are most abundant on the sea banks and in the coastal dales that occur on sea cliffs and nitrogen-rich sites. The vivid and vibrant pinks are beacons among the washed-out colours of late winter vegetation. The flower-heads are composed of five cleft petals, the pinks of which can vary in depth; on occasion white-flowered plants, which are either male or female, can be produced. The female plants are easily recognised by the inflated seed capsules. The stems can be stickily-downy and the lance-shaped leaves, with long-winged stalks, sit opposite each other.

In Britain it prospers in lightly shaded habitats such as copses, hedgerows and woodland clearings and is also known to survive in deep shade, so dark that the plant's flowering will be retarded. Sheltered coastal habitats are also favoured, but it also has the ability to succeed on exposed but stable shingle. The name *Campion* is synonymous with *champion*, an epithet bestowed during Elizabethan times on account of its upright grandeur while its Latin name refers to Silenus the drunken and merry god of the woodlands.

3) Valerian (*Valeriana officinalis*)   Valerian family
Cat-trail

Height to 120cm; flowers June to August. Local and occasional in Orkney (8/28); not easy to find.

While Valerian is found throughout Britain in a variety of damp habitats including woodland, in Orkney it is invariably found alongside the burns that are at the core of most of the county's best examples of 'treeless woodland'. Never common, this graceful perennial, has a restricted distribution and can be found only on Hoy, Rousay and in the West Mainland. It is one of the tallest wildflowers occurring in the county and usually appears head and shoulders above its neighbours such as Wild Angelica and Broad Buckler-fern. The spear-shaped leaves, which are bluntly-toothed, lie opposite each other along the leaf stalk. However, it is the flower-heads which attract most attention and the umbels are packed with delicate funnel-shaped flowers, softly pink, the colour of apple-blossom.

Its medicinal properties have been widely recognised. In bygone days, 'herb-women' collected it in quantity and armed with sedative properties it was, and still is, used for the treatment of insomnia, nervous tension, excitability and stress. Such is this herb's importance that it has attained a place on the *British Pharmacopeia*, the definitive collection of standards of pharmaceutical products. The smell of the root of the plant has a strong hold on some animals – cats are attracted to it as are rats; this along with pipes, helped the Pied Piper of Hamelin to achieve success. In many parts of Europe, Valerian tea is still a common drink.

4) Foxglove (*Digitalis purpurea*)   Figwort family
Trowie girs, **Trowie gliv** – *Fairy bells, Fairy fingers, Fairy's thimbles, Elves gloves, Witch's thimble*

Height to 150cm; flowers June to September. Local and frequent in Orkney (13/28); easy to find.

In the wild, Orkney represents this familiar and stately plant's most northerly station in Britain. True it does grow in Shetland but history tells us that it was introduced there. In fact, it is not universal within Orkney and is seemingly absent from most of the north isles with the exception of Rousay and Eday. Typically it grows in Orkney's 'treeless woodland' but it may also be found within areas of disturbed peaty ground, such as old peat cuttings or rabbit scrapes, often sharing with Rosebay Willowherb. Throughout the rest of Britain, it is frequently found in hedgerows, open woodlands, recently felled forestry plantations and 'waste land'; it shuns alkaline soils. The single unbranched stem may have anything from 20 to 80 pink-purple tubular or bell-shaped flowers. Dark purple spots are peppered over the white inside of the tube and its large leaves are oval and softly downy.

Foxgloves are powerful medicinal plants. They are extremely poisonous and the potent drug digitalis, which is used in the treatment for disorders of the heart, is obtained from the leaves. More locally in Scotland it was mixed with Hemlock and hog's lard as an ointment for cuts or its roots were crushed and applied as a hot poultice to treat internal swellings. It is also a plant steeped in folklore – a perennial that is linked inextricably with fairies, goblins, witches and trows the length and breadth of Britain evidenced by the numerous names from different regions – *Fairy bells, Fairy fingers, Fairy's thimbles, Elves gloves, Witch's thimble* and, of course, the Orkney names *Trowie girs* and *Trowie gliv*. In the Scottish Borders Foxgloves were placed in cradles to keep new born babies from being bewitched.

Ferns

There are over twenty different species of fern in the county; some, such as Wilson's Filmy-fern (*Hymenophyllum wilsonii*) and Wall-rue (*Asplenium ruta-muraria*), are very rare and require extremely specialised conditions to grow. Other ferns such as Sea Spleenwort (page 74), Hard Fern (page 158) and Polypody (page 131) are more widespread and well-known. Within Orkney's sheltered dales habitat larger feathery ferns occur and these include: Bracken (page 150), Male Fern (*Dryopteris filix-mas*), Lady Fern (*Athyrium filix-femina*), Scaly Male-fern (*Dryopteris affinis*), Hay-scented Buckler-fern (*Dryopteris aemula*), Northern Buckler-fern (*Dryopteris expansa*) and Broad Buckler-fern. The most widespread in Orkney is this last-named perennial and it is generally, according to Elaine Bullard, the only fern to be found on uninhabited islands. However, despite its widespread status it appears yet to be recorded from either Papa Westray or Sanday.

5) Broad Buckler-fern (*Dryopteris dilatata*)   Fern family

Height to 60cm; spores ripen July to September. Widespread and abundant in Orkney (20/28); easy to find.

Ditches that cross heathland or are adjacent to heathy roadside verges often provide conditions that mimic Orkney's natural dales and Broad Buckler-fern is often present in abundance. While many ferns can appear very similar, the scales around the base of the stem of the Broad Buckler-fern have a conspicuous dark stripe which makes for easier identification.

Pages 136/137:
1. Primrose at Burn of Hammars, Evie
2. Red Campion at Comlybank, Harray
3. Valerian at Lyde Road, Firth

       4. Foxglove at the Harray men's graves, Queenamidda, Rendall
       5. Broad Buckler-fern at Garth, Stromness

141

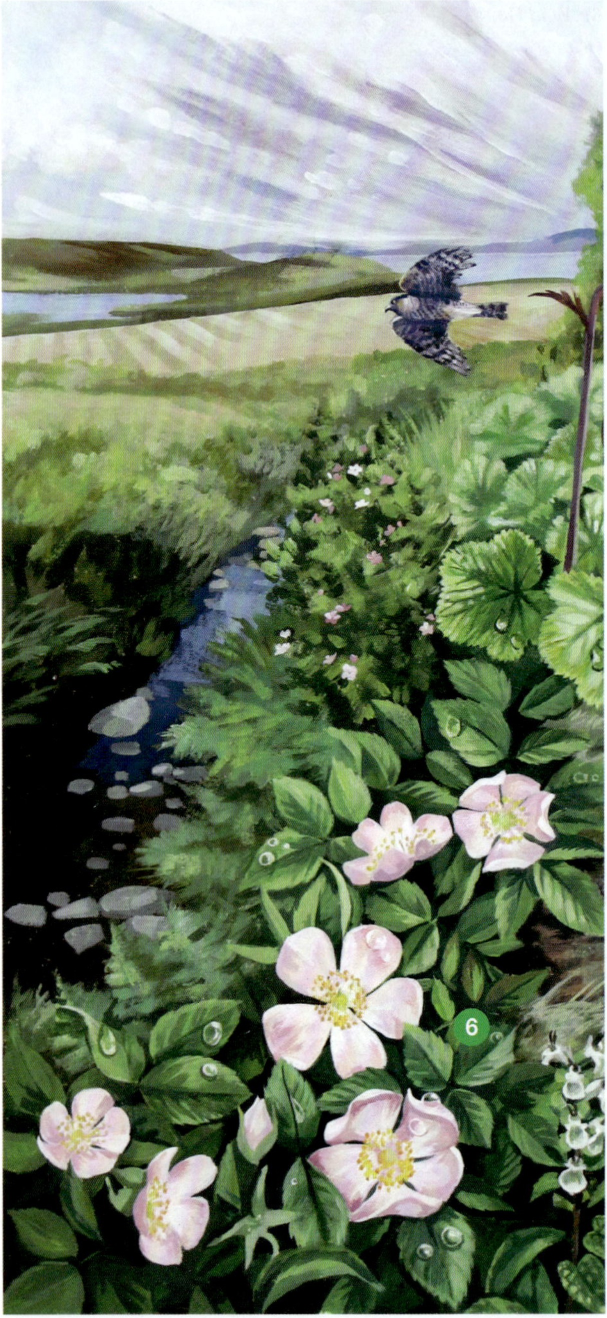
6

6) *Wild Roses* (Rosa agg.)   Rose family

Height to 300cm; flowers June to July. Local and occasional in Orkney (10/28); not easy to find.

The two main groups of Wild Roses that occur in the county are Dog Roses and Downy Roses. Dog Roses have smooth leaves and fruits, tend to sucker and form thickets; Downy Roses, have rougher leaves and appear bush-like. Three species occur in Orkney: Glaucous Dog-rose (*Rosa caesia*), Sherard's Downy Rose (*Rosa sherardii*) and Soft Downy Rose (*Rosa mollis*). However there are in addition a confusing number of hybrids and garden escapes.

Glaucous Dog-rose (*Rosa caesia*)

Occurring on Hoy, South Ronaldsay, Burray and in both the West and East Mainland, Glaucous Dog-rose is by far the commonest Wild Rose in Orkney. Long-term botanical records indicate that some individual plants have been known for more than one hundred years. While frequently occurring in dales, it is not unusual to find them along burnsides in upland areas and on sheltered sea cliffs. The flowers of the Orkney plants are usually pink and the hips red or orange red

The hips of Wild Roses have long been gathered and used in the making of jellies, jams, wines and a digestive tea. It is high in vitamin C and during the Second World War when citrus fruits were unavailable, the Ministry of Health established a rose-hip collection scheme specifically for the production of syrup for children and expectant mothers. Apparently the rose-hips of Scotland were highly prized for they contained more vitamin C than the hips of further south. Folklore tells us that in the Borders the belief was that if Birch and Dog-rose grew together on the graves of departed lovers, then death had not divided them. Thanks to Bonnie Prince Charlie, the Wild Rose is also a powerful symbol of Scottish nationalism – this '*White Cockade of the Jacobites*' adorned the Pretender's bonnet.

6. Wild Roses at Burn of Castlehill, Rousay

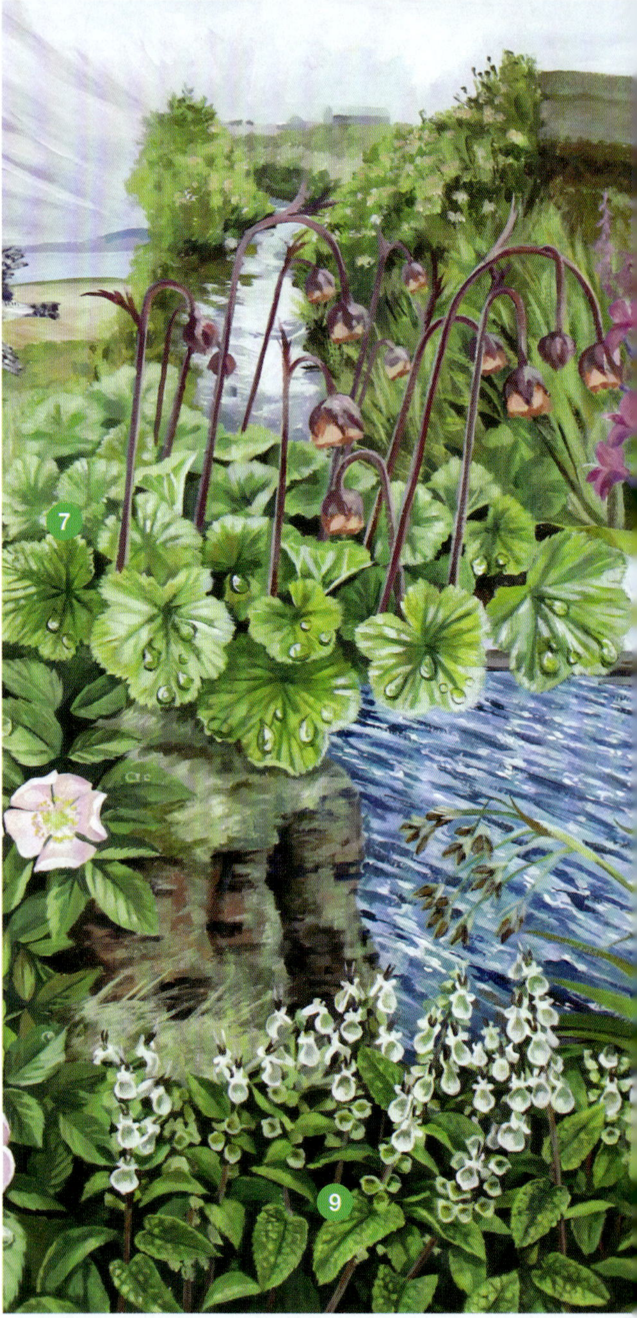

7
9

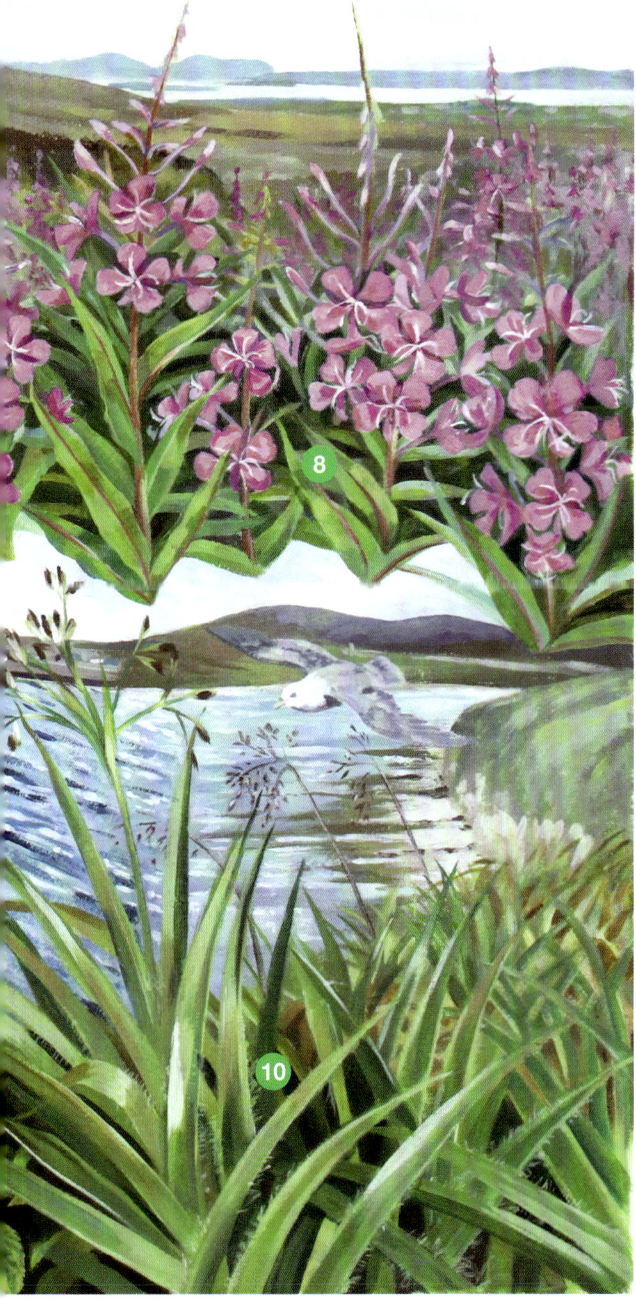
8
10

7) Water Avens *(Geum rivale)* — Rose family
Billy button, Soldiers buttons

Height to 45cm; flowers April to July. Local and occasional in Orkney (10/28); fairly easy to find.

This handsome perennial is never far away from water. Consequently in some parts of Britain, particularly central and southern England, it has undergone severe declines due to drainage of wetlands. It has experienced losses within Orkney especially during the period after the Second World War when agricultural 'development' programmes affected the well-being of many of the county's wetlands. However it may still be found flourishing in Orkney's dales, along the edges of lochs and burns and often in abandoned peat cuttings.

Its leaves are hairy and feature a large and generous, round terminal leaf which is edged with small, sharp teeth. The drooping flower-head which nods on a lengthy stalk, is both distinctive and subtle and would surely have made the most fitting headwear for 'the little people'. The flower's petals are orange-pink and shielded by eye-catching, dusky purple sepals. Grigson (1958) describes them as 'drooping, swarthy Egyptian blossoms'. Medicinally it has been utilised as an astringent and a stomach tonic.

8) Rosebay Willowherb
(Chamerion angustifolium) — Willowherb family
Fireweed

Height to 150cm; flowers June to September. Widespread and abundant in Orkney (22/28); easy to find.

It is difficult to believe that this slender and striking perennial, with its tall magenta spikes crowded with four-petalled flowers, was little known in Britain until the latter part of the 19th Century. Prior to its 20th Century rampage it occurred sparsely either in a few upland locations or in woodland. The Industrial Revolution was this plant's turning point; the making of railways, roads and industrial wasteland and the felling of woodland created the right conditions for the flourishing of this now familiar splash of colour. Its advance was accelerated by bombs; more disturbed earth helped it prosper and this vigorous, adaptive and conquering species positively thrives on ground that has been burnt – hence *Fireweed*. It was considered to be a shy woodland rarity in the 19th Century, and within Orkney it is the sheltered dales that provide it with a similar habitat. However, tall swathes may often be seen on the hill and indicate where controlled muirburn or wild fires have occurred.

There is little evidence of its use in Britain which contrasts with its status in North America where the Blackfoot consume its young leaves as greens, the Saanich drink its tea and the Inupiat utilise the pith as a sweetener. Linnaeus considered that the young shoots could be eaten like asparagus and in his country, Sweden, it was known as the Herb of Heaven. In the northwest Highlands of Scotland the boiled root was used to heal equine ailments and wounds.

9) Wood Sage (*Teucrium scorodonia*)   Dead-nettle family
Gulsick girse

Height to 25cm; flowers July to September. Local and rare in Orkney (6/28); hard to find.

Rousay, where it is found growing sparingly on sheltered rock outcrops or 'hammars', is this subtle and understated perennial's most northerly location in Britain. Elsewhere in the county it is equally scarce and can be found only on Hoy and in both the East and West Mainland where besides growing in dales also frequents sheltered gullies and geos along sea cliffs. In bygone Orkney its medicinal properties were used as a treatment for jaundice; in the Outer Hebrides it was considered a salve of headaches and in Gloucestershire, the fresh pink leaves were picked in spring to counter rheumatism. Throughout much of Britain it was valued as a bittering agent in home brewing.

It is the unshowy flowers that create this plant's subtlety. They are the colour of straw with a hint of green and appear phantom-like in the heavily shaded dells in which they can often be found. The inflorescence rises like a narrow church spire with the flowers in opposite pairs. The downy, stalked and pointed leaves are heavily wrinkled and edged throughout with numerous blunt teeth. It has little of the aroma of its cultivated cousin the Garden Sage.

10) Great Wood-rush (*Luzula sylvatica*)   Rush family

Height to 80cm; flowers May to June. Widespread and frequent in Orkney (16/26); easy to find.

There are two characteristics of dales habitat that suit this tussocky, mat-forming perennial. Dales normally provide shade and dampness and Great Wood-rush appears to flourish where such conditions persist; indeed in other parts of Britain it is frequently found in lowland woods. The other characteristic relates to grazing of which this plant is intolerant; dales can often be quite difficult to access and within them are gullies, ledges and all sorts of nooks and crannies where it is free to prosper. Furthermore, changes in agricultural practices have been responsible for the spread of Great Wood-rush over many parts of Orkney's open hill land. Until fairly recently, it was practice to over-summer cattle on the hill; with the demise of this custom, Great Wood-rush has been given licence to spread and is now an obvious feature of the hills on Hoy, the Mainland, Rousay and Eday. Many of the upland slopes in these areas are extensively clothed with Great Wood-rush; dark green carpets in the springtime, pale copper in the autumn.

It is the largest of Britain's wood-rushes. The shiny, bright-green leaves are numerous, broad, sharply pointed and sparsely hairy along the edges. The stems are long and slender supporting a loose spread of tiny florets in close clusters.

Pages 144/145:
7. Water Avens at Blubbersdale, Rendall
8. Rosebay Willowherb at Dale of Corrigall, Harray
9. Wood Sage at Inganess Bay, St Ola
10. Great Wood-rush at Waulkmill Bay, Orphir

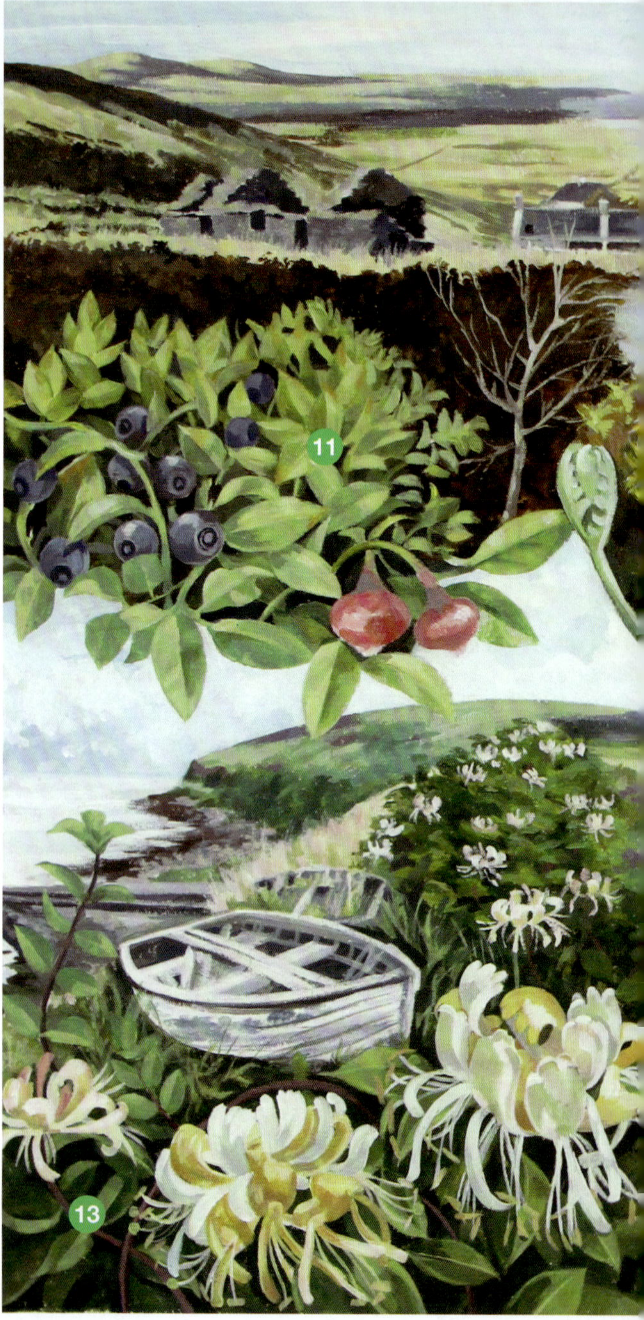
11
13

149

11) Blaeberry (*Vaccinium myrtillus*) — Heath family
Bilberry, Blueberry, Hurtleberry

Height to 50cm; flowers April to June. Widespread and frequent in Orkney (17/28); fairly easy to find.

With its wealth of names, it is evident that this shrub has played an important part in the cultural traditions the length and breadth of Britain. *Vaccinium myrtillus* is known variously as *Bilberry, Blackberry, Blueberry, Cowberry, Hartberry, Heatherberry, Hurtleberry, Whortleberry, Wimberry and Mossberry*. As we all know the berries make for excellent eating whether raw, in jelly, jam, tart or pie and Blaeberry Sunday, the nearest Sunday to 1st August, was a significant date in the calendar. It was the beginning of harvest and as the festival of the first fruits was one of the four quarterly feasts and synonymous with Lammas when a loaf of bread was offered to God. However, as with many rural customs, its strength has waned due in part to the removal of many areas of lowland heath where Blaeberry would have been abundant.as a consequence of agricultural intensification.

In Orkney it is uncommon and absent from some of the north isles but elsewhere, especially on Hoy, Rousay and the Mainland can be found in many areas of heath and dale. Initially it is the flat and bright green, oval leaves competing with the heather that draw the attention, and closer examination reveals that the leaves have teeth and the stems are four-angled. The urn-shaped flowers are greenish pink and sit on stems that emerge from the leaf axils. Other than providing a succulent berry rich in vitamin C, Blaeberry has been used in the Western Isles as treatment for dysentery and diarrhoea while its leaves have been dried as a substitute for tea. It has significant dyeing properties and is also highly regarded in the ophthalmic world for eye treatments.

12) Bracken (*Pteridium aquilinum*) — Fern family

Height to 180cm; spores ripen July to August. Local and occasional in Orkney (14/28); not easy to find.

This is one of the most well-known and familiar of ferns. However it is perceived as a nuisance; consequently few are fond of this vigorous perennial. Bracken can be poisonous to livestock if eaten in quantity but is normally avoided by cattle, sheep or rabbits aiding its spread at the expense of their grazing. The 20th Century witnessed a marked increase in its British distribution; given the right conditions it can become prolific and more intensive sheep grazing combined with more frequent burning of hill vegetation provided these conditions – in the 1970s it was invading more than 10,000 hectares of agricultural land annually.

However, its status within Orkney is entirely different. Here it is not particularly abundant although it has been known from pre-Neolithic times. Indeed it would appear that most of Orkney's current patches of bracken have been known and recorded since the county's early botanists first put pen to paper. Fertile spores are rarely seen and consequently Orkney has experienced little, if any, of the invasion experienced elsewhere. It is the tallest of the ferns and its Latin name literally means 'winged eagle' a reference to the appearance of the unfurling young fronds.

13) **Honeysuckle** (*Lonicera periclymenum*)   Honeysuckle family

Stems may reach 600cm; flowers June to September. Widespread and frequent in Orkney (15/25); easy to find.

Despite occurring throughout much of Orkney, some sources consider that this perennial, clockwise climber is only native to Hoy, the South Isles and Orphir. In all other localities within the county, it is believed to have been introduced. Whatever its origin it is typically found in dales situations, either inland or at the coast, where it scrambles over shrubs, rocks and even the rusting machinery that so often finds its way into coastal gullies. The older stems are woody, the younger ones, along which oval leaves lie opposite each other, are fleshy. Growing plants have the wherewithal to squeeze saplings into a spiral. The exotic flower-heads appear in whorls of cream-yellow trumpets which deepen to orange once they have been pollinated.

Honeysuckle has had a long history of superstitious association in rural areas. To avert the evil powers that were abroad on May Day, boughs were hung in byres to protect the cow, the milk and the butter. Its tough stems were put to practical uses throughout Britain; the making of baskets was widespread but in the Outer Hebrides, Honeysuckle bridles were fashioned for pack ponies. The beauty industry has long sought its petals and scents.

14) **Wood Horsetail** (*Equisetum sylvaticum*)   Horsetail family

Height to 80cm; cones ripe April to May. Local and frequent in Orkney (11/28); not easy to find.

Orkney's commonest Horsetails, Water Horsetail (page 70), Marsh Horsetail (page 70) and Field Horsetail (page 99) may be found in a wide variety of damp to very damp situations. Wood Horsetail is very particular in its requirements and is confined in general to the dales where shady peaty soils are kept permanently damp by flushing. Dales vegetation is primarily found in the south and west of the county and the distribution of this perennial follows suit such that the plant is unknown from the northern islands other than toeholds on Rousay and Westray.

The branches of the stem are themselves branched; these branches droop, thereby imparting a delicate and feathery appearance to the plant. It may often be found in colonies among heather where the wispy plumes can be seen standing higher than the surrounding vegetation. At the tip of the fertile stems is an oval cone which ripens in April and May.

Pages 148/149:
11. Blaeberry at Russadale, Stenness
12. Bracken at Hobbister, Orphir
13. Honeysuckle at Sandwick, South Ronaldsay
14. Wood Horsetail at Deep Dale, Holm

15) Wild Angelica (*Angelica sylvestris*) — Carrot family
Spoot girs

Height to 150cm; flowers July to September. Widespread and abundant in Orkney (24/28); easy to find.

'Statuesque' best describes the finest examples of Wild Angelica; even in winter, their skeletons make a striking addition to the landscape. The late Elaine Bullard was of the opinion that many of Orkney's plants were significantly larger than equivalents further south and cited the county's long summer daylight as the cause of this gigantism. Whether referring to Orkney or not, Geoffrey Grigson describes this perennial as 'an umbellifer of distinction and size'. The dome-shaped flower-heads, which are revered by nectar-seeking insects, are near-geometric perfection and are packed with tens of rays that carry tiny white or pink flowers. Grigson waxes lyrical once more by describing them as 'umbels dipped in claret'; these splendid umbels emerge from the upper leaves which remain as protective sheaths. The stem is robust, hollow and purple while the deep-green triangular-shaped leaves are sharply-toothed. Although common in the Orkney dales, Wild Angelica also inhabits heathland, sea cliffs and in some places even links.

It has long been a significant plant of childhood and has been used variously as peashooter, telescope and water gun. In the 18th Century a decoction from the roots was used for the treatment of cattle distemper by crofters in the west Highlands of Scotland, while in Shetland it was gathered to provide a black dye. Mention must be made of the much bigger **Garden Angelica** (*Angelica archangelica*) which grows sparingly. It is a sweetener and healer and much valued in Scandinavia from where it was probably brought to Orkney by Norse traders. Some fine examples can be found around Pierowall on Westray.

15. Wild Angelica at Muckle Eskadale, Harray

15

The peat hill heaths and blanket bogs

Of the ten habitats included in this volume, 'the peat hill' covers more of Orkney than any other and it can be found from near the coast to the summits of some of the county's highest hills. Although peat is far less abundant on some of the north islands such as Sanday and Stronsay and non-existent on North Ronaldsay, most of the other islands and parishes still have substantial areas of the peat hill; islands such as Eday, Hoy and Rousay are 'peat' islands and parishes such as Birsay, Firth and Orphir are similarly well-endowed. Indeed some of the best peat hills are nationally and internationally designated sites most notably the Orphir and Stenness Hills, Keelylang Hill and Swartaback Burn, the West Mainland Moorlands and of course, Hoy.

Terrestrial Orkney from space is two-coloured – brown and green; nowadays, broadly speaking, it is the high ground that is brown and

The Cuppers of Vacquoy, Rousay – background Loch Wasbister, Saviskaill Bay and Westray

the lowland that is green. Yet the extent of the modern day heather hill is but a fraction of what it once was – but for small pockets of links, woodland and agriculture, the heather blanket would have covered most of the 'peaty' islands, both at high level and low level. Over the last two hundred years there has been a significant decrease in the extent of the hill and its heather – it is estimated that during the 20th Century Orkney lost 50% of its hill to the plough and agricultural 'improvement'.

Dominating the peat hill are the heathers – Ling, Bell Heather and Cross-leaved Heath – in late summer of course, the heathers bloom and the 'brown' hill gives way to a 'purple' hill. Among the heathers are numerous mosses including sponge-like Sphagnum, ferns (such as Hard Fern) and occasionally clubmosses. The bright yellow flowers of Tormentil and the pale pink of Lousewort are lasting flowers and can be found for much of the spring and summer while in wetter areas stands of Bog Asphodel are a welcome addition later in the season. The insect-eating plants which include Butterwort and two types of sundew are worth looking for; the fleshy green stars of the former are easy to locate while the latter often requires a bit more work.

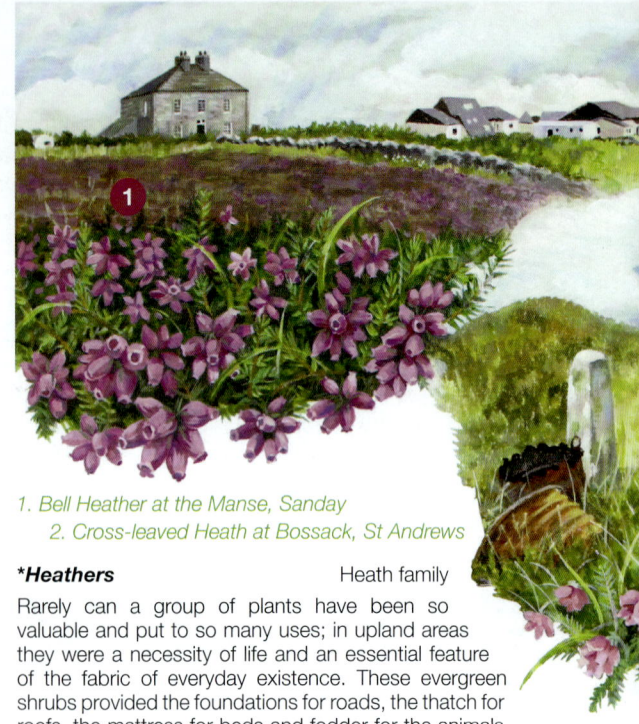

1. Bell Heather at the Manse, Sanday
2. Cross-leaved Heath at Bossack, St Andrews

Heathers — Heath family

Rarely can a group of plants have been so valuable and put to so many uses; in upland areas they were a necessity of life and an essential feature of the fabric of everyday existence. These evergreen shrubs provided the foundations for roads, the thatch for roofs, the mattress for beds and fodder for the animals. It was also turned into ropes, baskets and brushes, yielded a yellow dye for wool, flavoured beer and acted as both a diuretic and sedative. Pot scrubbers known as *heather rings* were particularly effective and popular. There are three species in Orkney: Ling, Bell Heather and Cross-leaved Heath. During the 20th Century all have declined due to changing agricultural practices, a change that has been mirrored throughout Britain where heathland has been lost not only to agriculture but also to forestry, mineral extraction and scrub.

1) Bell Heather (*Erica cinerea*) — Heath family

She heather

Height to 40cm; flowers July to September. Widespread and abundant in Orkney (23/28); easy to find.

Whereas Ling is generally found across the whole hill, Bell Heather has a distinct preference for well-drained locations on the drier parts of the heath. The conspicuous flowers are bell-shaped and adorn the hill with pinks, crimsons and purples and as with other heathers, white flowers are not unknown. The leaves are in whorls of three and are slightly unusual in that the edges are tightly rolled and covered in a protective cuticle to conserve moisture – an adaptation more typically seen in plants that exist in extremely dry conditions. A gentler plant than Ling and in the Borders known as *She heather,* Bell Heather was

3. Ling at Mor Stein, Shapinsay

destined to be turned into softer brushes and brooms. Its honey is considered by apiarists to be thinner, darker and more strongly flavoured than Ling honey.

2) Cross-leaved Heath (*Erica tetralix*)   Heath family

Height to 25cm; flowers July to September. Widespread and abundant in Orkney (22/28); easy to find.

Superficially Cross-leaved Heath resembles Bell Heather – there is similarity in both flower shape and leaf shape. However, Cross-leaved Heath, arguably the prettiest of Orkney's heathers, is a lover of wet ground. Bell Heather seeks out the drier sites on the hill, Cross-leaved Heath gravitates to the lower-lying wet hollows and may be found growing in standing water. It is also often the first of the heathers to recover after a heath fire.

The leaves are very distinctive. Looked down from above the whorls of four leaves appear as crosses the length of the stem – hence its Latin name *tetralix* which incorporates the Greek word for four. The rose-pink flower-heads are clustered at the head of the stem imparting an umbel-like appearance, and as with the other heathers, white flowers are occasionally observed.

3) Ling (*Calluna vulgaris*)   Heath family

Heather, He heather

Height to 40cm; flowers July to September. Widespread and abundant in Orkney (25/28); easy to find.

Of the three members of the Heath family in Orkney, Ling is not only the commonest but also the principal flowering plant of the hill; it can be found county wide but is absent from some of the smaller uninhabited islands that are or have been heavily grazed. It is a bushy evergreen shrub with densely packed spikes of small pink-purple flowers. The leaves are tinier than the flowers and sit opposite each other on a wiry and twisted woody stem. White-flowered forms are fairly frequent; much more infrequent are the forms that exhibit white woolly leaves. Its name derives from the Anglo Saxon word *'Lig'* meaning fire and recalls the importance of heather as fuel. Its utility is remembered through its Latin name *Calluna* which comes from the Greek meaning 'to brush'. *Ling* is a tough, wiry and durable plant and in the Borders is known as *He heather*.

4) Hard Fern (*Blechnum spicant*) — Fern family

Height to 75cm; spores ripen June to August. Widespread and frequent in Orkney (18/28); easy to find.

Suitable habitat occurs over much of Orkney and this evergreen, with its double-sided comb-like leaves, may be found upon the acid soils in upland and lowland areas of most parishes and most islands. However, because of its reliance upon peaty soils, it is not known from the peat-less islands of Papa Westray, North Ronaldsay or Sanday. Hard Fern is one of the few ferns in Britain to bear separate sterile and fertile fronds. Lying flat on the ground in rosette form are the sterile fronds which die back in winter while standing erect, and having the appearance of a fish backbone, are the thinner, fertile spore-carrying fronds that remain evergreen.

4. Hard Fern at Knowes of Trotty, Harray

5) Tormentil (*Potentilla erecta*)　　　　　　　　　　　Rose family
Bark**, **Hill bark**, **Smero

Height to 25cm; flowers May to October. Widespread and abundant in Orkney (27/28); easy to find.

The bright yellow flower-heads of Tormentil are a familiar sight in Orkney – the hills are studded with them for six months of the year. They also light up the county's lowland heaths and the maritime heaths and grasslands that border the coast – very wet places and cultivated ground are inhospitable. It is a creeping perennial with thin wiry stems and five-fingered leaves that are shiny, toothed, deep green and without stalks. By contrast the flowers are on long stalks and it is one of the few members of the Rose family with just four petals.

Historically Tormentil has been harvested for a variety of reasons. The roots are rich in tannins and the plant was used extensively in the leather industry throughout Britain and Europe. In Faroe its role in tanning leather continued until the 1950s and in Scotland during the 19th Century its over-exploitation led to collecting bans on Coll and Tiree. Medicinally it had a variety of uses including remedy for colic, diarrhoea and cystitis in humans and scour in cattle. Orkney went one better – the roots were boiled in milk and drunk to expel intestinal worms. Across the Minch it passed as a cure for cold sores and was applied as a poultice for corns.

5. Tormentil at Rushacloust, Eday

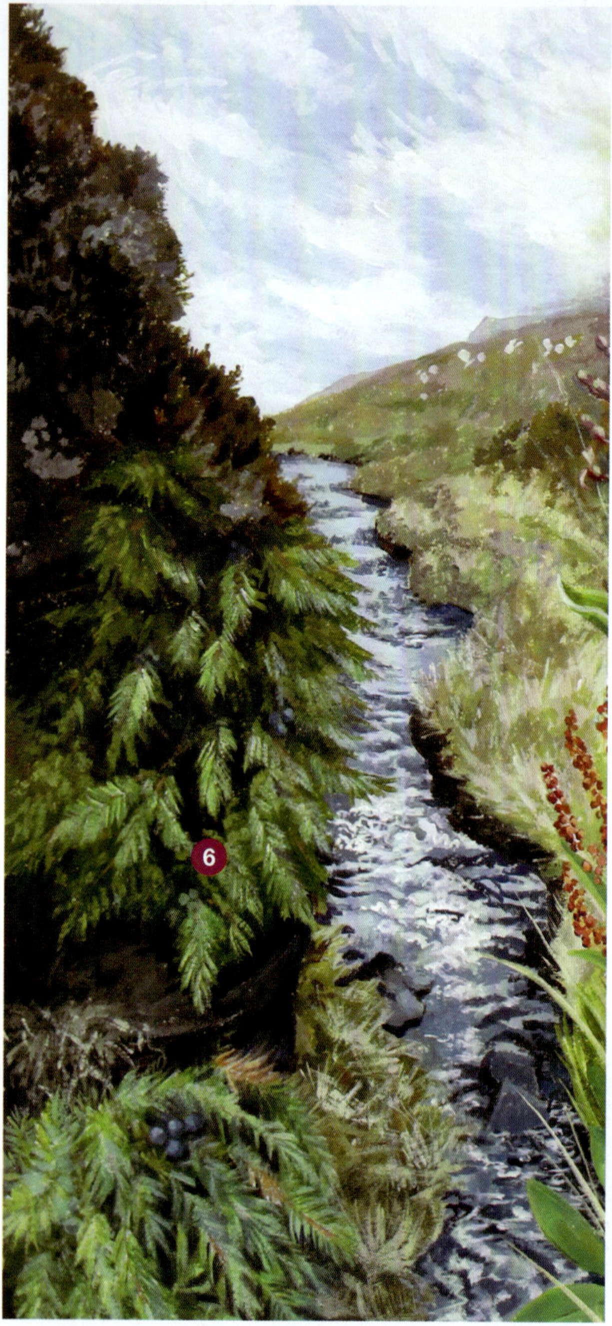
6

6) Prostrate Juniper (*Juniperus communis* subsp. *nana*)
Juniper family

Height rarely to 100cm; flowering May to June; fruits September to October. Local and rare in Orkney (6/28); hard to find.

In Britain, Common Juniper may grow as tall as 10 metres. In Orkney, it occurs as a low shrub, and the subspecies known as Prostrate Juniper is subjected to such severe wind-pruning that it rarely attains more than a metre in height. The shrubs are typically twisted and are covered in dense and sharply-pointed blue-green leaves in whorls of three which have a broad white stripe on their inside surface. The berries are initially green but turn blue-black by late summer. Bushes live on average for about 100 years.

Its distribution within the county has lessened over the last two centuries as a result of agricultural changes, muirburn and grazing; the best remaining examples are found on rock outcrops safe from fire or teeth. Hoy is undoubtedly its stronghold but it retains a weak presence in both the East and West Mainland, Rousay, Shapinsay and South Ronaldsay.

Throughout Scotland, all parts of the Juniper tree have been put to use. The wood was burned to fumigate houses, its cleansing properties were considered to ward off the plague. Meat and kippers were smoked with the reek of Juniper and creels were fashioned from its roots. The berries provided flavouring for game or a refreshing tea and they were gathered commercially for the gin industry; during the 17th Century Highland berries were exported to Holland for the production of *jenever gin*. It is a very powerful diuretic and has a dark side; known as savin, it was administered to induce abortions.

6. Prostrate Juniper along Burn of Greenheads, Hoy

7. Lesser Twayblade at Stromness reservoir, Stromness
8. Heath Spotted-orchid at Costa Head, Evie

7) **Lesser Twayblade** (*Neottia cordata*) — Orchid family

Height to 10cm; flowers July to September. Local and occasional in Orkney (10/28); hard to find.

Unquestionably this perennial is one of Orkney's most insignificant looking and inconspicuous plants. It is as shy and retiring as its bigger sibling, Common Twayblade (page 32), is bold. *Tway* is an archaic form of *two* and often it is merely the glimpse of its two tiny oval leaves in amongst Ling, Blaeberry or Sphagnum that gives its presence away. Without an obvious flower this tiny Orchid gives more than a passing imitation of a newly-emerged seedling. Even in flower it is still very difficult to see; the slender reddish stem and the brownish flowers are a camouflage match for the colours of the heather understorey. Elaine Bullard delighted in finding one plant growing from the cup of leaves that are so characteristic of Heath Rush.

Quite possibly Lesser Twayblade is under-recorded not just in Orkney, but throughout heathery Britain. It is a wildflower that requires 'a nose to the ground approach'. We do know of course that it has been lost from many sites in Britain due to habitat destruction in relation to agriculture and forestry developments of the 20th Century.

8) Heath Spotted-orchid (*Dactylorhiza maculata*)   Orchid family
Eve, Puldery – Moorland Spotted-orchid

Height to 20cm; flowers June to August. Widespread and frequent in Orkney (21/28); fairly easy to find.

Many, if not all, Orchids hybridise freely. The Heath Spotted-orchid does not buck the trend and hybridises with the Northern Marsh-orchid (*Dactylorhiza purpurella*) – the Orkney *Eve* and the Orkney *Adam*. Orchids can look very similar but this one's preference for acidic soils helps set it apart from others and although occurring most frequently on the hill, it is not uncommon to find it growing in flushes and bogs. During the 20th Century, plants of the heath and the wetlands have diminished through habitat destruction and drainage – the decline of this Orchid is similarly reflected.

Occasionally all-white forms are happened upon but generally the flowers are pale pink and decorated with streaks and lines rather than dots. The flower spike is distinctly pointed and the flower's bottom lip is wavy and made up of three lobes – the shallow mid-lobe has a rounded and toothed lobe on either side. The lance-shaped leaves are pointed and adorned with circular purple spots.

9) Sheep's Sorrel (*Rumex acetosella*)   Dock family
Soorick

Height to 20cm; flowers May to August. Widespread and frequent in Orkney (20/28); fairly easy to find.

The smaller of the two Sorrels that occur in Orkney, Sheep's Sorrel is also far less frequently found than its bigger brother Common Sorrel. It occurs on the hill where plants can be especially easy to see on peat tracks and in abandoned peat cuttings. The leaves are spear-shaped having two lobes at the base which spread or point forwards unlike the backward pointing lobes of Common Sorrel (page 89). The dull red male and female flowers of this perennial are quite inconspicuous and borne on separate plants.

Both of the Sorrels are known by the colloquial name *Sooricks*. They have also been put to similar uses in their medicinal and culinary histories. Folk remedies include them in treatments for diarrhoea and scurvy; latterly it has been a primary ingredient in a cancer treatment commonly referred to by the name *Essiac*. Its charred seeds were revealed during excavations at the Neolithic site of Howe, near Stromness and in the kitchen, the lemony leaves have been gathered for centuries either for salads or as a curdling agent.

9. Sheep's Sorrel at Burray Ness, Burray

10) Heath Speedwell (*Veronica officinalis*) Figwort family
Common speedwell

Height to 15cm; flowers May to August. Widespread and frequent in Orkney (17/28); fairly easy to find.

Two other of Orkney's Speedwells, Field Speedwell and Germander Speedwell (page 107), are mostly restricted to cultivated land. Heath Speedwell has slightly different requirements and is usually located in the soils associated with dry grassland and heath. There is a tendency for this perennial to occur in very short turf or on rock outcrops where there is the thinnest of soils, in much the same manner as one often finds Wild Thyme. The four-petalled lilac flowers are clustered on slender spikes and sit well above the oval leaves which are themselves neat, hairy and shallowly-toothed.

Various reasons have been presented for its name. The *officinalis* part of its Latin label suggests that the plant was part of the apothecary's stock-in-trade. Supposedly Heath Speedwell had the ability to cure a long list of ailments – chronic skin complaints (including leprosy), tuberculosis, wounds, coughs, stomach upsets and arthritis; its all-round healing properties would have ensured that it was a standard item on the shelf.

10. Heath Speedwell at 12 hour Tower, Rousay

11) Stone Bramble (*Rubus saxatilis*) Rose family

Height to 25cm; flowers June to August; fruits August to September. Local and occasional in Orkney (8/28); not easy to find.

This wild relative of both the Strawberry and Raspberry has a very restricted distribution within Orkney being found solely in both the West and East Mainland, Hoy, South Ronaldsay and Rousay - Hoy has the greatest abundance by far. Although occurring in the hill, Stone Bramble, a biennial, favours shady areas on rocky ground where the soils are more alkaline than acid. It is a low, creeping plant with long runners and erect downy and slightly prickly, flowering stems. The toothed and downy leaves are in threes; two are opposite and stalk-less while the terminal leaf is stalked. Like many from this family, the flowers are white; the Stone Bramble has narrow petals which are no longer than the sepals. The edible fruits are a rich scarlet which Grigson (1955) compared to *'cabochon garnets'* (precious stones polished or uncut) and the leaves can be dried and used as a tea substitute.

Clubmosses

Orkney is home to five different species of Clubmoss: Fir Clubmoss (*Lycopodium selago*), Stag's-horn Clubmoss (*Lycopodium clavatum*), Interrupted Clubmoss (*Lycopodium annotinum*) and Alpine Clubmoss (*Diphasiastrum alpinum*) all occur on the hill and Lesser Clubmoss (*Selaginella selaginoides*) which, while occurring on the hill, is also at home in the wetlands of fens and flushes.

12) Stag's-horn Clubmoss (*Lycopodium clavatum*) Clubmoss family

Trailing to 100cm; spores ripe June to September. Local and rare in Orkney (5/28); hard to find.

11. Stone Bramble at Nowt Bield, Hoy
12. Stag's-horn Clubmoss at North Kews, Evie
13. Fir Clubmoss at Fibla Fiold, Rendall

Stag's-horn Clubmoss is as prostrate as Fir Clubmoss is upright. Its shoots trail and creep across nearby vegetation and in so doing, it sends out roots. At regular intervals it is branched and these have a silvery grey-green appearance caused by the hair tips on the crowded leaves; the leaves on the stem are significantly bigger than the leaves on the cone-bearing stalks. The cones, which usually occur in pairs, are bright green in early summer becoming a very noticeable pale yellow by late autumn. Bright yellow spores emanate from the cones and this substance, known as Lycopodium powder, is used as an absorbent in surgery and as a component of fireworks. The long, trailing but very slow growing stems of this evergreen perennial were popular as a table decoration for Harvest Homes and winter dances.

13) Fir Clubmoss (*Huperzia selago*)   Clubmoss family

Height to 10cm; spores ripe June to August. Local and occasional in Orkney (9/28); fairly easy to find.

Resembling a diminutive fir tree or even a cactus, these evergreen perennials occur among the heather, on bare ground or rock ledges. The stems, which fork from the main trunk and are largely equal in size, are stiffly erect and have strong and prickly leaves. Changes in agriculture practices which have resulted in the loss of hill ground have consequently affected the abundance of Fir Clubmoss in Orkney. Nowadays its distribution is quite limited occurring solely on the uplands of Hoy, West Mainland, South Ronaldsay, Rousay and Westray; however it has a mere toe-hold on the last three.

Its range of uses is quite eclectic. In Canada the Nitinaht of Vancouver

Island employed it as a purgative and in druidic Britain, it was burned to produce a medicinal smoke for eye disorders.

Milkworts

Rogation flower, Procession flower, Cross-flower

The two Milkworts that occur in Orkney, Heath and Common, are both perennials, both quite small and both of quite similar appearance. Historically they have been linked to increased milk production in cattle and humans but such is their similarity, that it is doubtful whether any differentiation has been made in the past. In rural Scotland, the presence of Milkwort in pastures was considered to increase the yield from the cow and in the Gaelic world it was known as *lus a bhianne*, milk plant. Elsewhere in Europe, authors of herbal tracts indicated that an infusion of Milkwort was supposed to increase the flow of a nursing mother's milk. There is religious significance connected to Milkwort in that it was picked and carried in the processions during Rogation week, hence the alternative names *Rogation flower* and *Procession flower* when the bounds were beaten and the crops were blessed. During the parade a cross, decorated with Milkwort, was carried – hence another of its names, *Cross-flower*.

14) Heath Milkwort (*Polygala serpyllifolia*) Milkwort family

Thyme-leaved milkwort

Height to 15cm; flowers May to August. Widespread and frequent in Orkney (18/28); fairly easy to find.

In Orkney, this is the Milkwort most frequently met with on the hill where it seems to flourish in old peat cuttings and on recently muirburned areas. It was noted that it became particularly abundant immediately after the 1984 fire on Hoy. Creeping up through the heather its flowers are studs of vivid blue against the backdrop of heather browns; occasionally flowers of pink and white are produced.

14. Heath Milkwort on Greeny Hill, Birsay
15. Common Milkwort on Greeny Hill, Birsay
16. Heath Bedstraw at Craw stone, Westray

The main point of differentiation between these two Milkworts is that in this species the oval-shaped leaves sit opposite each other especially towards the base of the slender stem.

15) Common Milkwort (*Polygala vulgaris*)   Milkwort family

Height to 15cm; flowers May to September. Local and occasional in Orkney (11/28); not easy to find.

Although it can be encountered on the hill, Common Milkwort is not a flower of acid soil. Its likely situation on the hill is in among flushes or close to outcrops and crags. The flower colour is generally blue but like Heath Milkwort, the stems may be dressed in pink or white blooms. The major difference is in the leaves which are overall smaller than Heath Milkwort and sit alternately along the stem. In addition, as one travels up the stem, the leaves get appreciably larger and longer.

16) Heath Bedstraw (*Galium saxatile*)   Bedstraw family

Height to 12cm; flowers June to September. Widespread and abundant in Orkney (22/28); easy to find.

While some overlapping is always going to be the case, the four commonest Bedstraws in Orkney can generally be found in their four distinct habitats: Cleavers on the shore, Lady's Bedstraw on the links, Common Marsh-bedstraw in freshwater and Heath Bedstraw on the hill. All of them are low growing and have a tendency to sprawl or creep, some more so than others. Heath Bedstraw is however the Bedstraw that creeps least and unashamedly spends its season more or less prostrate growing in among Heathers and on heathy grasslands. With its white clusters of very small four-petalled flowers this perennial has similarities to Common Marsh-bedstraw but structurally it is more robust and closer to Lady's Bedstraw. The white flowers are grouped in conspicuous short-stalked clusters along the stem and are far more obvious than those of Common Marsh-bedstraw as are the leaves which lie in whorls of four to six. Botanists consider that Heath Bedstraw is a useful indicator of unimproved hill land.

17) Heath Rush (*Juncus squarrosus*)   Rush family
Moss rush, Goosecorn

Height to 25cm; flowers June to July. Widespread and abundant in Orkney (22/28); easy to find.

The presence of Heath Rush in the hill is often cited as an indicator of previous unsympathetic heathland management. It can be abundant in areas where sheep grazing is heavy and in Orkney it is commonly seen on bare areas along hill tracks. It is a wiry perennial that forms dense tufts from which the stiff and, usually leafless, stems emerge. Similarly wiry but also grooved are the leaves which lie in a rosette. Having pale margins to the clustered dark brown flowers bestows a silvery appearance and in the autumn the fruits are brown and egg-shaped.

In 18th Century Orkney, Heath Rush was known as *Moss rush* or *Goosecorn* - the seed heads were fed to domestic geese. In Shetland, the plant was fashioned into pot scrubbers and hearth brushes; additionally, a common belief was that chewing the stems, known as *Burri-stikkels*, could result in a hare-lip. It obviously featured large in Shetland life where there was an oft-used piece of health and safety advice – '*Stramp fair on da Burra* (Heath Rush)*, keep wide a da floss* (Soft Rush)'.

18) Fairy Flax (*Linum catharticum*)   Flax family
Purging flax

Height to 10cm; flowers June to September. Widespread and occasional in Orkney (21/28); not easy to find.

Considering it is such a small plant, it is capable of packing a substantial punch. The clue is in its alternative name *Purging Flax* but caution must be exercised since large quantities, taken internally, are deemed to be extremely poisonous. In the Gaelic world, the plant goes by the name *miosach* meaning *monthly* which relates to its use

17. Heath Rush on the Taing, Wyre
18. Fairy Flax in Russadale quarry, Stenness
19. Round-leaved Wintergreen on Moss of Sheepal, Rousay

in female medicine; it is documented that women in 18th Century Mull and Skye suppressed periods with infusions of Fairy Flax and Lesser Meadow-rue.

This wiry and tiny annual is often found in the drier parts of the hill. However, it frequently occurs in a wide range of habitats especially those that are rich in calcium including rock outcrops and flushes. The stems have the appearance of fine wire along which oval single-veined leaves sit opposite each other, with five-petalled white flowers in loose clusters atop the stem.

19) Round-leaved Wintergreen (*Pyrola rotundifolia* ssp. *rotundifolia*)

Height to 30cm; flowers June to September.   Wintergreen family
Local and rare in Orkney (1/28); hard to find.

One of Orkney's rarest wildflowers of the hill, Round-leaved Wintergreen is confined now to Rousay. Previously, it was far more widespread and occurred also on Hoy and in the West Mainland; its decline can be attributed to muirburn, grazing and the winning of peat. Since this perennial evergreen is so uncommon, it is likely too that it requires some specialised soil and moisture conditions – generally it appears to grow well amongst Sphagnum. When in flower, it can be very conspicuous with a stem of ivory-white goblet-shaped flowers rising above the surrounding vegetation – the flowers are quite similar to the well-known garden plant Lily of the Valley. Equally conspicuous are the dark green leaves which are large, round and with long stems.

As in Orkney, the species has declined in Britain especially since the 1930s due to agricultural changes, afforestation and wetland management.

20) Slender St John's-wort (*Hypericum pulchrum*)
St Peter's wort — St John's-wort family

Height to 30cm; flowers June to August. Widespread and frequent in Orkney (20/28); fairly easy to find.

As a family, the St John's-worts are one of the most important in European traditions; they play an integral part in white magic and are some of the chief herbs of St John the Baptist. This Christian festival was a festival of fire whereby the herbs of St John which included Mugwort, Greater Plantain, Yarrow, Corn Marigold, Danewort, Ivy, Orpine and Vervain, were purified by smoke in order to strengthen them in their tasks to combat the devil and witchcraft. Latterly, in the Gaelic world, it was worn by men and women under the left armpit to ward away enchantment and death.

Throughout Britain this delicate perennial may be found on heaths, in open woodlands and hedgerows. In Orkney, heaths provide the medium for this traditionally important plant to cast its spell. Its petals are butter-yellow with a hint of red and a closer look reveals red and black spots. The round and slender reddish stem is erect and the oval leaves, which are decorated with translucent spots, lie opposite each other.

21) Green-ribbed Sedge (*Carex binervis*) — Sedge family

Height to 60cm; flowers June; fruits July. Widespread and abundant in Orkney (21/28); easy to find.

Tall and slender and towering over its neighbouring heath vegetation, Green-ribbed Sedge is possibly one of the easiest of the sedges to recognise. Although this perennial is found throughout the hill in Orkney, it is often more conspicuous on the open and drier slopes. The dark green leaves have wine red blotches and the flower-head consists of a male spike above two or three female spikes which are well-spaced down the stem. The fruits are very distinctive being purple-brown and having two prominent green ribs.

20. Slender St.John's-wort on Golta, Flotta

22) *Lady's-mantles* (Alchemilla spp.)   Rose family
Dew-cup

This notoriously difficult group totals 14 species in Britain, two of which are generally considered to have been introduced. Perhaps the most familiar and widespread of the Lady's-mantles is the vigorous and aggressively spreading Garden Lady's-mantle (*Alchemilla mollis*) which is also the largest having leaves at times in excess of 15cm. This species can be found occasionally in Orkney in locations where garden refuse has been deposited. In the wild however, there are considered to be two species in the county, both of which may be found in the hill: Hairless Lady's-mantle appears to prefer damp soils and seeping water, while Southern Lady's-mantle is more likely on rock outcrops. Both have large palm-shaped leaves and frothy clusters of tiny lime-green flowers.

Alchemilla means *Little alchemist* and the plant was very important in magic. Alchemists believed that the morning dew collected from the leaves had magical properties – this 'celestial water' was considered most powerful. The name Lady's-mantle refers to the Virgin Mary and historically it has been used for restoring a woman's virginity and sagging bosoms to their former shape.

Southern Lady's-mantle (*Alchemilla filicaulis*)

Height to 30cm; flowers May to September. Local and occasional in Orkney (7/28); not easy to find.

The backs of the flowers are hairy as are both sides of the leaves.

Hairless Lady's-mantle (*Alchemilla glabra*)

Height to 15cm; flowers May to September. Widespread and frequent in Orkney (15/28); fairly easy to find.

Generally larger than Southern Lady's-mantle and almost hairless except for some appressed hairs on the leaf stalk.

21. Green-ribbed Sedge on Wideford Hill, St Ola

22. Lady's-mantle on the hill, Egilsay

23. Bog Asphodel at Burn of Sowardee, Sandwick
24. Sphagnum at Blubbersdale, Rendall
25. Marsh Violet at Glenrae, Orphir

23) **Bog Asphodel** (*Narthecium ossifragum*) — Lily family
Pulderuck *– Maiden hair, Lancashire asphodel*

Height to 25cm; flowers July to September. Widespread and frequent in Orkney (21/28); easy to find.

Clumps and swathes of flowering Bog Asphodels bring a surprisingly vivid and intense yellow to the hill in summer. It is normal to see wet hollows full of these upright perennials but some of the shallow valleys between spurs are packed so tightly that from a distance in July and August, some of Orkney's hills appear to have flowing yellow rivers. The six-petalled flowers are star-shaped while the long blade-like leaves are wafer-thin. Bog Asphodel continues to colour the hill in autumn when the dying leaves cast a warm glow of peach; by mid-winter the leaves have gone and it is just the stems that rise bone-white over the hill. The first part of its Latin name *Narthecium* refers to the 'rod-like' appearance of these stems. The second part of its name literally translates as 'bone breaking'. For many years it has been believed the eating of it causes brittleness of bones in sheep. In actuality, this bone weakness is much more likely to be caused by the lack of mineral salts in the soil where the plant grows.

Throughout much of upland Britain it has been employed as a dye for fabrics. However in Lancashire, it was used specifically for a hair dye by the women of the county and was known either as *Maiden hair* or *Lancashire asphodel*. It has also seen service as a substitute for Saffron in medicine and cooking.

24) *Sphagnum (*Sphagnum* spp.)　　　　　　　　　　　　　　　　Moss
Bog-moss

Height to 10cm. Widespread and abundant in Orkney; very easy to find.

With their ability to absorb prodigious amounts of moisture, the multi-coloured swathes of Sphagnum mosses that clothe the wetter parts of the hill in carpets, cushions and hummocks play a very important role in the creation of peat bogs. The Sphagnum layer is composed of hundreds of individual fragile and feathery plants packed closely together so providing support for each other. Water is held in their spongy forms long after the surrounding soil has dried out. In this way the plants continue to provide essential nutrients to the soil and help prevent the decay of dead plant material which over hundreds of years gets compressed to form peat. There are at least 26 species of Sphagnum moss growing in Orkney commonest of which is Red Bog-moss (*Sphagnum capillifolium*). Other fairly abundant species include Cow-horn Bog-moss (*S. denticulatum*), Lustrous Bog-moss (*S. subnitens*), Blunt-leaved Bog-moss (*S. palustre*) and Papillose Bog-moss (*S. papillosum*). The species range in colour from red and pink to orange and green.

In Canada, Native North Americans have gathered Bog-moss for bedding (which included the linings to cradles), nappies and wound dressings. Its importance as a dressing was recognised during wartime and in its heyday during the First World War, the harvesting of Sphagnum was an industry in Scotland producing 500,000kg per month.

25) Marsh Violet (*Viola palustris*)　　　　　　　　　　　　Violet family

Height to 10cm; flowers April to July. Widespread and occasional in Orkney (15/28); not easy to find.

175

Like its close relative the Common Dog-violet (page 77), it flowers early in the spring; however unlike its relative, its flowering period is brief. It is regarded as a perennial herb of wet areas, bogs, heaths or marshes but it particularly favours acid soils where there is flushing. In Orkney it prefers peaty, shady areas and is often associated with Sphagnum mosses. Records indicate that it can be found, sometimes sparingly, in every Orkney parish and island except for North Ronaldsay and Sanday.

The pale lilac flowers are similar to those of the Common Dog-violet but the petals are blunt, have dark purple veins and lack the Dog's blue quality. Both species are scentless. However, it is the leaves that provide the obvious difference; those of the Marsh Violet are quite rounded or kidney-shaped, those of the Common Dog-violet are heart-shaped.

26) Marsh Lousewort (*Pedicularis palustris*) — Figwort family
Red Rattle

Height to 25cm; flowers May to September. Widspread and frequent in Orkney (18/28); fairly easy to find.

Superficially Marsh Lousewort is very similar to Lousewort in looks and in habits. Both of them are part-parasites and latch on to the roots of grasses in order to extract mineral salts and water. Furthermore it also shares its unwelcome reputation of being a supplier of lice and liver-fluke. Marsh Lousewort is a tall and erect annual with a single upright and purplish stem. The green fern-like leaves, which are also tinged purplish, are divided into a series of toothed and separate lobes like two rows of leaflets. The pink-purple flower-heads are composed of a narrow upper lip and a broad lower. Marsh Lousewort is not uncommon in Orkney but is far less abundant and widespread than Lousewort. Although seemingly suitable habitat occurs, it does not appear to be present in Eday, North Ronaldsay, Papa Westray, Rousay or Shapinsay.

Culpepper considered that the plant had a great influence on moods and humours and suggested that it should be boiled in wine and drunk to stabilise the uneasy balance in man of black bile, blood, choler and phlegm.

27) **Lousewort** (*Pedicularis sylvatica*)   Figwort family

Money-in-the-purse, …-the-box, …-the-basket, …-the-rattle.

Height to 15cm; flowers April to July. Widespread and abundant in Orkney (21/28); easy to find.

The belief that this pretty perennial infests cattle and sheep with lice and liver fluke has been prevalent for centuries – hence its unfortunate name. Indeed recognition of this supposed ability no doubt accounts for the first part of its Latin name which means *louse*. The case for spreading lice is not proven but transmission of liver-flukes is possible. The plant succeeds in the poorest of wet and heathy soils; any browsing animals that have been sentenced to find nutrition in such conditions are in all probability likely to struggle and be susceptible to the water-borne liver-fluke embryos. Much better press is forthcoming from the Outer Hebrides where it is considered to increase the milk yield of goats and in Shetland where children used to seek out its sweet 'honey' flowers.

In Orkney it is most frequently found among heathers where it has a distinct preference for the wetter areas. Like its close relative Yellow Rattle (page 32) it is a part-parasite of roots, but unlike its close relative it occurs only on acidic soils. The many stems spread from the base and carry prettily crimped leaves while the fairly large Snapdragon-like flowers are composed of two dark pink petals the upper lip longer than the lower. As with many flowers, white-flowered forms are encountered sporadically. The inflated coin-like seed capsules, which persist into winter, are the reason for its other names *Money-in-the-purse, …the-box, …the-basket* and *…the-rattle*.

26. Marsh Lousewort at Grip of Black Craig, Stromness
27. Lousewort on West Hill, Graemsay

28. Great Sundew at Dwarfie Stane, Hoy
29. Round-leaved Sundew at Burgar Hill, Evie

*Sundews

There are three species of Sundew in Britain and Orkney is home to two of them – Round-leaved and Great. Their Latin name *Drosera* derives from the Greek meaning 'dew' or 'dewdrops' which refers to the drops of glistening fluid which tip the hairs that sprout from the leaves. It was believed that Sundews were capable of retaining their 'dew' in full sunlight – hence their name. Sundews live on nutrient-deficient soils and the sticky fluid traps insects that, once digested, supplement the plant's nitrate nutrition (midges are attracted to the dewdrops, mistaking them for water in which to lay their eggs). The tiny, white, five or six-petalled flowers rarely open and are most usually found in bud form; this suggests that these perennials can fertilise even when the buds are closed. Like the other insect-eater of the hill, the Butterwort, Sundews were used as curdling agents and as a medicine for respiratory agents. The 'dew' was used to counter sunburn, freckles and whooping cough and was considered to be at its most potent if harvested before sunrise. Its strength was further increased by distilling with wine and this is possibly the derivation of the liqueur *Rossolis*. As with many specialities of heathland, there have been notable declines in lowland areas due to habitat destruction.

28) Great Sundew (*Drosera anglica*)   Sundew family

Height to 12cm; flowers July to August. Local and rare in Orkney (3/28); hard to find.

With its upright and orange-coloured leaves, Great Sundew is noticeably more conspicuous than its smaller cousin. However, it is far more restricted in its distribution than the Round-leaved Sundew and can be encountered only on Hoy and at one location in the West Mainland. It favours the wetter parts of blanket bogs and base-rich mires and may often be seen in standing water.

29) Round-leaved Sundew (*Drosera rotundifolia*)   Sundew family
Common sundew

Height to 8cm; flowers June to August. Widespread and occasional in Orkney (15/28); not easy to find.

Round-leaved Sundew holds its circular leaves flat and is found growing on wet peat. Invariably it grows in close proximity to Sphagnum mosses where it can easily be overlooked due to the similar red colours in both species. Its distribution within Orkney is restricted to East and West Mainland, Hoy, Rousay, Shapinsay and South Ronaldsay. Other than a single record on Eday, it is absent from the rest of the North Isles.

*Cottongrasses
Lucky Minni's oo, Massa kruppan

The Latin name that is common to the three species of cottongrass that grow in the county is *Eriophorum* meaning 'bearing wool'. Broad-leaved Cottongrass is the rarest of the three that grow in Orkney having been found only on Hoy. These plants of wet and peaty ground have been harvested in the past; their silky fibres have been used extensively in Scotland not only for the manufacture of cloth and as stuffing for pillows and mattresses but also in the creation of clothing such as shirts and socks. In some parts of Scotland, tradition was that the bride knitted a pair of bedsocks from cottongrass wool which would be worn on her first married night. Another use for the fluffy heads was as wicks for candles. Among sheep farmers it had a high reputation as a spring tonic – sheep that had been feebled by a long winter were turned out on to the moss where recovery was almost guaranteed after a few days of cropping cottongrass. It is a useful plant for the traveller – its presence indicates boggy areas that are best avoided. Habitat loss, especially in lower-lying areas, has led to its decrease.

30. Hare's-tail Cottongrass at Norseman, Firth

30) Hare's-tail Cottongrass (*Eriophorum vaginatum*)   Sedge family

Height to 50cm; flowers May to July. Widespread and frequent in Orkney (15/28); easy to find.

Although, this tussock-forming perennial, like its near-relative Common Cottongrass, is typical of wet and peaty moorlands, it can often be found in slightly drier parts of the hill where Ling is invariably its nearest neighbour. More definitely though Hare's-tail Cottongrass is easily distinguished by its single flower spikes and its much narrower and thread-like leaves. It is an exceptionally hardy plant, not only capable of surviving after the severest of burning, but also capable of rapid increase.

31) Common Cottongrass (*Eriophorum angustifolium*) Sedge family

Height to 50cm; flowers May to July. Widespread and abundant in Orkney (25/28); easy to find.

Of the three cottongrasses that grow in the county, Common Cottongrass is the one that can often be found in the wettest parts of the hill. Indeed this perennial has a distinct preference for growing in standing water and that trait helps protect it from muirburn. All the cottongrasses have similarities but Common Cottongrass is easily separated by the fact that it has three to five drooping flower-heads and narrow keeled leaves, which have a three-sided point at the tip and are often tinged purple.

31. Common Cottongrass at Redbanks, St Andrews

32) Butterwort (Pinguicula vulgaris)   Butterwort family
Klepsy girs*, *Eccle grass – *Butter mixer, Cheese plant, Bog violet*

Height to 12cm; flowers May to July. Very widespread and frequent in Orkney (24/28); easy to find.

The many and various names by which this insectivorous perennial is known give some indication of its significance in Britain. It is afforded great importance in Hebridean folklore where it is known as *mòthan* and has the status of a holy plant capable of protecting ordinary folk from witches and the arrows of elves, cows from fairies, travellers from harm and women during childbirth. Additionally it was held that drinking milk from a cow that had grazed on *mòthan* would protect a newborn child and grant the drinker immunity from danger. However, its chief application among many cultures is as a rennet substitute whereby the leaves were wrapped in muslin and added to milk to curdle and thicken it. This practice was widespread and recorded from much of Scotland, including both Orkney and Shetland, and from Lapland.

Wet heaths seem to be its prime location but it also occurs among Sphagnum moss, in flushes and on permanently wet rock faces. After overwintering as a tiny rootless bud, a star-like rosette of oval, fleshy, sticky yellow-green leaves develops which is designed to attract and trap insect visitors. A thin stalk rises from the centre on top of which is a violet flower complete with a white throat patch. As with many heathland plants, losses have occurred in lowland areas due to agricultural intensification and drainage.

32. Butterwort at Brinkie's Brae, Stromness

32

33. Creeping Willow at Community Hall, Graemsay

33) Creeping Willow (*Salix repens*)   Willow family

Height to 150cm; flowers April to May; fruits June and July. Widespread and abundant in Orkney (25/28); easy to find.

It was a difficult decision to include this tree in the text and illustrations. However, Creeping Willow is a characteristic plant of Orkney's heathland whether it is coastal or inland. It can also be less 'tree-like', and more 'flower-like' than the other Willows that grow in Orkney; Creeping Willow is often seen low to the ground with wiry and flexible, far-reaching branches that trail among the stems of heathers and Crowberry. During April and May heathy ground is dotted with bright yellow catkins on silvery grey stems. The male flower-heads are slightly bigger than the female while the oval leaves appear later and are adorned with white silky hairs on the underside.

Willow has long been an essential ingredient in the country medicine chest; infusions of willow bark were remedies for the ague and chills and it is not difficult to imagine Creeping Willow being chewed in bygone times to alleviate ills and ailments. Willows are the source of salicylic acid which was isolated and developed into aspirin in the late 19th Century. It had other uses as well; on St Kilda the stems were twisted into barrel hoops.

34) Cloudberry (*Rubus chamaemorus*)   Rose family

Heatherberry, Hillberry, Nowtberry

Height to 18cm; flowers May to August. Local and rare in Orkney (2/28); hard to find.

This Arctic-alpine almost squeezed into the next habitat section *The High Hill;* Grigson states that this perennial 'is found on the highest mountains in the north where it lives in the clouds'. However, 'cloud'

35. Bog Bilberry on Klondyke, Burray
34. Cloudberry on Rowamo, Harray

comes from the Old English *clud* meaning 'hill' so essentially it is hillberry. In reality it occurs on moorland or blanket bog above 600 metres however, oddly, in the extreme south of its range, North Wales, it can be found just below 100 metres. In Orkney it is a real rarity and is known from only two locations, Harray, where it was discovered in 1949 and Hoy, where it was found in 1963. There may be other unfound clumps in the county since it has a fairly short growing season with the plant dying away by early August. The wrinkled and downy leaves are rounded with half a dozen lobes while the single, large, five-petalled white flower appears in May.

In Scandinavia the berries are harvested in large quantities – in Norway they are known as *Blotta berries* and in Lapland, the Sami bury them to preserve supplies. In Scotland it is the badge of the MacFarlane clan and in Yorkshire, where it is considered to taste of 'nowt', it is known as *Nowtberry*. The raspberry-like berries, which start off red but turn golden orange, are uncommon in Britain and have not been seen in Orkney.

35) Bog Bilberry (*Vaccinium uliginosum*) Heath family

Height to 50cm; flowers May to July; fruits August and September. Local and rare in Orkney (5/28); hard to find.

This plant's distribution within Britain is distinctly Scottish. Other than for a handful of sites in Cumbria, and a remarkable record on Exmoor in Somerset, all other locations are in northern and western Scotland, Orkney and Shetland. It occupies similar habitat to its near relative Blaeberry (page 150) but it would appear that Blaeberry is more suited to well-drained heaths while Bog Bilberry prefers very acidic peaty soils. In Orkney its presence is confined to Burray, Hoy, Rousay and West Mainland where it may be found usually on the higher hills, but also in 'some curious odd corners elsewhere' Bullard (1995). On the high hills this perennial normally mixes in with the heathers to form a prostrate mat of upland vegetation; at lower levels it will appear as a bush up to 50cm in height.

Blaeberry has twigs that are green and four angled; Bog Bilberry has twigs that are round, brown and woody. It can be recognised from a distance by its leaves which are blue-green, this gives the plant a glaucous aura. The undersides of the leaves are heavily netted with veins and the finely turned urn-shaped flowers are a delicate pink.

36) Black Bog-rush (*Schoenus nigricans*) Sedge family

Height to 75cm; flowers May to June; fruits July to August.
Widespread and frequent in Orkney (21/28); easy to find.

Although sedges and rushes in general are indicative of wetlands, Black Bog-rush is most frequently found among the base-rich flushes that can proliferate in some parts of the hill. Its presence in the hill indicates an alkaline fen and this perennial is easily recognised by a sweep of grey and seemingly washed-out tussocks occupying damp areas in among the dark heather. Close up it yields leaves that are at least half the length of the stems and at the base, the sheaths are black and shiny. The flowering head is readily recognisable too, being oval, dense and, like the sheaths, black.

37) Yellow Saxifrage (*Saxifraga aizoides*) Saxifrage family

Height to 20cm; flowers July to September. Local and rare in Orkney (1/28); hard to find.

There are three wild true Saxifrages in Orkney, Starry, Purple and Yellow. Hoy is blessed with them all but the first-named, Starry, is

36. Black Bog-rush at Loch of Banks, Birsay

known from just one site. The other two species are more widespread in the north of the island with clusters of records around the Cuilags, Quoyawa and Nowt Bield. Purple Saxifrage (page 191) appears to occur at slightly higher altitudes than either of the other two and consequently, for this book, can be found in the High Hill section.

Yellow Saxifrage is chiefly found growing in lime-rich stony flushes or by running water where this perennial's bright yellow flowers are like beacons among the surrounding heathers and hill grasses. It is not uncommon to find the wide-spaced petals dotted with red or occasionally orange while the near stalk-less leaves are narrow and toothed.

38) Deergrass (*Trichophorum germanicum*)　　　　Sedge family

Height to 25cm; flowers May to June. Widespread and frequent in Orkney (17/28); easy to find.

Nothing else in Orkney looks like Deergrass and it is debatably the easiest of all the 'grasses' to identify. It normally manifests itself as a symmetrical and brush-like tussock covered with erect and extremely slender, smooth, round stems. The stems of this perennial are leafless except for a single short, strap-like leaf near the base while at the top is a single yellow-brown, egg-shaped spikelet.

It succeeds in the most adverse of hill conditions and positively thrives in burnt areas or where the ground has been heavily trampled or grazed. Its claim to fame is that it features prominently on the badge of Clan Mackenzie.

37. Yellow Saxifrage at Nowt Bield, Hoy

38. Deergrass at Mosshouse, Holm

The high hill and stony tops

Orkney is generally low-lying with gently undulating and rounded hills that are a feature of both the West and East Mainland, Eday, Rousay and Westray, The highpoints are Mid Hill in the West Mainland (275m), Gaitnip in the East Mainland (101m), Ward Hill on Eday (101m), Kierfea on Rousay (235m) and Fitty Hill on Westray (169m). Hoy is the exception with much of the northern part of the island above 200 metres and the highest summits of Ward Hill and the Cuilags at 479m and 433m respectively. It is on the high Hoy hills that Orkney's tundra-like vegetation is most obvious and has established through a combination of exposure and cool oceanic summers. On the tops of these high hills, strong winds have sculpted terraces and hill dunes of thin soil interspersed with bare stone pavements – only the most hardy and drought-resistant species can survive here.

However, these plants are not strictly confined to the tops. Exposed conditions are prevalent throughout Hoy and the tundra type vegetation can occur at relatively low altitudes - Alpine Bearberry

Ward Hill, Hoy – background Cuilags, Sandy Loch and Hoy Sound

grows in profusion at an elevation of only 100 metres. In the lower corries Purple Saxifrage descends towards sea level whereas elsewhere in Scotland it is normally confined to much higher altitudes. As Berry (2000) asserts, 'There is probably no other place in the world where the vegetation zones are so telescoped altitudinally. It is possible to stand on Hoy at just over 1000 feet in Arctic-type tundra with dwarf vegetation sheltering in the lea of wind-formed terracing and look down on farm crops below'.

While Hoy is the obvious place for Orkney's tundra-type vegetation, there are other locations within the county where examples can be found. On both Rousay and Westray, and to a lesser extent the West Mainland, tundra-type vegetation occurs on the tops of the high hills and on the thin soils that are characteristic of the exposed *hammars*. On Westray, Moss Campion mingles with Scottish Primrose at an altitude of only 82 metres and on Rousay, Alpine Bearberry exists on the tops of Knitchen Hill, Blotchnie Fiold and Kierfea.

1. Trailing Azalea on Mel Fea, Hoy

1) Trailing Azalea (*Loiseleuria procumbens*) Heath family

Trailing to 25cm; flowers May to July. Local and rare in Orkney (1/28); hard to find.

In Orkney, as with many wildflowers of this habitat, Trailing Azalea can only be found on Hoy. In Britain, it can only be found in Scotland where its preferred locations are exposed stony mountain heaths, ridges and plateaux. Normally it grows at altitudes of between 500 and 900 metres, but as we move further north in Scotland, it may be found at much lower levels culminating in Shetland where it may be found at 240 metres on Ronas Hill. Hoy's plants occur on the hills in the north of the island at altitudes of above 300 metres.

Trailing Azalea is a tiny mat-forming shrub densely covered with very small evergreen leaves that are oval, have rolled-under edges and sit opposite each other on woody stems. The pink five-petalled flowers are small and funnel-shaped and flowering generally commences in early May.

2) Bearberry (*Arctostaphylos uva-ursi*) Heath family

Trailing to 150cm; flowers May to July; fruits July to September. Local and rare in Orkney (2/28); hard to find.

Bearberry's distribution in Orkney is restricted to Hoy. It clings to the ground on the island's high hills and is typically found in areas that are open and well-drained. Many fine mats of this handsome and conspicuous shrub with its thick-barked, long trailing stems of evergreen leaves can be found alongside the footpath to the Old Man of Hoy from Rackwick. The oval and untoothed leathery leaves are dark green and broadest at the tip and it is this mass of luxuriant foliage which draws the eye first and foremost. In amongst this luxuriance are clusters of pink-tinged, white bell-shaped flowers and an array of edible berries that turn from green to ruby red. Its name

2. Bearberry above the Burn of Greenheads, Hoy

derives from the supposed fondness of bears for the fruit; indeed its Latin name *uva-ursi* means 'grape of the bear'.

Bearberry occurs in North America, Greenland, Iceland and Northern Europe and has been put to use in a multitude of ways throughout its geography and history; it has had a widespread career as a tanning agent. The leaves have been used for centuries as a tonic for urinary, bladder and kidney ailments among the Cherokee and Okanagan people of North America and in Scotland, the powdered leaves treated kidney stones. Mixed with tobacco, the leaves were smoked by the Nitinaht of Vancouver Island in Canada.

3) Purple Saxifrage (*Saxifraga oppositifolia*) Saxifrage family

Height to 15cm; flowers March to May and occasionally again. Local and rare in Orkney (1/28); hard to find.

This early-flowering perennial appears to flourish in the harshest of exposed environments and it is known from the most northerly botanical area on earth, the north coast of Greenland. Purple Saxifrage is generally found at high altitudes, but at higher latitudes it is often located at sea level. In Orkney, the hills of Hoy are its only known location. Flowering has been known for February but generally an excursion into the glens and ghylls of Ward Hill in March and early April will be rewarded by the presence of plenty of plants in their full glory. It tends to favour stony ground such as cliff ledges and cliff faces where the soil is moist, at its thinnest and most base-rich – newly exposed rock is a great favourite.

The trailing stems are densely covered with tiny, dark-green and fleshy, oval leaves which sit opposite each other along the stems. The tips of the leaves are invariably and characteristically coated with lime. Overall Purple Saxifrage is a small plant whose brilliant rosy-purple, five-petalled flowers appear quite large in comparison. Grigson (1955), who describes the plant as 'one of the most exquisite natives' considers it should be renamed to celebrate its beauty and proposes *Mountain Emperor* or *Snow Purple*. He even suggests *Ingleborough Beauty* to acknowledge its discovery in 1668 by John Ray on the Yorkshire hill of that name.

4) Alpine Bearberry (*Arctostaphylos alpinus*)   Heath family
Mountain bearberry, Black bearberry, Arctic bearberry

Trailing to 60cm; flowers May to August; fruits Aug to Oct. Local and rare in Orkney (6/28); hard to find.

This woody perennial is one of Britain's scarcest plants, growing only in Scotland, but well represented in Orkney. Within the county it is more common and more widespread than Bearberry, yet since the loss of a small colony on Westray due to cultivation, it is still found only on Hoy and Rousay. Generally it grows on mineral soils or occasionally in blanket bog at altitudes above 1000 metres but at Orkney's latitude, it may be found at just 100 metres. It may often be seen on windswept ridges among low Heather and Crowberry. Such is Orkney's importance for the plant that in 2002 *Plantlife* (the organisation that is solely dedicated to saving wild plants and their habitats) selected Alpine Bearberry as the flower emblem of the county.

Despite the similarities, it is not conclusive as to whether Alpine Bearberry was employed in the same manner as Bearberry. The

3. Purple Saxifrage in Glen of the Horn, Hoy

former is sufficiently different in that its leaves are deciduous and its berries are black. Additionally, the bright green, finely-toothed, netted leaves of Alpine Bearberry turn deep crimson in the autumn. It does however have similar white, bell-shaped flowers although these lack the pink tone so evident on Bearberry. Orkney's 18th Century naturalist George Low referred to this plant as the *Mountain Strawberry-tree*.

5) Moss Campion (*Silene acaulis*)   Campion family

Height to 8cm; flowers June to August. Local and rare in Orkney (2/28); hard to find.

In general and throughout Europe, Moss Campion is a plant of the mountains that is typically found on ledges, plateaux and cliff slopes where the substrate is base-rich. However, it can crop up where similar conditions occur at much lower altitudes and is known from some areas of stabilised sand dune. The distribution of Moss Campion in Orkney, as with all the other plants in this section, is restricted; it is known only from Hoy and Westray. Like most of its kind it grows at high levels; however, on occasion, as on Westray, plants may be found near sea level where it is known to flower on coastal grassland and been seen to rub shoulders with *Primula scotica*. At times its appearance at lower levels is due to being dislodged by severe weather and washed down from higher rock.

It is a very distinctive and striking wildflower characterised by dense green and rounded cushions of leaves on top of which are solitary, five-petalled pink flowers on short stalks – like a diminutive Red Campion on a hassock of Thrift-like leaves.

4. Alpine Bearberry on Blotchnie Fiold, Rousay

5. Moss Campion on Bloody Tuaks, Westray

6) Dwarf Cornel (*Cornus suecica*) — Dogwood family

Height to 20cm; flowers July to August. Local and rare in Orkney (1/28); hard to find.

In the stakes of rarity within the county, Dwarf Cornel ranks very highly, alongside that of Mountain Avens. As far as Orkney's botanists know, this low and creeping perennial herb can only be found at a single locality on Hoy, on difficult to access ledges high up on the Kame. Neither is it common in Britain; apart from some isolated records in Yorkshire, Northumberland and Shetland, the vast majority of locations are in Scotland's highest lands.

At a distance it appears to have four ivory-white petals; these are in fact petal-like bracts which encompass the flowers and are small, blackish-purple and may number anything between eight and 25. The unstalked leaves, which taper to a rounded point and have well defined ribs, are positioned opposite to each other along the erect stem. In Gaelic it is known as *Lus-a-chrais* 'the plant of gluttony' since it was considered that its red and round fruits stimulated the appetite.

7) Common Cow-wheat (*Melampyrum pratense*) — Figwort family

Height to 50cm; flowers May to Oct. Local and rare in Orkney (2/28); hard to find.

In many respects, it could be considered that Common Cow-wheat's appearance in this division is slightly inappropriate. It is an annual that may be found throughout Britain in a number of habitats that include woodland, hedgerows and heathland on poor, acidic soils. In Orkney, it is found exclusively on Hoy, and only found at height in the north of the island; previously it was also known from the Orphir hills up until 1920. Like its near relatives, Yellow Rattle, Marsh Lousewort and Lousewort, it is a parasite and attaches itself to the roots of grasses to extract water and minerals. Its name derives from the belief that grazing cows upon the plant would result in the finest and yellowest butter. Folklore considered that if pregnant women eat flour from its seeds, they would bear male children.

It is an erect plant that grows in rather loose sprawling patches. The leaves are spear-shaped and arranged opposite each other along the stem while the two-lipped lemon-yellow flowers are in pairs and all are on the same stem facing the same direction. The upper lip is shaped like the ridge of a roof and the mouth of the flower is closed by an arched-up lower lip. Grigson is lyrical about the plant's colours choosing to express the yellow against the green as 'delightfully cool' and to describe the colour of the lips as 'yolk gold in the mouth and pale yellow to almost white on the outside'.

8) Mountain Avens (*Dryas octopetala*)   Rose family

Height to 10cm; flowers May to July. Local and rare in Orkney (1/28); hard to find.

Another gem of Orkney's high and stony places and now found solely on a very few outcrops of rock in the hills of Hoy. It is likely that Mountain Avens (which is the national plant of Iceland) was one of the first plants, along with mosses, lichens, willows and dwarf birch to take over the almost bare and rocky surface of the earth when the last ice-age retreated. It is a lime-loving evergreen plant and in Britain is rare everywhere, only occurring with any degree of abundance on ledges and in rock crevices of the mountains of northwestern Scotland and on the limestone of the Burren in western Ireland. However, its need for lime means that where the conditions are suitable it may be found on shell sand at the coast. Because of this dependency on lime it is likely to be vulnerable when sites become more acidic through increased rainfall.

The distinctive leaves of this low and creeping shrub are dark green above, woolly and silver below. They have been likened to oak leaves and this accounts for the first part of its Latin name, *Dryas*, after Dryad the nymph of the oak tree. The centre of the flower is gold and more often than not, it has eight white petals, hence the second part of its scientific name *octopetala*; occasionally plants occur with twice that number. When flowering is over, the wind quickly disperses the feathery hairs of the seed head.

9) Alpine Saw-wort (*Saussurea alpina*)   Daisy family

Height to 40cm; flowers August to September. Local and rare in Orkney (2/28); hard to find.

In a British context, this thistle-like, but prickle-free perennial of the mountains is rare; in England it occurs solely in the Lake District, high Pennines and Cheviots; in Wales it is exclusive to Snowdonia and in Ireland to the highest hills in the west. Its stronghold is mainland Scotland where it can be found in the Highlands from Argyll in the south to Sutherland in the north with outposts in the Southern Uplands, the Inner and Outer Hebrides, the Caithness coast, Orkney and Shetland. It can usually be found at altitude on damp cliffs, rock outcrops or scree but on occasion, having been washed down hillsides, may become established at much lower levels. In Orkney its distribution is restricted to the highest islands, Hoy and Rousay. On Hoy its favoured locations include the glens and slopes of Ward Hill while on Rousay it is found on the summit of Kierfea Hill.

The fragrant florets are purple and sit in a compact cluster on a cottony stem. Its name derives from the appearance of the leaves which are lance-shaped and toothed. Gerard described them as being 'somewhat snipt about the edges like a sawe'. The uppersides are hairless while the undersides are, like the stem, covered in down.

196

197

10) Mountain Sorrel (*Oxyria digyna*)　　　　　　　　　　Dock family

Height to 20cm; flowers July to August. Local and rare in Orkney (1/28); hard to find.

One of Orkney's rarest plants, this perennial is known only from some of the most inaccessible gullies and ledges that gird the eastern sides of Ward Hill and the Cuilags on Hoy – in fact it is as rare as its cousin Common Sorrel is routine. Neither is it unprepossessing and by late summer the vibrant colours of its reddening leaves flame like beacons against the sandstones. These leaves, initially green, are kidney-shaped, fleshy and can be the size of an 'old penny'. The flowers, typically dock-like, are insignificant while the stem is almost leafless.

Elsewhere in Britain it has a restricted distribution and can only be found among the mountains of Cumbria, north Wales and the Scottish Highlands. Although occasionally found at sea-level in Scotland, it is more likely to occur above 150 metres especially on damp and ungrazed mountain ledges.

Pages 196/197:

6. Dwarf Cornel on Enegars, Hoy

7. Common Cow-wheat on Enegars, Hoy

8. Mountain Avens on Ward Hill, Hoy

9. Alpine Saw-wort on Haist, Hoy

10. Mountain Sorrel on Haist, Hoy

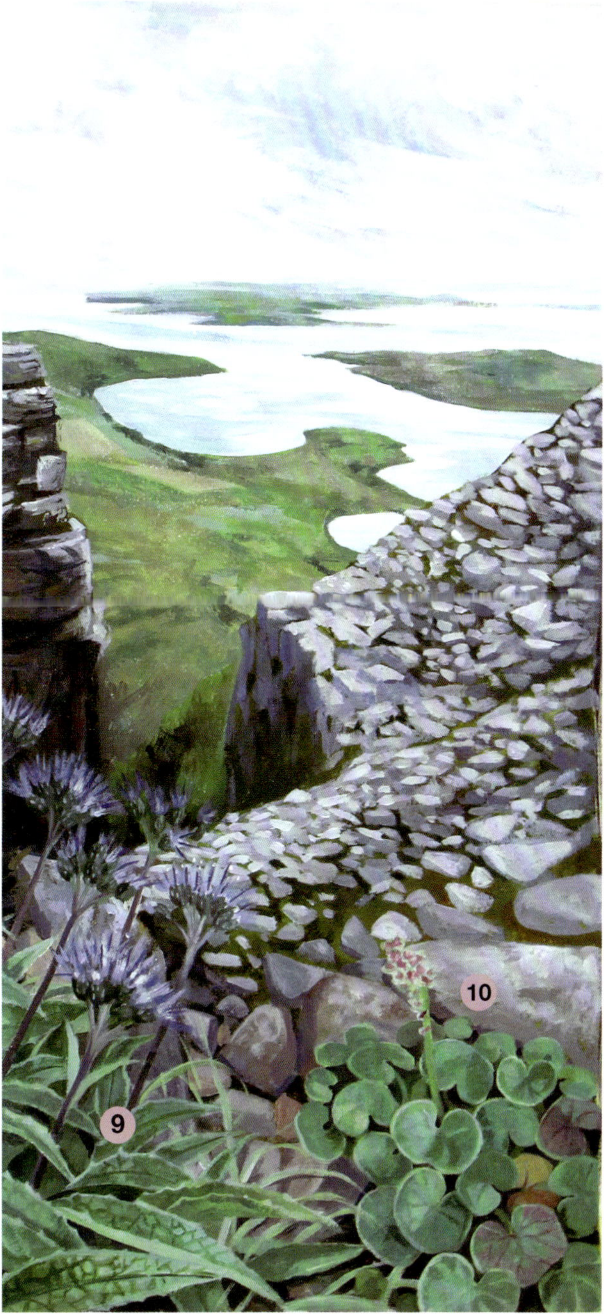
10
9

Bibliography

Berry, R.J. (2000) *Orkney Nature*. T & A.D. Poyser

Berry, R.J. (1985) *The Natural History of Orkney*, William Collins and Co. Ltd

Blamey, M., Fitter, R. and Fitter, A. (2003) *Wildflowers of Britain and Ireland*, A. & C. Black

Brand, J. (1701) *A Brief description of Orkney, Zetland, Pightland Firth and Caithness*

Bullard, E.R. (1995) *Wildflowers in Orkney, a new checklist*. Elaine R. Bullard

Bullard, E.R. *Planticru*, in litt.

Butler, K. and Crossan, K. (2009) *Wildflowers of the North Highlands of Scotland*. Birlinn

Clapham, A.R., Tutin, T.G. and Warburg, E.F. (1962) *Flora of the British Isles*. Cambridge

Dobson, F.S. (2005) *Lichens, an illustrated guide to the British and Irish species*. Richmond Publishing Co. Ltd

Dony, J., Perring, F.H. and Rob, C.M. (1980) *English Names of Wildflowers*. BSBI

Flaws, M and Woodford, B. (1997) *Teeos and tea-flooers*. Pinnsvin

Gear, S. (2008) *Flora of Foula*. Foula Heritage

Grigson, G. (1955) *The Englishman's Flora*. J.M. Dent & Sons Ltd

Grigson, G. (1974) *A Dictionary of English Plant Names*. Allen Lane

Lamb, G. (2004) *Orcadiana*. Bellavista

Lamb, G. (1995) *Orkney Wordbook*. Byrgisey

Loudon, J.C. (1848) *Encyclopaedia of Gardening*.

Mabey, R (1998) *Flora Britannica*. Chatto and Windus

Malcolm, D. (2003) *Shetland's Wildflowers, a photographic guide*. The Shetland Times Ltd

McClintock, D. (1966) *Companion to Flowers*. G. Bell and Sons, London

Milliken, W. and Bridgewater, S. (2004) *Flora Celtica*. Birlinn Ltd

Neill, P. (1806). *A tour through some of the islands of Orkney and Shetland*.

Phillips, R. (1994) *Grasses, Ferns, Mosses and Lichens of Great Britain and Ireland*. MacMillan

Phillips, R. (1977) *Wildflowers of Britain*. Pan

Preston, C.D, Pearman, D.A, and Dines, T.D. (2002) *New atlas of the British and Irish Flora*. Oxford University Press

Rose, F. (2006) *The Wildflower Key.* Frederick Warne

Spence, M. (1914) *Flora Orcadensis*. D. Spence

Stewart, A., Pearman, D.A. and Preston, C.D. (1994) *Scarce Plants in Britain.* JNCC

Tait, C. (1999) *The Orkney Guide Book.* Charles Tait, Photographic, Orkney

Wallace, J. (1700) *An Account of the Islands of Orkney*. London

Appendices

Location of habitats by parish and island

- **i) Sand and shingle shores**
- **ii) Salt marshes**
- **iii) Dunes, links and dry grasslands**
- **iv) Lowland freshwater - lochs, burns, marshes and wet grasslands**
    - a) Lochs
    - b) Burns
- **v) Plantation woodlands**
- **vi) Wild woods and dales**

Because of their widespread nature, there are no specific locations listed for the following habitats: *Sea cliffs, coastal grasslands and coastal heaths; Arable fields, waysides and disturbed ground; The peat hill – heaths and blanket bogs.* Conversely, because of its limited distribution, there are no specific locations listed for *The high hill and stony tops* which are restricted to small areas of Hoy, Rousay and Westray.

i) Sand and shingle shores

Birsay	Mar Wick Bay	Birsay Bay
Burray	Bu Sands	Sutherland
	No 4 barrier	
Deerness	Sand of Ouse	Sandside Bay
Eday	Bay of London	Bay of Greentoft
	Sealskerry Bay	Sands of Mussetter
Egilsay	Mae Banks	
Evie	Evie	Aikerness
Firth	Bay of Firth	
Flotta	Curries Firth	Kirk Bay
Glims Holm	Weddell Sound	
Graemsay	Bay of Sandside	
Holm	Sandber	Sandoyne
	Cornquoy	Wester Sand
Hoy	Rack Wick	Melberry
North Ronaldsay	South Bay	Linklet Bay
Orphir	Waulkmill	Swanbister
Papa Stronsay	Bight of Stackaback	
Papa Westray	Bay of Moclett	South Wick
Rendall	Bay of Puldrite	Waas Wick
Rousay	Berrihead	Saviskaill
St Andrews	Rerwick	Sand of Ness
St Ola	Scapa Bay	
Sanday	Bay of Lopness	Bay of Newark
	Backaskaill Bay	Doun Helzie
	Otterswick	Sandquoy Bay
Sandwick	Bay of Skaill	
Shapinsay	Sandy Geo	Veantrow Bay
South Ronaldsay	Newark Bay	Sand Wick
	Ayre of Cara	No 4 barrier
South Walls	The Ayre	
Stenness	Bay of Ireland	
Stromness	Warebeth	
Stronsay	Cumley Bay	Mill Bay
	Inganoust	Sand of Rothiesholm
	Stursy	Sands of Odie
Westray	Grobust	Bay of Skaill
	Bay of Swartmill	Bay of Tafts
	Mae Sand	
Wyre	Bay of Whelkmulli	

Echnaloch Bay	Weddell Bay
Dingieshowe	Newark
Sandyland	Green Bay
Sands of Doomy	
Ayre	Howes Wick
Bay of Creekland	The Ayre
North Wick	
Oyce of Isbister	
Tresness Bay	Sty Wick
Scar	Whitemill Bay
Bay of Sowerdie	Bay of Scuthvie
Bay of Furrowend	Bay of Sandgarth
Honeysgeo	Sand of Wright
Sand of the Crook	Bight of Scarma
Bights of Bomasty and Baywest	St Catherine's Bay
Brae Geo	
The Ouse	Bay of Brough
Bay of Tuquoy	Bay of Garth

ii) Salt marshes

Deerness	Sandisand	
Firth	The Ouse	Oyce of Rennibister
Holm	Bay of Sandoyne	
Hoy	Myre Bay	Wyng Strand
	North Bay	Little Ayre
	Lyrawa Bay	Pegal Bay
Orphir	Waulkmill	Orphir Bay
Papa Stronsay	Bight of Stackaback	
Rendall	Oyce of Isbister	
Rousay	Bay of Ham	
St Andrews	Swarsquoy	Mill Sand
Sanday	Tor Ness and Quivals Creek	Cata Sand
	Black Rock Marsh	Otterswick
Shapinsay	Ouse	Veantrow Bay
South Ronaldsay	Oyce of Quindry	Oyce of Herston
Stenness	Cumminess	Brig o' Waithe
Stromness	Congesquoy	Hamnavoe
Stronsay	Oyce of Huip	
Westray	Bay of Tuquoy	The Ouse

iii) Dunes, links and dry grasslands

Birsay	Birsay Bay	
Burray	Bu Sands	Sutherland
Deerness	Sand of Ouse	Sandside Bay
Eday	Green Bay	Bay of Greentoft
	Sands of Mussetter	Sands of Doomy
Egilsay	Mae Banks	
Evie	Aikerness	
Glims Holm	Weddell Sound	
Graemsay	Bay of Sandside	
Hoy	Rack Wick	Melberry
North Ronaldsay	South Bay	Linklet Bay
Papa Westray	Bay of Moclett	South Wick
Rousay	Links of Scockness	Saviskaill
St Andrews	Sand of Ness	
St Ola	Scapa	
Sanday	Bay of Lopness	Bay of Newark
	Backaskaill Bay	Doun Helzie
	Otterswick	Sandquoy Bay
Sandwick	Bay of Skaill	

The Ayre	Saltness
Ore Bay	Mill Bay
Swanbister Bay	
Sandisand	Bay of Suckquoy
Little Sea	Lama Ness
Knockhall	
Clestrain	
Day of Okaill	

Weddell Bay	No 4 barrier
Newark	Dingieshowe
Sandyland	Sealskerry Bay
Bay of London	
Bay of Creekland	The Ayre
North Wick	
May Sand	
Tresness Bay	Sty Wick
Scar	Whitemill Bay
Bay of Sowerdie	Bay of Scuthvie

Shapinsay	Sandy Geo	Bay of Sandgarth
South Ronaldsay	Newark Bay	Sand Wick
	Ayre of Cara	No 4 barrier
Stromness	Warebeth	
Stronsay	Cumley Bay	Mill Bay
	Inganoust	Sand of Rothiesholm
	Stursy	Sands of Odie
Westray	Grobust	Bay of Skaill
	Bay of Swartmill	Bay of Tafts
	Mae Sand	

iv) Lowland freshwater a) Lochs (including upland lochs)

Birsay	Loch of Isbister	Loch of Banks
	Bigbreck Quarry	Loch of Boardhouse
Burray	Echna Loch	Northfield Quarry
Deerness	Loch of Ouse	Eves Loch
Eday	Sealskerry Loch	Mill Loch
	Loch of London	
Egilsay	Loch of the Graand	Manse Loch
Evie	Looma Shun	Lowrie's Water
Firth	Loch of Wasdale	Verigens
Flotta	Stanger Head	
Harray	Loch of Bosquoy	Parro Shun
Holm	Black Loch	Loomi Shun
Hoy	Suifea lochs	Loch of Grutfea
	Water of the Wicks	Loch of Torness
	Hoglinns Water	Heldale Water
	Sands Water	Lochs of Withigill
	Little Loch	
North Ronaldsay	Trolla Vatn	Dennis Loch
	Ancum Loch	Hooking Loch
Orphir	Loch of Kirbister	Lochs of Griffyelt
Papa Stronsay	Mill Loch	
Papa Westray	Loch of St Tredwell	Loch of Hyndgreenie
Rendall	Loch of Brockan	
Rousay	Muckle Water	Peerie Water
	Loch of Loomachun	Loch of Sacquoy
	Loch of Scockness	Loch of Jan Janet
St Andrews	Loch of Swarsquoy	Loch of Messigate
	Loch of Hestecruive	

Honeysgeo	Sand of Wright
Sand of the Crook	Bight of Scarma
Bights of Bomasty and Baywest	St Catherine's Bay
Brae Geo	
The Ouse	Bay of Brough
Bay of Tuquoy	Bay of Garth

Loch of Sabiston	The Loons
Loch of Hundland	Loch of Swannay
Southfield Quarry	
Loch of Carrick	Loch of Doomy
Loch of Watten	Loch of Welland
Peerie Water	Loch of Vastray
The Shunan	
Loch of Ayre	Loch of Graemeshall
Loch of Stourdale	Sandy Loch
Loomi Shuns	Berry Lochs
Kit Loch	Muckle Lochs
Water of Hoy	Lochs of Geniefea
Loch of Sjaivar	Loch of Garso
Loch Gretchen	Brides Loch
Loch of Wasbister	Loch of Moan
Loch of Wasday	Loch of Knitchen
Loch of Withamo	
Loch of Lakequoy	Loch of Tankerness

St Ola	Kirkwall Reservoir	Loch of Carness
Sandwick	Mill Dam of Voy	Loch of Skaill
	Manmogila	Arburn
	Orr Shun	
Sanday	Bea Loch	Roos Loch
	Loch of Brue	Westayre Loch
Shapinsay	Vasa Loch	Mill Dam
South Ronaldsay	Trena Loch	Gairy Lochs
	Sounds Loch	Graemston Loch
South Walls	Loch of Greenhill	
Stenness	Loch of Stenness	Loch of Harray
Stromness	Stromness Reservoir	The Loons
Stronsay	Loch of Matpow	Gricey Water
	Muckle Water	Little Water
	Blan Loch	
Westray	Loch of Garth	Muckle Water
	Loch Saintear	Loch of the Stack
Wyre	Loch of Oorns	Loch of the Taing

iv) Lowland freshwater b) Burns

Birsay	Burn of Warth	Burn of Gueth
	Burn of Durkadale	Burn of Boardhouse
	Burn of Kithuntlins	Burn of Teema
	Burn of Gyron	Burn of Swartageo
	Burn of Etherigeo	Burn of Whitemire
Burray	Burn of Sutherland	
Deerness	West Burn of Denwick	East Burn of Denwick
Evie	Burn of Evrigert	Burn of Woodwick
	Burn of Ennisgeo	Burn of Millhouse
	Burn of Woo	Burn of Eunalias
Fara	Back Burn	
Firth	Burn of Rossmyre	Burn of Grimbister
	Burn of Syradale	Burn of Wasdale
	Burn of Holland	Burn of Redland
Flotta	Mill Burn	
Graemsay	Quoys Burn	
Harray	Burn of Netherbrough	Burn of Nettleton
Holm	Burn of Deepdale	Graemeshall Burn
	Burn of Gangsta	
Hoy	Burn of Hellia	Burn of Rebitoe
	Braebuster Burn	Burn of Dale

Loch of Stenness	Loch of Clumly
Mill Dam of Rango	Loch of Rosemire
North Loch	Loch of Rummie
Loch of Langamay	
Lairo Water	Loch of Sandside
Loch of Lythe	Liddel Loch
Burwick Loch	Vensilly Loch
Bruce's Loch	Lea Shun
Straenia Water	Loch of Rothiesholm
Cuppin o' Cheor	Loch of Burness
Loch of Swartmill	Craig Loch

Burn of Beaquoy	Burn of Kirbuster
Burn of Swannay	Burn of Rusht
Burn of Kirkgeo	Burn of Hillside
Burn of Lushan	Burn of Durkadale
Burn of Deith-hellia	
Burns of Savegarth	Burn of Upperhass
Burn of Pow	Burn of Rumerdale
Burn of Desso	Berry Burn
Burn of Stennadale	Maitland's Burn
Burn of Geo	Burn of Vinden
Leisburn	Burn of Bluebrae
Lyde Burn	Burn of Corrigall
Burn of Button	Cot Burn
Burn of Stourdale	Burn of the Kame
Upper Hedal	Mill Burn

Hoy cont.	Blind Burn	North Burn of Quoys
	Burn of the Nowt Bield	South Burn
	Burn of Segal	Rackwick Burn
	Burn of Hoglinns	Burn of Greenheads
	Burn of Ore	Burn of Longigill
	Burn of Withigill	Burn of Bailliefea
	Pegal Burn	Lyrawa Burn
	North Burn of Sneuk	Burn of Runcigill
Orphir	Burn of Fidge	Gyre Burn
	Cupwillo Burn	Burn of Naversdale
	Mill Burn	Burn of Vam
	Burn of Russa	Burn of Westquoy
	Burn of Greenigoe	
Rendall	Burn of Cruan	Burn of Dale
	Burn of Hackland	Burn of Nearhouse
	Burn of Grimisdale	Burn of Orquil
Rousay	Burn of Tafts	Limmers Burn
	Burn of Quoys	Suso Burn
	Burn of Oldman	Burn of Wasdale
St Andrews	Burn of Culdiegeo	Burn of Voy
	Mill Burn	
St Ola	Burn of Hestigeo	Burn of Cottland
	Crantit Canal	Burn of Fingerack
	Burn of Hatston	Willow Burn
Sandwick	Burn of Uppadee	Burn of Stanyknowe
	Brough Burn	Burn of Yeldadee
	Burn of Lyking	Burn of Bakataing
	Burn of Vetquoy	Burn of Hackland
	Burn of Hackland	Burn of Roo
	Burn of Cruaday	
Shapinsay	Burn of Housa	BurnTrolldgeo
South Ronaldsay	Oback Burn	Burn of Stane
	Filiber Burn	Olad Burn
	Burn of Liddel	Graemston Laik
South Walls	Burn of Barkquoy	Mill Burn
Stenness	Burn of Ireland	Burn of Ottersgill
	Burn of Burralie	Burn of Vean
	Housequoy Burn	Muckle Burn of Stenness
	Burn of Lyradale	
Stromness	Burn of Cringlegeo	May Burn
	Burn of Deepdale	Burn of Ha

South Burn of Quoys	Whaness Burn
Water Glen	Burn of Redglen
Burn of Berriedale	Burn of the Sale
Burn of Forse	Burn of Heldale
Burn of Moifea	Burn of Westdale
Mill Burn	Burn of the White Horse
Blind Burn	Summer Burn
Burn of Rinnigill	
Burn of Swanbister	Burn of Effradale
Burn of Lerquoy	Burn of Heatheryquoy
Burn of Drumie	Black Burn
Burn of Swartaback	Burn of Clummar
Burn of Blubbersdale	Burn of Sweenalay
Northgue Burn	Burn of Ellibister
Burn of Claybank	Burn of Myres
Burn of Trumland	Burn of Cruar
Burn of Castlehill	
Burn of Quoykea	Burn of Langskaill
Burn of Caldale	Lingro Burn
Gill Burn	Burn of Wideford
Burn of Langadee	Burn of Cruland
Burn of Unigarth	Burn of Snusgar
Burn of Blutshun	Burn of Grudgin
Burn of Hourston	Burn of Clett
Grip of Grunkahowe	Burn of Ess
Berriedale Burn	Newark Burn
Cool Burn	Sandwick Burn
Oback Burn	
Burn of Redkirk	
Burn of Villas	Burn of Jockasey
Burn of Russadale	Little Burn
Burn of Heddle	Burn of Rickla
Boltifar Burn	Burn of Sunardee
Burn of Quholmslie	Burn of Streather

Stromness cont.	Burn of Dykeside	Burn of Eastalet
	Burn of Mousland	Burn of Una
	Burn of Dale	Burn of Clovigarth
Stronsay	Mill Burn	Burn of Millgrip
Westray	Burn o' Cheor	Sink of Hagock
	Grips of Hestigeo	

v) Plantation woodlands

Mainly deciduous		Mainly coniferous
Eday	Carrick	**Birsay**
Evie	Woodwick	**Eday**
Firth	Binscarth	**Firth**
Hoy	Melsetter	**Flotta**
Kirkwall	Willows	**Holm**
Orphir	Gyre	**Hoy**
Rendall	Queenamidda	**Hoy**
Rousay	Trumland	**Hoy**
Shapinsay	Balfour	**Hoy**
St Ola	Berstane	**Hoy**
St Ola	Muddisdale	**St Andrews**
St Ola	Wideford Burn	
South Ronaldsay	Cools	
South Ronaldsay	Olav's Wood	
South Ronaldsay	Roeberry	
South Ronaldsay	South Cara	
Stenness	Happy Valley	
Stromness	Oglaby	
Westray	Fribo	

vi) Wild woods and dales

Birsay	Durka Dale	
Deerness	Dale of Helzie	
Eday	Leenies Dale	Dale of Carpoquoy
Evie	Durrisdale	Dale
Firth	Kings Dale	Lyra Dale
	Dale of Redland	Stennadale
	Muckle Eskadale	Little Eskadale
Harray	Dale of Corrigall	Dale
Holm	Deepdale	

Burn of Selta	Burn of Helliaclov
Burn of Lyregeo	Burn of Garth
Burn of Sowadee	
Grip of Monivey	Grip of Juber

Ravie Hill
Vinquoy
Redland
Sutherland
Netherbutton
Hoy Forest
Hoy Lodge
Lyrawa
Wee Fea
White Glen
Langskaill

Cott of Dale	Airsdale
Turrie Dale	Heatherdale
Wasdale	Syradale
King's Dale	

Hoy	Berriedale	Lenders Dale
	West Dale	North Dale
	Deep Dale	Dale
Orphir	Naversdale	Rams Dale
	Dale (Smoogro)	North Dales
	Ferndale	Dale of Oback
Papa Westray	Dale o' Caman	
Rendall	Blubbersdale	Varme Dale
	Aviedale	
Rousay	North Dale	Quendale
	Brendale	Ervadale
St Ola	Muddisdale	Caldale
Sandwick	Voydale	Savedale
South Ronaldsay	Berriedale	Berriedale (Windwick)
South Walls	Aithsdale	
Stenness	Russa Dale	Stoursdale
	Summers Dale	
Stromness	Deepdale	Mousland Dale
	The Dale	
Westray	Muslandale	Old Berriedale

Burn of Dale	Smerr Dale
Heldale	Grims Dale
Quoy-i-dale	
Linna Dale	The Dale
Scorra Dale	Effra Dale
Grimis Dale	Dale of Redland
Knowe of Dale	Swandale
Wasdale	
Lesliedale	Sunnydale
Dale (Dale Moss)	
North Dales	Sunny Dale
Burn of Dale	Dry Dale
Swinedale	

Botanical descriptions of some of Orkney's best sites – SSSIs, SACs, LNRs, RSPB, SWT

A brief description of some of Orkney's pre-eminent sites, including the species and habitats for which they are designated, follows. Please bear in mind that some of these sites hold impressive and rare species; their rarity may preclude them from featuring in this book.

Deerness
Mull Head LNR

The spectacular coastline of the Mull Head LNR in the northeastern corner of Deerness is home to extensive tracts of maritime heath and maritime grassland. Typical plants on the site include Spring Squill, Thrift, Sea Plantain, Grass-of-Parnassus, Buck's-horn Plantain, Kidney Vetch, Ling, Bell Heather, Crowberry and cottongrasses. The vegetated sea cliffs support Scots Lovage and some plants typical of 'dales' vegetation can be found in the sheltered and lush cliff geos.

Hoy
Hoy SSSI and SAC, part RSPB
Notified for blanket bog, dystrophic loch, upland assemblage, upland oak woodland

The extensive uplands on Hoy, which rise to 479m, are of great botanical importance. There has been little grazing and little burning for nearly half a century which is an uncommon state of affairs for hill land in Britain. On the exposed summits are alpine and subalpine heaths with Arctic-alpine plants such as Bearberry, Alpine Bearberry, Trailing Azalea and Dwarf Willow (*Salix herbacea*). Down in the valleys are woodland areas including Berriedale, Britain's most northerly natural woodland, where trees such as Rowan (*Sorbus aucuparia*), Downy Birch (*Betula pubescens*), Aspen (*Populus tremula*), and Hazel (*Corylus avellana*) occur.

Areas of Blanket bog are characterised by swathes of undisturbed Sphagnum moss among which can be found species such as Great Sundew while the wet heath habitats contain numerous lichens and Cross-leaved Heath.

Some of Hoy's scarcest wildflowers occur where the soils are rich in calcium. Two of the richest areas are Quoyawa and Nowt Bield where the following specialities occur: Holly Fern (*Polystichum lonchitis*), Alpine Meadow-grass (*Poa alpina*), Hoary Whitlow Grass (*Draba incana*), Mountain Sorrel, Mountain Avens, Alpine Saw-wort, Roseroot, Purple Saxifrage, Alpine Meadow-rue, Yellow Saxifrage, Starry Saxifrage (*Saxifraga stellaris*), Purging Flax, Few-flowered Spike-rush

h) Waulkmill SSSI, part RSPB
Notified for maritime cliff, salt marsh

Situated on the north side of Scapa Flow in the parish of Orphir, Waulkmill Bay, regarded as one of the county's finest beaches, is important nationally for its salt marsh and cliff vegetation. The salt marsh is by far the largest in Orkney and within it grow Sea Milkwort, Sea Arrowgrass, Saltmarsh Rush, Saltmarsh Flat-sedge (*Blysmus rufus*) and One-glumed Spikerush (*Eleocharis uniglumis*), Glasswort, Lesser Sea-spurrey, Greater Sea-spurrey and Long-bracted Sedge (*Carex extensa*). On the herb and fern rich cliffs the only natural colony of Aspen on Orkney Mainland can be found alongside uncommon plants such as Wood Sage, Hay-scented Buckler Fern and Stone Bramble, whilst Pyramidal Bugle used to occur here.

i) West Mainland Moorlands SSSI, part RSPB
Notified for blanket bog, upland assemblage

From Birsay in the north to Firth in the south, the West Mainland Moorlands extend almost 13kms making it the second largest block of moorland in Orkney. The hill ground is essentially acidic; heath, both wet and dry, and blanket bog covers much of the site. However, where springs bubble to the surface, the alkaline conditions mean the occurrence of plants such as Alpine Meadow-rue and Black Bog-rush. The site's many sheltered dales are rich with tall herbs such as Valerian, Water Avens and ferns such as Male Fern and Broad Buckler-fern. Willow scrub, mainly Eared Willow (*Salix aurita*), with Grey Willow (*Salix cinerea*) also evident in patches and the site is also the location for scarce plants such as Moonwort (*Botrychium lunaria*), Frog Orchid, Lesser Twayblade, Chickweed Wintergreen (Trientalis *europaea*) and hybrid Horsetail.

Westray
West Westray SSSI, part RSPB
Notified for maritime cliff

Extensive areas of maritime grassland and maritime heath occur along the western cliffs of Westray.

Within both habitats can be found colonies of the Scottish Primrose and other uncommon species such as Alpine Meadow-rue and Alpine Bistort (*Persicaria alpina*). Moss Campion can be found on the wetter rock ledges and communities of ferns including Sea Spleenwort, Brittle Bladder-fern (*Cystopteris montana*) and Male Fern occur in among the shelter of rocks.

Local Nature Conservation Sites in Orkney

regular font = habitats found in the Orkney Book of Wildflowers

italics = features of interest as defined in Orkney Islands Council Local Plan 2004

Birsay

Brough of Birsay – sea cliff (*maritime cliff and slope, maritime heath, maritime grassland*)

Burn of Ess – freshwater (*burns and canalised burns*)

Loch of Banks – freshwater, hill (*upland heath*)

Loch of Boardhouse – freshwater, hill (*lowland fens, mesotrophic lochs, upland heath, burns and canalised burns*)

Loch of Hundland – freshwater, hill (*mesotrophic loch, lowland fens, upland heath, blanket bog, burns and canalised burns*)

Loch of Sabiston – freshwater, wild woods (*eutrophic standing waters, lowland fens, wet woodlands*)

Loch of Swannay – freshwater, hill (*lowland fens, mesotrophic lochs, upland heath, burns and canalised burns*)

Vias Moss – freshwater, plantation woodland (*broad-leaved plantation, lowland fens*)

Deerness

Eves Loch – salt marsh, freshwater (*coastal salt marsh, saline lagoons*)

Loch of the Ouse – dune, freshwater, hill (*lowland fens, lowland dry acid grassland, upland heath, mesotrophic loch, links*)

Mirkady Point – shore, salt marsh (*salt marsh, coastal vegetated shingle*)

Taracliff to Point of Ayre – sea cliff (*maritime cliff and slope*)

Evie

Costa Hill – freshwater, sea cliff, hill (*upland heath, Crowberry heath, maritime heath, maritime cliff and slope, maritime grassland, upland fens, flushes, swamps*)

Hill of Dwarmo – freshwater, hill (*upland heath, species-rich heath, lowland calcareous grassland, lowland fens and inland rock outcrop and scree*)

Links of Aikerness – dune (*aeolianite*)

Loch of Vastray – freshwater (*mesotrophic loch*)

Mainland coast – shore, salt marsh (*inter-tidal mudflats, coastal salt marsh, strandline*)

Peerie Water – freshwater, hill (*blanket bog, oligotrophic and dystrophic lochs*)

Firth

Barebrecks – freshwater, wild wood, hill (*blanket bog, basin bog, lowland fens, wet woodlands, burns and canalised burns*)

Bridgend – freshwater, wild wood, hill (*lowland fens, wet woodlands, blanket bog, lowland dry acid grassland, burns and canalised burns*)

Heddle – freshwater, wild wood, hill (*lowland meadows, lowland calcareous grassland, lowland dry acid grassland, lowland fens, upland heath, blanket bog, upland willow scrub, burns and canalised burns*)

Hewing – freshwater (*basin bog, burns and canalised burns*)

Keelylang – freshwater, plantation woodland, hill (*lowland fens, upland fens, flushes and swamps, wet woodlands, upland heath, species-rich heath, blanket bog, burns and canalised burns*)

Loch of Wasdale – freshwater, hill (*lowland meadows, lowland dry acid grassland, lowland fens, mesotrophic lochs, upland heath, blanket bog*)

Rennibister – freshwater (*marshy grassland*)

Rossmyre – freshwater, wild wood, hill (*lowland fens, wet woodlands, basin bog, burns and canalised burns*)

The Ouse – salt marsh (*coastal salt marsh, saline lagoon, inter-tidal mudflats*)

Harray

Breckan – freshwater (*marsh*)

Corrigall – freshwater, hill (*blanket bog, upland heath, burns and canalised burns*)

Knowes of Trotty – freshwater, hill (*lowland dry acid grassland, upland heath, lowland fens, blanket bog*)

Loch of Bosquoy – freshwater, hill (*eutrophic standing water, lowland meadows, lowland dry acid grassland, lowland fens, upland heath, species-rich heath*)

Netherborough – freshwater (*lowland meadows, lowland dry acid grassland, lowland fens, burns and canalised burns*)

Quoyer – freshwater (*lowland meadows, lowland dry acid grassland, lowland fens, eutrophic standing water*)

Setter – freshwater, hill (*lowland fens, wet woodlands, upland heath, basin bog, burns and canalised burns*)

The Shunan – freshwater, hill (*eutrophic standing waters, mesotrophic lochs, lowland fens, upland heath*)

Holm

Breckquoy – freshwater, hill (*lowland fens, upland heath, Crowberry heath, lowland meadows, burns and canalised burns*)

Gaitnip Hill – freshwater, sea cliff, hill (*upland heath, Crowberry heath, lowland fens, blanket bog, burns and canalised burns, maritime cliff and slope, maritime grassland*)

Heathery Howes – freshwater, hill (*upland heath, blanket bog, oligotrophic and dystrophic loch*)

Loch of Ayre – freshwater (*mesotrophic loch*)

Loch of Graemeshall – freshwater (*lowland fens, reed beds, eutrophic standing water*)

Notster – sea cliff, hill (*upland heath, maritime heath, lichen heath, maritime cliff and slope, maritime grassland*)

Rose Ness – sea cliff, hill (*upland heath, Crowberry heath, maritime cliff and slope, maritime grassland*)

Orphir

Burn of Greenigoe – freshwater, hill (*blanket bog, upland heath, Crowberry heath, burns and canalised burns*)

Loch of Kirbister – freshwater, wild wood, hill (*eutrophic lochs, lowland fens, wet woodland, blanket bog, burns and canalised burns*)

Orphir hills, southern fringe – freshwater, wild wood, hill (*lowland meadows, lowland fens, upland fens, flushes and swamps, reed beds, wet woodlands, upland heath, species-rich heath, blanket bog, lowland dry acid grassland, burns and canalised burns*)

The Fidge – salt marsh, freshwater, sea cliff, hill (*lowland meadows, lowland calcareous grassland, lowland dry acid grassland, lowland fens, maritime heath, blanket bog, eutrophic standing waters, burns and canalised burns, coastal salt marsh*)

Rendall

Burn of Ellibister – freshwater, hill (*lowland fens, blanket bog, burns and canalised burns*)

Como – freshwater, hill (*upland heath, species-rich heath, lichen heath, lowland fens*)

Loch of Brockan – freshwater, hill (*eutrophic standing waters, upland heathland*)

Quoyhenry – freshwater, hill (*lowland fens, basin bog, upland heath*)

Rendall Moss – freshwater, wild wood, hill (*wet woodlands, upland heath, blanket bog, basin bog, lowland fens, burns and canalised burns*)

St Andrews

Bay of Suckquoy – salt marsh, hill (*salt marsh, intertidal mud flats, upland heath*)

Blown, Culdigeo and Whitemoss – freshwater, hill (*upland heath, lowland fens, blanket bog, upland fens, flushes and swamps, oligotrophic and dystrophic lochs, burns and canalised burns*)

Greenock – freshwater, hill (*lowland fen, blanket bog, basin bog, upland heathland*)

Heathery Howes – freshwater, hill (*oligotrophic and dystrophic lochs, blanket bog, basin bog, upland heathland*)

Loch of Tankerness – freshwater, wild wood (*mesotrophic loch, wet woodlands*)

Long Ayre – shore, salt marsh (*coastal salt marsh, coastal vegetated shingle, saline lagoon*)

Mill Sand – shore, salt marsh, freshwater, sea cliff, hill (*inter-tidal mudflats, eutrophic standing water, coastal salt marsh, maritime grassland, upland heath, species-rich heath, vegetated shingle*)

Mossclair – hill (*upland heath*)

Redbanks – hill (*upland heath, blanket bog, basin bog*)

Rerwick – sea cliff (*Crowberry heath, maritime cliff and slope, maritime grassland*)

St Peter's Pool – salt marsh, dunes, hill (*lowland dry acid grassland, upland heath, Purple Moor-grass and rush pasture, coastal sand dunes, inter-tidal mud flats, coastal salt marsh*)

Swart Howe – freshwater, hill (*upland heath, lowland fens, upland flushes fens and swamps, blanket bog*)

Veddertownmail – freshwater, hill (*wet heath, grassland*)

Yinstay Loch – freshwater, sea cliff, hill (*upland heath, Crowberry heath, basin bog, eutrophic standing water*)

St Ola

Berry Hill – hill (*blanket bog*)

Caldale – freshwater, hill (*blanket bog, upland heath, burns and canalised burns*)

Head o' Work – sea cliff, hill (*upland heath, Crowberry heath, lichen heath, maritime cliff and slope, maritime grassland*)

Loch of Carness – freshwater (*eutrophic standing water*)

Loch of Work – freshwater (*marsh*)

Wideford Burn – freshwater, wild wood, hill (*wet woodland, upland heath, lowland fens, Purple Moor-grass and rush pasture, eutrophic standing water, burns and canalised burns*)

Wideford Hill – hill (*upland heath, blanket bog*)

Sandwick

Breck of Linkquoy – freshwater, hill (*upland heath, lowland fens, lowland meadows, burns and canalised burns*)

Borwick – freshwater, sea cliff (*lowland fens, maritime grassland*)

Clumly Breck – hill (*upland heath, species-rich heath*)

Decca Station – freshwater (*marsh*)

Hestwall – freshwater (*marsh*)

Loch of Clumly – freshwater, hill (*mesotrophic lochs, upland heath*)

Loch of Rosemire – freshwater (*eutrophic standing waters, marsh*)

Loch of Skaill – freshwater (*eutrophic standing waters, lowland meadows, lowland fens*)

Mill Dam of Rango – freshwater (*eutrophic standing waters, lowland fens, lowland meadows, lowland dry acid grassland, burns and canalised burns)

Orr Shun – freshwater (*lowland fens, mesotrophic lochs, burns and canalised burns*)

Reed Meadow – freshwater (*reed beds, lowland meadows*)

Row Head – sea cliff (*maritime cliff and slope, maritime heath, maritime grassland*)

Stones of Via – lowland freshwater (*eutrophic standing waters*)

Tronston – freshwater (*lowland fens, eutrophic standing water*)

Unigarth – freshwater (*lowland meadows, lowland fens, eutrophic standing water*)

Stenness

Anderswick – freshwater, wild wood, hill (*lowland fens, upland fens, flushes and swamps, reed beds, ponds, wet woodlands, upland heath, blanket bog, lowland dry acid grassland, burns and canalised burns*)

Bigswell – freshwater, hill (*upland heath, basin bog, burns and canalised burns*)

Brig o' Waithe – salt marsh (*coastal salt marsh, inter-tidal mudflats*)

Brodgar – freshwater, hill (*lowland meadows, upland heath, lowland fens, species-rich heath, mesotrophic lochs*)

Harray Road End – freshwater, hill (*upland heath, blanket bog, lowland fens, burns and canalised burns*)

Stromness

Brinkies Brae – hill (*upland heath, Crowberry heath, lichen heath, outcrops*)

Brunt Hill – freshwater, hill (*mesotrophic lochs, upland heath, Crowberry heath, species-rich heath, blanket bog, upland fens, flushes and swamps*)

Deepdale – freshwater (*burns and canalised burns*)

the Loons – freshwater, hill (*lowland fens, lowland meadows, upland heath, basin bog, burns and canalised burns*)

Quholm – freshwater (*burns and canalised burns*)

Warebeth – dunes (*aeolianite*)

Burray

Burray Ness – sea cliff, hill (*maritime cliff and slope, maritime heath, maritime grassland, upland heath, lowland dry acid grassland*)

Echna Loch – freshwater (*eutrophic standing water*)

Klondyke – hill (*upland heath, blanket bog, basin bog, lichen heath, Crowberry heath*)

North Links – dunes (*coastal sand dunes, links*)

South Links –dunes (*coastal sand dunes, links, lowland meadows*)

Sutherland Links – dunes, freshwater (*lowland meadow, links, burns and canalised burns*)

Cava

Sea cliff, hill (*upland heath, blanket bog, maritime cliff and slope, maritime grassland*)

Eday

Bomo – hill (*upland heath, blanket bog, Crowberry heath*)

Braehead – freshwater, hill (*upland heath, blanket bog, oligotrophic and dystrophic lochs*)

Dale – freshwater, hill (*lowland fen, blanket bog*)

Fersness Hill – wild wood, hill (*upland heath, blanket bog, upland willow scrub*)

Loch of London – freshwater, sea cliff, hill (*upland heath, blanket bog, oligotrophic and dystrophic lochs, Crowberry heath*)

Mussetter, Doomy and London – dunes, freshwater, hill (*upland heath, blanket bog, oligotrophic and dystrophic lochs, coastal sand dunes, burns and canalised burns*)

Red Head and Vinquoy Hill – freshwater, seacliff, hill (*upland heath, blanket bog, basin bog, maritime heath, Crowberry heath, eutrophic stamnding waters, maritime cliff and slope*)

Resting Hill – hill (*upland heath, blanket bog*)

Sealskerry – freshwater, sea cliff (*eutrophic standing water, maritime grassland, maritime cliff and slope*)

Skaill – hill (*upland heath, basin bog*)

Stennie Hill – hill (*upland heath, blanket bog*)

Ve Ness – hill (*upland heath, Crowberry heath, blanket bog*)

Vinquoy Wood – plantation woodland (*conifer*)

Ward Hill and Chapel Hill – hill (*upland heath, Crowberry heath, blanket bog*)

Egilsay

Lochs of Watten and Welland – freshwater (*eutrophic standing waters, lowland fens, reed beds, lowland meadows*)

Manse Loch – freshwater (*eutrophic standing waters, lowland fens*)

Fara

sea cliff, hill (*upland heath, blanket bog, maritime cliff and slope*)

Flotta

Calf of Flotta – sea cliff (*maritime cliff and slope, maritime grassland*)

Golta Peninsula – sea cliff, hill (*upland heath, blanket bog, maritime cliff and slope, maritime grassland*)

Western Moors – hill (*upland heath, blanket bog*)

Gairsay

freshwater, sea cliff (*maritime cliff and slope, upland heath, maritime heath, maritime grassland, lowland fens*)

Glims Holm

dunes, freshwater, sea cliff, hill (*maritime cliff and slope, coastal sand dunes, upland heath, maritime grassland*)

Graemsay

Graemsay Hill (west and east) – freshwater, hill (*lowland fens, upland heath*)

North coast – freshwater, hill (*upland heath, species-rich heath, lowland fens, lowland meadows, upland calcareous grassland, inland rock outcrops and scree*)

Hoy and Walls

Aith Head – sea cliff, hill (*upland heath, maritime heath, maritime cliff and slope, maritime grassland*)

Brims – freshwater, sea cliff (*lowland meadow, maritime heath, lowland fens, maritime cliff and slope, maritime grassland*)

Bu, Moaness – wild wood (*upland willow scrub*)

Crockness – hill (*upland heath, blanket bog*)

Fea Heath – hill (*upland heath*)

Hoy and North Walls moorland fringes including Binga Fea, Lyrawa Hill, Moi Fea, North Lyrawa, Pegal Hill, Pegal Bay, Shell Hill, Wee fea and Burn – salt marsh, freshwater, sea cliff, wild wood, plantation, hill and high hill (*upland heath, blanket bog, Crowberry heath, upland flushes, fens and swamps, upland birchwood, upland willow scrub, conifer plantation, burns and canalised burns, oligotrophic and dystrophic lochs, maritime cliff and slope, coastal salt marsh*)

Loch of Greenhill – freshwater, hill (*upland heath, lowland fen*)

Melsetter Coast – dunes (*links*)

Newhouse Heath – hill (*upland heath, blanket bog*)

Quoy – freshwater, hill (*upland heath, lowland meadows, lowland fens*)

Quoys Glen – freshwater, wild wood, hill (*upland birchwood, upland heathland, burns and canalised burn*)

Tui Fea – wild wood, hill (*upland birch wood, upland willow scrub, upland heathland*)

Whaness Burn – freshwater, wild wood, hill (*upland willow scrub, upland heathland, burns and canalised burns*)

Witter, Braebuster Burn and Hoy Lodge Marsh – freshwater, sea cliff, wild wood, hill (*upland heath, lowland fens, upland flushes, fens and swamps, lowland calcareous grassland, treeless woodland and dales, maritime cliff and slope, maritime grassland, maritime heath, Crowberry heath*)

Hunda

sea cliff, hill (*upland heath, Crowberry heath, maritime heath*)

North Ronaldsay

Ancum Loch – freshwater (*lowland fen, eutrophic standing water*)

Bride's Loch – freshwater (*eutrophic standing water*)

Gretchen Loch – dunes, freshwater (*eutrophic standing water, machair*)

Hooking Loch – freshwater (*eutrophic standing water*)

Kirbist Mire – freshwater (*marsh*)

Loch of Garso – freshwater (*eutrophic standing water*)

North Ronaldsay – shore (*strandline*)

Papa Stronsay

Mill Loch – shore, freshwater (*eutrophic standing water, coastal vegetated shingle*)

Papa Westray

Loch of Ness – dunes, freshwater (*lowland meadow, lowland fen, coastal sand dunes*)

Loch of Via – freshwater (*eutrophic standing water*)

Mayback – freshwater (*marsh, swamp*)

St Tredwell and Moclett Links – dunes, freshwater (*lowland meadow, eutrophic standing water, links*)

Wellpark – freshwater (*marsh, swamp*)

Rousay

Loch of Skockness – freshwater (*eutrophic standing waters*)

Loch of Wasbister – freshwater (*lowland fens, eutrophic standing waters*)

Saviskaill – sea cliff (*maritime cliff and slope, maritime heath, maritime grassland*)

Scabra Head – freshwater, sea cliff, hill (*maritime cliff and slope, maritime heath, maritime grassland, upland heath, species-rich heath, upland calcareous grassland, lowland fens*)

Shingly Hill – hill (*upland heath, blanket bog*)

Swandale – freshwater, sea cliff, hill (*maritime cliff and slope, maritime heath, maritime grassland, upland heath, species-rich heath, lowland fens, lowland calcareous grassland*)

Rysa Little

freshwater, sea cliff, hill (*maritime cliff and slope, upland heath, blanket bog, lowland fens*)

Sanday

Bea Loch – dunes, freshwater (*eutrophic standing waters, reed beds, machair*)

Braeswick – shore, freshwater (*lowland fens, vegetated shingle*)

Cleat – salt marsh, dunes, freshwater (*lowland fens, machair, saline lagoons, coastal salt marsh*)

Doun Helzie – dunes, seacliff (*maritime cliff and slope, coastal sand dunes, links*)

Grunavi Head – freshwater, sea cliff, hill (*upland heath, maritime cliff and slope, maritime heath, Crowberry heath, lowland fens*)

Holms of Ire – shore, sea cliff (*maritime cliff, vegetated shingle, maritime grassland*)

Little Over-the-Water – salt marsh, freshwater, hill (*saline lagoons, lowland fens, upland heath, coastal salt marsh*)

Lyre Cliffs – sea cliff, hill (*maritime cliff and slope, upland heath, Crowberry heath, maritime heath, lichen heath, lowland dry acid grassland*)

Mires of Whip – freshwater (*eutrophic standing waters, lowland fens*)

Roos Loch – shore, freshwater (*vegetated shingle, eutrophic standing water*)

Sanday School – hill (*upland heath, species-rich heath*)

Tofts Ness – dunes (*machair*)

Warsetter – sea cliff (*maritime cliff and slope, maritime heath, maritime grassland, lowland meadows*)

West Brough – freshwater (*wetland with open water*)

Whitemill Point – dunes, freshwater (*eutrophic standing waters, reed beds, lowland fens, lowland meadows, machair*)

Shapinsay

Banks of Runabout – freshwater, sea cliff, hill (*upland heath, Crowberry heath, lowland dry acid grassland, lowland fens, maritime cliff and slope, burns and canalised burns*)

Greenwall – freshwater, sea cliff, hill (*upland heath, Crowberry heath, lowland fens*)

Lairo Water and the Ouse – shore, salt marsh, freshwater, sea cliff (*eutrophic standing waters, maritime heath, maritime grassland, coastal vegetated shingle, coastal salt marsh*)

East Hill – sea cliff, hill (*upland heath, Crowberry heath, lichen heath, maritime cliff and slope, maritime heath, maritime grassland*)

The Galt – sea cliff, hill (*upland heath, Crowberry heath, maritime heath, maritime grassland*)

Vasa Loch – freshwater (*eutrophic standing waters*)

South Ronaldsay

Aikers – freshwater (*eutrophic standing water, lowland fens*)

Ayre of Cara – dunes (*coastal sand dunes*)

Barth Head – freshwater, sea cliff, hill (*maritime cliff and slope, upland heath, maritime heath, lichen heath, lowland fens*)

Blows Moss – freshwater, woodland, hill (*lowland fens, wet woodland, upland heathland*)

Burn – freshwater, hill (*upland heath, burns and canalised burns*)

Loch of Burwick – freshwater (*marsh, fen*)

Dale Moss – freshwater, hill (*basin bog, upland heathland*)

Dam of Collie – freshwater (*lowland fens*)

Dam of Hoxa – freshwater (*reed bed, lowland fens, lagoon*)

Gairy – freshwater, sea cliff, hill (*eutrophic standing waters, upland heath, Crowberry heath, lichen heath, species-rich heath, lowland fens*)

Loch of Graemston – freshwater (*lowland fens, eutrophic standing waters*)

Green Head – freshwater, sea cliff (*maritime cliff and slope, lowland fens, lowland meadows, maritime heath, Crowberry heath, maritime grassland*)

Grimness and Honeysgeo – salt marsh, sea cliff, hill (*maritime cliff and slope, upland heath, maritime heath, lichen heath, Crowberry heath, maritime grassland, coastal salt marsh*)

Hoston Bay – sea cliff (*maritime cliff and slope, maritime heath, lowland meadow*)

Hoxa – woodland, sea cliff, hill (*maritime cliff and slope, upland heath, upland willow scrub, Crowberry heath*)

Loch of Lythe – freshwater (*eutrophic standing water*)

Lower Olad – freshwater, sea cliff, hill (*upland heath, lowland fens, upland flushes, fens and swamps, Crowberry heath, lichen heath, maritime heath*)

Lynegar – sea cliff, hill (*upland heath, Crowberry heath*)

Newark Bay – dunes (*coastal sand dunes*)

Olad summit – freshwater, sea cliff, hill (*upland heath, lowland fens, Crowberry heath, species-rich heath*)

Sandwick – sea cliff, woodland, hill (*upland willow scrub, upland heath, maritime cliff and slope*)

Southeast coast S.Ronaldsay – freshwater, sea cliff, hill (*upland heath, maritime heath, lichen heath, Crowberry heath, maritime cliff and slope, maritime grassland, lowland fens, eutrophic standing waters, mesotrophic lochs*)

Stews – sea cliff (*maritime cliff and slope, maritime grassland*)

Ward Hill (east) – freshwater, sea cliff, hill (*upland heath, Crowberry heath, upland flushes, fens and swamps*)

Ward Hill (north) – freshwater, hill (*upland heath, lowland fens*)

Ward Hill – freshwater, sea cliff, hill (*upland heath, Crowberry heath, species-rich heath, lowland fens*)

Stronsay

Bruce's Loch – freshwater (*eutrophic standing waters*)

Burgh Head and Little Water – freshwater, sea cliff, hill (*upland heath, maritime heath, species-rich heath, maritime grassland, maritime cliff and slope, lowland fen, eutrophic standing water*)

Burial Ground Loch – freshwater (*eutrophic standing water*)

Lea Shun – dunes, freshwater (*eutrophic standing water, links*)

Loch of Matpow – dunes, freshwater (*eutrophic standing water, links*)

Loch of Rothiesholm and Blan Loch – dune, freshwater (*eutrophic standing waters, mesotrophic lake, lowland fen, coastal sand dune, machair*)

Meikle Water – freshwater (*lowland fen, eutrophic standing water*)

Rothiesholm – freshwater, sea cliff, hill (*upland heath, Crowberry heath, upland flushes, fens and swamps, oligotrophic and dystrophic lochs, maritime cliff and slope, basin bog*)

Southeast Coast – shore (*strandline*)

Westray

Ayre of Roadmire – shore, freshwater (*coastal vegetated shingle, saline lagoons, reed beds*)

Backaskaill – shore, freshwater (*shingle, swamp, marshy grassland*)

Fribo Marsh – freshwater (*grassland, marshy grassland*)

Kirbist – freshwater, sea cliff (*maritime cliff and slope, maritime heath, maritime grassland, lowland fens, lowland calcareous grassland, inland rock outcrops and scree*)

Loch of Burness – freshwater (*eutrophic standing water*)

Loch of Garth – dunes, freshwater (*coastal sand dunes, links*)

Loch of Saintear – freshwater (*eutrophic standing water*)

Loch of Swartmill – freshwater, hill (*eutrophic standing water, upland heath*)

Loch of Tuquoy – freshwater (*marsh*)

Point of Burrian – sea cliff (*maritime cliff and slope*)

South Westray Coast – shore (*intertidal mud flats, strandline*)

Taftend – freshwater (*marsh*)

The Ouse – shore (*intertidal mudflats, coastal vegetated shingle*)

West Aikerness – freshwater, sea cliff (*maritime cliff and slope, maritime heath, maritime grassland, eutrophic standing water*)

Wyre

Bay of Cott – freshwater (*lowland fens*)

Helziegetha – freshwater, hill (*lowland fens, lowland meadows, upland heath, Purple Moor-grass and rush pastures*)

The Taing – salt marsh, freshwater, sea cliff, hill (*upland heath, Crowberry heath, maritime heath, maritime grassland, lowland dry acid grassland, eutrophic standing waters, coastal salt marsh*)

Index

(Page number refers to species text)

Alpine Meadow-rue	85
Alpine Bearberry	192
Alpine Saw wort	195
Amphibious Bistort	64
Annual Sea-blite	16
Autumn Gentian	31
Autumnal Hawkbit	80
Bearberry	190
Bell Heather	156
Bitter-cresses	116
Black Bog-rush	186
Blaeberry	150
Blood-drop-emlets	62
Bog Asphodel	174
Bog Pimpernel	52
Bogbean	51
Bog Bilberry	185
Bracken	150
Brackish Water-crowfoot	67
Broad Buckler-fern	140
Broad-leaved Dock	114
Brooklime	68
Buck's-horn Plantain	75
Bugloss	39
Bulbous Buttercup	41
Bush Vetch	112
Butterbur	60
Butterwort	182
Carnation Sedge	87
Cat's-ear	79
Charlock	104
Cleavers	6
Cloudberry	184
Clubmosses	166
Colt's-foot	100
Common Bird's-foot-trefoil	40
Common Chickweed	117
Common Cottongrass	181
Common Cow-wheat	194
Common Dog-violet	77
Common Fumitory	113
Common Hemp-nettle	100
Common Marsh-bedstraw	56
Common Milkwort	169
Common Mouse-ear	119
Common Ragwort	36
Common Ramping-fumitory	113
Common Saltmarsh-grass	17
Common Sorrel	89
Common Twayblade	32
Common Water-crowfoot	67
Corn Spurrey	96
Cottongrasses	180
Cow Parsley	110
Cowslip	29
Creeping Buttercup	98
Creeping Thistle	93
Creeping Willow	184
Cross-leaved Heath	157
Crowberry	86
Curled Dock	6
Curved Sedge	41
Daffodil	124
Daisy	92
Dandelion	94
Deergrass	187
Devil's-bit Scabious	88
Dwarf Cornel	194
Early Marsh-orchid	63
Eyebright	83
Fairy Flax	170
Ferns	140
Few-flowered Garlic	126
Field Forget-me-not	97
Field Gentian	30
Field Horsetail	99
Field Pansy	96
Field Speedwell	107
Fir Clubmoss	167
Forget-me-nots	52
Foxglove	139
Fumitories	113

Germander Speedwell	107
Glassworts	20
Glaucous Dog-rose	143
Glaucous Sedge	88
Goldenrod	86
Grass-of-Parnassus	28
Great Sundew	179
Great Willowherb	48
Great Wood-rush	147
Greater Bird's-foot-trefoil	68
Greater Plantain	118
Greater Sea-spurrey	19
Green-ribbed Sedge	172
Ground-elder	124
Ground-ivy	131
Groundsel	111
Hairless Lady's-mantle	173
Hairy Bitter-cress	117
Hard Fern	158
Hardheads	38
Hare's-tail Cottongrass	181
Heath Bedstraw	169
Heath Milkwort	168
Heath Speedwell	165
Heath Rush	170
Heath Spotted-orchid	163
Heathers	156
Hogweed	109
Honeysuckle	151
Horsetails	69
Hybrid Bluebell	132
Hybrid Woundwort	104
Ivy-leaved Water-crowfoot	67
Kidney Vetch	76
Lady's Bedstraw	25
Lady's-mantles	173
Lady's Smock	49
Lesser Burdock	34
Lesser Celandine	130
Lesser Meadow-rue	43
Lesser Sea-spurrey	18
Lesser Spearwort	58
Lesser Trefoil	98
Lesser Twayblade	162
Ling	157
Lousewort	177
Lyme Grass	27
Mare's-tail	64
Marram	26
Marsh Arrowgrass	58
Marsh Cinquefoil	63
Marsh Cudweed	59
Marsh Horsetail	70
Marsh Lousewort	176
Marsh Marigold	46
Marsh Pennywort	50
Marsh Ragwort	55
Marsh Thistle	60
Marsh Violet	175
Marsh Willowherb	50
Meadow Buttercup	71
Meadow Vetchling	112
Meadowsweet	47
Milkworts	168
Monkeyflowers	62
Moss Campion	193
Mountain Avens	195
Mountain Everlasting	84
Mountain Sorrel	198
Mouse-ear Hawkweed	28
Northern Dead-nettle	103
Northern Marsh-orchid	65
Opposite-leaved Golden-saxifrage	132
Oraches	10
Oxeye Daisy	108
Oysterplant	4
Perennial Sow-thistle	8
Pineappleweed	116
Pink Purslane	125
Polypody	131
Prickly Sow-thistle	95
Primrose	138
Prostrate Juniper	161
Purple Ramping-fumitory	113
Purple Saxifrage	191
Ragged Robin	46
Red Bartsia	35

Red Campion	138
Red Clover	37
Red Dead-nettle	103
Ribwort Plantain	119
Rosebay Willowherb	146
Roseroot	81
Round-leaved Sundew	179
Round-leaved Wintergreen	171
Salmonberry	125
Saltmarsh Rush	17
Sand Sedge	24
Scentless Mayweed	110
Scots Lovage	76
Scottish Primrose	78
Scurvygrass	14
Sea Arrowgrass	15
Sea Aster	20
Sea Bindweed	43
Sea Campion	5
Sea Ivory	83
Sea Mayweed	8
Sea Milkwort	18
Sea Plantain	16
Sea Rocket	7
Sea Sandwort	11
Sea Spleenwort	74
Selfheal	42
Sheep's Sorrel	164
Shepherd's-purse	102
Silverweed	9
Slender St John's-wort	172
Smooth Sow-thistle	95
Sneezewort	54
Snowdrop	130
Soft Rush	54
Southern Lady's-mantle	173
Spear Thistle	92
Speedwells	106
Sphagnum	175
Spring Squill	82
Stag's-horn Clubmoss	166
Stinging Nettle	101
Stone Bramble	166
Sundews	178
Sun Spurge	105
Sweet Cicely	108
Sweet Rocket	106
Tansy	115
Thread-leaved Water-crowfoot	67
Thrift	74
Tormentil	159
Trailing Azalea	190
Tufted Forget-me-not	52
Tufted Vetch	114
Valerian	139
Water Avens	146
Water-crowfoots	67
Water Forget-me-not	53
Water Horsetail	70
Water Mint	47
Water-cress	56
Wavy Bitter-cress	117
White Clover	38
Wild Angelica	152
Wild Pansy	24
Wild Roses	143
Wild Thyme	79
Wood Anemone	124
Wood Horsetail	151
Wood Sage	147
Yarrow	33
Yellow Iris	57
Yellow Rattle	32
Yellow Saxifrage	186

Notes

Notes

Notes

Notes

Notes

Sacquoy Head
Faraclett Head
Rousay
Saviskaill Bay
Kierfea Hill
Muckle Water
Peerie Water
Trumland RSPB
Costa Head
Eynhallow
Brough of Birsay
Loch of Swanney
Birsay Parish
Evie Parish
Loch of Boardhouse
Loch of Hundland
Marwick Head RSPB
The Loons RSPB
Birsay Moors RSPB
Tingwall
Loch of Banks RSPB
Dounby
Cottascarth and Rendall RSPB
Rendall Parish
Sandwick Parish
Bay of Skaill
Loch of Skaill
Harray Parish
Loch of Harray
Wide Firth
Brodgar RSPB
Finstown
Firth Parish
Loch of Stenness
Stromness Parish
Stenness Parish
Keelylang Hill
Stromness
Loch of Kirbister
Orphir Parish
Hobbister RSPB
Mid Hill
Waulkmill Bay
Hoy Sound
Graemsay
Moaness
Bring Deeps
Scapa Flow
Ward Hill
Hoy RSPB
Cava
Rora Head
Rackwick Bay
Hoy
Fara
Lyness
Flotta
Hoxa Head
Car Ferry to/from Scrabster
Heldale Water
Hoglinns Water
Switha
Longhope
South Walls
Cantick Head
Torness
Brims
Swona
Car Ferry to/from Gills Bay